Youth Gangs and Community Intervention

YOUTH GANGS AND COMMUNITY INTERVENTION

Research, Practice, and Evidence

EDITED BY

ROBERT J. CHASKIN

Columbia University Press   *New York*

Columbia University Press
Publishers Since 1893
New York   Chichester, West Sussex
Copyright © 2010 Columbia University Press
All rights reserved

Library of Congress Cataloging-in-Publication Data
Youth gangs and community intervention : research, practice, and evidence /
edited by Robert J. Chaskin.
p. cm.
Includes bibliographical references and index.
ISBN 978-0-231-14684-5 (cloth : alk. paper) —
ISBN 978-0-231-14685-2 (pbk. : alk. paper) —
ISBN 978-0-231-51931-1 (ebook)
1. Gang prevention—United States—Citizen participation.
2. Gangs—United States.
3. Gang members—Rehabilitation—United States.
4. Community organization—United States.
I. Chaskin, Robert J.   II. Title.
HV6439.U5Y68   2010
364.1'0660973—dc22   2009040101

Columbia University Press books are printed on permanent and durable acid-free paper.
This book is printed on paper with recycled content.
Printed in the United States of America

References to Internet Web sites (URLs) were accurate at the time of writing.
Neither the author nor Columbia University Press is responsible for URLs that may
have expired or changed since the manuscript was prepared.

Contents

Acknowledgments

This book brings together papers on the theory behind, evidence for, and nature of community approaches to addressing the youth gang problem. The papers were written in honor of Irving A. Spergel, who spent a long and productive career developing scholarship and testing intervention approaches to address this problem. Spergel is a well-known gang and community intervention scholar who has had significant influence on the field during his long tenure. Having worked with gang youth while at the New York City Youth Board and having studied with Richard Cloward and Lloyd Ohlin at Columbia University in the 1950s, Spergel came to the University of Chicago in 1960 to join the faculty of the School of Social Service Administration. He was named the George Herbert Jones Professor in 1993, and in addition to an influential body of published scholarship, he is the principal architect of a comprehensive community-based model that has been adopted by the Office of Juvenile Justice and Delinquency Prevention as the Comprehensive Community-Wide Approach to Gang Prevention, Intervention, and Suppression. Over the course of his career, Spergel has played many roles—youth worker, scholar, teacher, program designer, evaluator, mediator, activist. He embodies a particular orientation to scholarship in the world, and a particular drive to build knowledge that has a real and practical effect on critical social problems of the day.

Acknowledgments

The book is based on papers delivered at a Festschrift held at the University of Chicago in honor of Irving A. Spergel upon his retirement. The Festschrift itself was an effort to generate dialogue (in the spirit of Spergel's scholarship and engagement in the field) among a broad range of people involved in various ways with youth gangs, gang intervention, and community practice. The event provided an opportunity to raise, consider, and debate some of the key issues and important (and underexamined) points of contention among people oriented toward the problem from significantly different perspectives, including the police, city government, community leaders, faith-based institutions, schools, community youth workers, researchers, and, to some extent, youth themselves.

Many of the papers are based on presentations given at the Festschrift; others were written after this event to round out and enhance the coherence and completeness of the volume. Thanks go both to the contributing authors whose work is assembled here and to the other participants and organizers of the symposium and the production of this book, including James Burch, Roberto Caldero, Robert Fairbanks, Luis Gutierrez, Waldo Johnson, Malcolm Klein, Jeanne Marsh, Barbara McDonald, Charles Ramsey, Emilie Schrage, Bill Sites, Jamie Stanesa, Randolph Stone, Herman Warrior, Father Bruce Wellems, Celeste Wojtalewicz, Phelan Wyrick, Dan Zorich, and the many people who work with young people in communities in Chicago in a broad range of roles who participated actively in the discussions that the presentations generated, lending their perspective, wisdom, and understanding of challenges to the debate.

orientations. There have also been shifts in the extent to which such interventions dealt largely with individual and group behavior and intervention versus concentrating on more collective, community-based orientations.

Thus there is a rich history of, and a substantial literature on, various aspects of the phenomenon of youth gangs. Much of this literature seeks to build theory that explains or provides empirical evidence of the sources and determinants of delinquency; the influences that foster the emergence of gangs as social groupings; the attractions, incentives, and pressures that draw particular young people to become involved in gangs; the specific organization and behavior of particular gangs (their membership, structure, economy, activities); or the emergence of new dynamics in the proliferation of gangs, the nature of gang violence, and the effects of gang activities on young people and the communities in which they live. Some, though a good deal less, of this literature deals explicitly with intervention (Curry and Decker 2003; Klein 1971; Klein and Maxson 2006; Spergel 1966, 1995, along with a set of program-specific evaluations of particular interventions)—on what works, what has failed, and what policy directions should be considered to more effectively address the conditions that shape gang formation and the detrimental effects of gang behavior. There is, however, much more ground to cover on this front—on how to think about, implement, understand, and apply knowledge about the effects of gang prevention and intervention policy and practice.

The Volume

This volume contributes to filling that gap by bringing together current scholarship that explicitly targets the ideas behind, approaches to, and evidence for the relative effectiveness of community-based youth gang interventions. It is not meant to provide a comprehensive assessment of gang intervention approaches, and although critical attention is paid to policies and initiatives that rely, for example, on suppression strategies, the emphasis of the chapters that follow is more fundamentally about multifaceted, community-based approaches in which suppression is (or may be) one component.

The rationale for this focus on community-based interventions as responses to gangs and gang violence is straightforward: Although there now exists a range of different kinds of program and policy responses to integration of theory, research, and program implementation to build both knowledge and effective programs.

In chapter 6, James Short and Lorine Hughes frame an argument for rethinking our approach to intervention research concerning youth gangs. They assert that we need to reorient our understanding of gangs and rethink the kinds of measures and evidence that we rely on to evaluate interventions that seek to address them. First, they interrogate the "problematic nature of gangs" and the similarly problematic relationship between scientific observation and measurement, on the one hand, and gangs and gang programs, on the other. Then, partly on the basis of a new analysis of some early research on youth gangs in Chicago, they argue that research integrity regarding gangs and gang intervention needs to take into account an understanding of social capital and collective efficacy, and the role that these constructs play (and could potentially play) within the context of youth gang interventions. Although they point out that additional work is needed to test the viability of this approach, they make a strong case that these constructs are justifiable both theoretically and empirically, and potentially generative of important insights that can improve intervention and our understanding of effectiveness.

In Part III, the volume moves from a review of evidence and consideration of knowledge building to a reconsideration of contexts, orientations, and intervention strategies in light of the current state of knowledge, and suggests additional potential directions for shaping future youth gang interventions. In chapter 7, James Diego Vigil argues for an ecological and developmental approach to engaging young people who are at risk of or involved in gang life. Building on the concept of "multiple marginality" that he developed in earlier work, Vigil draws on decades of ethnographic work with Latino gang youth to explore the processes through which young people are socialized into the gang lifestyle. He then outlines an orientation to gang intervention that takes into account the particular social and cultural circumstances under which such socialization occurs and that tailors intervention to the particular developmental stage at which different young people are confronted with choices regarding gang involvement.

Chapter 8 also argues for a developmental and community-embedded orientation to considering youth gang intervention. Here, Jeffrey Butts and Caterina Gouvis Roman focus on the importance of prevention and early-intervention strategies and lay the foundation for a conceptual framework that builds on comprehensive community approaches to addressing youth gangs by integrating the insights of positive youth development and community justice approaches. Positive youth development, they argue, provides a set of "practice principles" that can usefully guide the identification and provision of a range of developmental supports that may promote protective factors and counter risk factors faced by young people who are susceptible to gang involvement, and may encourage their positive development. Similarly, community justice models offer insight into the effective development of participatory, deliberative processes at the community level that can contribute to the effective implementation of comprehensive gang models.

In chapter 9, David Kennedy fundamentally reorients our consideration of youth gangs and intervention strategies to think about the critical ways in which "norms, narratives, and networks"—the essential underlying understandings, expectations, accounts, interpretations, and relationships that shape the interaction of youth, gangs, communities, law enforcement, and others—condition both our understanding of youth gangs and our responses to them. First, Kennedy shows how implicit norms and unspoken narratives play out among those on different sides of the youth gang issue and how the lack of examination and critical engagement across them creates barriers to understanding and moving past them. Drawing on the experience of, among other programs, a recent drug-market intervention, he then explores the possibility of using group processes to surface competing narratives and come to a collective understanding that allows communities to move beyond these institutionalized impasses and toward common ground.

Finally, Irv Spergel provides the last word. In chapter 10, he considers the implications of the chapters in this volume as a whole, and points to future directions toward more effective, evidence-based youth gang intervention. Framing his analysis with an overview of the scope of the youth gang problem (including the increasingly globalized nature of gang activity and gang proliferation), Spergel provides a critical review of explanations for the emergence of youth gangs, theories behind youth gang interventions and programs, and the three prevailing models guiding community-based youth gang programs—those focused on youth social development, deterrence and suppression, and integrated approaches. Finally, he discusses the challenges of evaluation within this realm and offers a set of recommendations, particularly for the implementation of large-scale demonstrations and effective partnerships among researchers, policymakers, and community actors at both the local and the national level.

Although pursuing different questions and drawing on different material to build their respective cases, the chapters reflect some recurring themes. One of these concerns the importance of community both as a context to be taken account of (shaping opportunity and providing conditions that may, in part, foster gang involvement or offer alternatives to it) and as a unit of action to be mobilized. Community processes—deliberative planning, relational networks, collaborative action—and community resources—programs, opportunities, organizations, institutions—play a central role here. Thus there is recognition in this work of the "embeddedness" of youth and gang activity in community, as well as the fact that community is itself contentious. This focus remains largely local. There is much here that moves beyond the individual (including tailoring intervention to individual needs within the context of community dynamics), but relatively little that moves beyond the community level to institutional factors and players (e.g., prisons) or broader factors that fundamentally shape the circumstances in which these communities find themselves, such as racism, structural changes in the economy, federal policy, broader dynamics of investment and disinvestment, and the distribution of public resources (e.g., for schools or affordable housing). This essentially local focus raises a question about the extent to which we may also need to address the broader "causal story" (Stone 1989) that lies behind the "gang problem" in particular communities, and its implications for both assigning responsibility and considering intervention. Although the local community is of central importance to understanding youth gangs and acting to address the problems associated with them, and although it is important to "engage" the community in such solutions, we need also to recognize the power of these broader structural forces that are at play and the limitations of relying completely on local intervention in light of them.

Another recurring theme concerns a particular focus on youth and the need to understand the role and circumstances of young people in all their complexity as both agents and objects, responding, at a particular stage of life, to differential opportunities, constraints, and pressures. This emphasis concerns, in part, how youth are perceived in general, and the nature of and assumptions about gang involvement among (some) youth in particular. One way in which these perspectives may play out is through a perceived predisposition among some—especially law enforcement—to make broader assumptions about gang involvement among youth in some communities than are warranted, and to view gang membership as an overarching condition that characterizes young people's social life, fundamentally shapes their interactions, and defines their existence. In contrast, many young people in these communities who may be perceived as gang members are not gang-involved, and many others may be involved only tangentially and temporarily, in the meantime engaging in a broad range of normative activities and relationships in school, with family, and with non-gang-involved peers. Further, this "stage of life" is itself graduated, entailing different opportunities and challenges as young people grow through adolescence. Thus we need to understand gang involvement in the broader context of youth development, relationships, and choices. Such an orientation suggests that a focus on gang-involved or at-risk youth needs to be grounded in an understanding of young people, not just an orientation toward gangs. It is also connected, as David Kennedy points out, to a focus on justice, not as a framework for retribution but more broadly as having to do with engagement, understanding, and responsible action.

Finally, there is a theme about knowledge and knowledge use—the limitations to it, ways to rethink it, the need to better connect it to intervention, policy, and practice—in the service of youth and communities and in response to the gang problem. This theme emphasizes, on the one hand, the ability and limitations of current research knowledge to provide the kinds of evidence needed to inform policy and practice and, on the other, the frequent disconnect between theory and program, between evidence and policy, and between producers of knowledge and those who might use such knowledge in deciding on policy priorities, resource distribution, and practice on the ground.

Taken together, the chapters in this volume synthesize current knowledge and provide new insight into what works, what might work, and what enduring challenges remain in addressing youth gangs and in building (and applying) knowledge to improve such approaches.

References

Cloward, R. and L. Ohlin. 1960. *Delinquency and Opportunity: Theory of Delinquent Gangs.* New York: Free Press.

Curry. G. D. and S. H. Decker. 2003. *Confronting Gangs: Crime and Community.* Los Angeles: Roxbury.

Delaney, T. 2006. *American Street Gangs.* Upper Saddle River, N.J.: Pearson/ Prentice Hall.

Hagedorn, J. M., ed. 2007. *Gangs in the Global City: Alternatives to Traditional Criminology.* Urbana and Chicago: University of Illinois Press.

Haskins, J. 1975. *Street Gangs Yesterday and Today.* New York: Hastings House Publishers.

Hay, D., P. Linebaugh, J. Rule, E. P. Thompson, and C. Winslow, eds. 1975. *Albion's Fatal Tree: Crime and Society in Eighteenth-Century England.* New York: Pantheon.

Jankowski, M. S. 1991. *Islands in the Street.* Berkeley: University of California Press.

Klein, M. W. 1971. *Street Gangs and Street Workers.* Englewood Cliffs, N.J.: Prentice Hall.

——. 1995. *The American Street Gang.* New York: Oxford University Press.

Klein, M. W., H. J. Kerner, C. L. Maxson, and E. Weitekamp, eds. 2001. *The Eurogang Paradox: Street Gangs and Youth Groups in the U.S. and Europe.* Dordrecht, The Netherlands: Kluwer Academic Publishers.

Klein, M. W. and C. L. Maxson. 2006. *Street Gang Patterns and Policies.* New York: Oxford University Press.

Massey, D. and N. Denton. 1998. *American Apartheid: Segregation and the Making of the Underclass.* Cambridge, Mass.: Harvard University Press.

Pearson, G. 1983. *Hooligan: A History of Reportable Fears.* New York: Schocken.

Sanders, W. B. 1970. *Juvenile Offenders for a Thousand Years.* Chapel Hill: University of North Carolina Press.

Shaw, C. R. and H. D. McKay. 1942. *Delinquency and Urban Areas.* Chicago: University of Chicago Press.

Short, J. F. and L. A. Hughes, eds. 2006. *Studying Youth Gangs.* Lanham, Md.: AltaMira.

Spergel, I. A. 1966. *Street Gang Work: Theory and Practice.* Reading, Mass.: Addison-Wesley.

——. 1995. *The Youth Gang Problem: A Community Approach.* New York: Oxford University Press.

Stone, D. 1989. "Causal Stories and the Formation of Policy Agendas." *Political Science Quarterly* 104 (2): 281–300.

Thrasher, F. M. 1927. *The Gang.* Chicago: University of Chicago Press.

Whyte, W. F. 1943. *Street Corner Society.* Chicago: University of Chicago Press.

Wilson, W. J. 1987. *The Truly Disadvantaged.* Chicago: University of Chicago Press.

Youth Gangs and Community Intervention

[Part I]

Framing the Youth Gang Problem

The Chicago School

A Context for Youth Intervention Research and Development

ROBERT J. CHASKIN

> These facts indicate that the source of much of our delinquency must be sought in the conditions of life surrounding children in the community and that methods of treatment and prevention must in some way or other cope with these conditions.
>
> — Rodney H. Brandon

In his foreword to the landmark publication *Juvenile Delinquency in Urban Areas* (Shaw and McKay 1942), Rodney Brandon, who at the time was the director of the Department of Public Welfare in Illinois, distilled the principal message from the most comprehensive study to date of the spatial distribution of juvenile delinquency in the United States. Focusing initially on Chicago and finally including twenty cities widely distributed geographically and varying significantly in size and other characteristics, the study demonstrated that variations in rates of delinquency across neighborhoods were highly correlated with factors such as neighborhood poverty, population mobility, physical deterioration, and minority (black and foreign-born) status, and that patterns of concentrated delinquency remained relatively stable across neighborhoods through the successive in- and out-migration of different groups. In light of these findings, the study argued, we can focus on delinquency neither as the product of culturally determined behavior fostered by particular ethnic groups nor as a purely individual phenomenon amenable to individual-level intervention alone. Instead, both the problem and the solution need to be framed in terms of structurally determined community characteristics and the dynamics of community organization and functioning.

Shaw and McKay's work was seminal to informing subsequent research and intervention concerning delinquency and crime, urban sociology, and community practice, and was itself informed by prior work that was at the heart of early American sociology and social work scholarship and practice. The nature and role of community in reflecting, shaping, and conditioning social interaction and access to resources and opportunity, and the relationship between community circumstances and dynamics and the status and well-being of its inhabitants—the children, young people, and families who make their homes there—are enduring themes to this day.

The purpose of this chapter is to draw on some of this seminal work as a basis for laying a broad foundation for the material that follows. I focus in particular on three issues. The first concerns assumptions about the nature of "community" and its potential role as a unit of analysis and action. The second has to do with young people in communities and approaches to community-based youth intervention. The third centers on the relationship between research and social intervention—policy and practice—and issues revolving around knowledge development and utilization in the context of community interventions.

In exploring these issues, I draw on some of the research and activities that have developed in Chicago, including work of the early "Chicago School" of the University of Chicago.[1] In doing so, I raise a set of questions about the possibilities, limitations, and enduring tensions that inhere in many community initiatives and community-based youth interventions.

I use Chicago as a point of departure because this work provides a kind of intellectual and practical touchstone for considering urban communities and approaches to community-based youth intervention research and development (including that focused on delinquency and youth gangs—the subject of this volume) and because stepping back to reconsider these beginnings—and some of the subsequent developments of theory and empirical research spawned by (or in response to) them—provides a useful point of reference for considering present orientations. Sociological inquiry spearheaded at Chicago focused on the urban environment and its relationship to human behavior generally (see Park 1925 for a version of this agenda as it was developing in the 1920s), and on sources and responses to delinquency and crime in particular.[2] Thus it provides a foundation for understanding some of the assumptions behind and critical elements of practice within community-based youth interventions addressing crime, delinquency, and gang involvement.

This orientation, however, is just that: a starting point to help frame a set of issues. I make no attempt here to provide a comprehensive analysis of the Chicago School. There have been a number of these, arguably beginning with Albion Small's 1916 history of sociology in the *American Journal of Sociology* and going through Andy Abbott's recent hundred-year retrospective (Abbott 1999; Small 1916; cf. Bulmer 1984; Deegan 1988; Faris 1967; Hawthorn 1976). There have also been a number of critiques (some of which I will draw on below), as well as at least one recent effort to rethink Chicago School scholarship with reference to contemporary criminology and the study of gangs in today's globalized context (Hagedorn 2007).[3] For current purposes, I draw selectively on this work as a kind of foundation for examining the three issues that are the topic of this chapter and that play out in different ways in subsequent chapters.

Community

Notions of community and investigations into urban dynamics and neighborhood life were an important component of early Chicago School endeavors. Several aspects of this work are relevant here, including an orientation to community as a tool and venue for knowledge development and social intervention, a theoretical framework describing urban growth and neighborhood formation, and an ongoing concern with the dynamics of neighborhood-level processes and interactions.

In the late nineteenth and early twentieth centuries, both sociology and social work in the United States were developing (as bodies of theory and practice and as professions) in the context of rapid societal change brought about by accelerating industrialization, urbanization, and demographic diversification resulting from high levels of immigration and increasing population mobility. The city of Chicago was emblematic of these changes—a dynamic, rapidly industrializing, rapidly growing city (it doubled in size between 1880 and 1900, doubled again in the next decade, and continued to grow by nearly 25 percent per decade through 1930). Scholars and social reformers working in Chicago had ready access to these dynamics as they played out on the ground, and they looked upon the city and its component neighborhoods as a kind of "laboratory or clinic" (Park 1925:46)—a venue for both observation and intervention, data collection, and practice informed by research and a scientific orientation to social problems.[4]

The basic research orientation that drove these investigations was a social survey approach to empirical investigation that relied heavily on fieldwork, mapping, and broadly ethnographic approaches, as well as the use of social statistics to describe, classify, and analyze the characteristics of neighborhoods, populations, and interactions among groups. These investigations included community-focused explorations—attempts to understand the particularities of place and the circumstances under which people lived there—and those concerned with particular social groups and social problems as they existed across neighborhoods.[5] The work was fundamentally empirical, seeking to gather and organize social facts to build our understanding of particular social phenomena and inform potential responses to social problems. It was also fundamentally oriented toward context—toward understanding social facts as they are situated in time and space and as they operate through processes of relationships and interaction (Abbott 1999).

This orientation clearly informed the work on urban growth and community dynamics that was a core focus of the early Chicago School, organized largely within the theoretical framework of urban ecology. Within this framework, patterns of urban growth and the differentiation of neighborhoods were seen as the outcome of organic processes of selection and competition for scarce resources, and of invasion and succession by different groups over time. Industrial development created functionally differentiated sub-areas of the city, social processes of cultural attraction and identity (as well as proximity to work and economic factors such as the price of rent) informed residential settlement, and the development and reproduction of locally based sentiments and symbols promoted community cohesion (Burgess 1925; Firey 1982 [1945]; McKenzie 1925; Park 1925, 1936; Zorbaugh 1929). These processes were seen to lead, in part, to a set of discrete residential neighborhoods (or "natural areas")—a "mosaic of little social worlds which touch but do not interpenetrate," in Robert Park's (1925) famous phrase. Neighborhoods emerged in this way within a broader pattern of urban growth that created, in part, areas of poverty within a "zone of transition" that occupied the space between central-city and industrial areas and more-stable residential neighborhoods farther from the center (Burgess 1925).

These transitional neighborhoods were the sites of high levels of mobility and change and, as a consequence, were characterized by high levels of social disorganization. They were also the neighborhoods in which crime, delinquency, and gang formation were most prevalent—seen as a "natural" outcome of urban dynamics described by the ecological framework. Reflecting this orientation, Frederic M. Thrasher, in his major (1927) study of gangs in Chicago, states:

> In nature foreign matter tends to collect and cake in every crack, crevice, and cranny—interstices. There are also fissures and breaks in the structure of social organization. The gang may be regarded as an interstitial element in the framework of society, and gangland as an interstitial region in the layout of the city. (1963 [1927]:21)

The communities that constitute these "interstitial regions" provide the local context—the physical environment, the nature of opportunity, the quality of schools and other institutions, the nature of interpersonal relationships, the degree of access to resources—to which young people respond in forming and joining gangs. In Thrasher's view, for example, gang formation is a response to the failure of society (instantiated in local contexts) to provide appropriate opportunity and diversion for young people. In its absence, he suggests, the gang provides both: "It fills a gap and affords an escape" (1963 [1927]:33). For Shaw and McKay, crime and delinquency in these areas are responses to the disjunction between the goals promoted by society and the opportunity to achieve them available to the residents (especially young people) of disadvantaged communities, as well as conflicting value orientations and weakened institutional sources of socialization and social control (e.g., through local organizations and associations) within them. Again, delinquency is an alternative, offering "the promise of economic gain, prestige, and companionship" based on the structure of opportunity and patterns of behavior available to young people in their immediate social world (1942:436).

Both of these analyses were grounded in an essentially urban ecological framework, which remains influential for understanding urban dynamics and community functioning today, although subsequent scholarship has both refined and challenged some of its basic claims. Two issues in particular are worth highlighting here. One concerns a fundamental challenge to the assumptions regarding the nature of "organic" change that drives urban processes, highlighting instead the critical roles played by particular forms of agency, conflict, and the dynamics of investment as promoted by both capital and policy actors (Castells 1977; Gottdiener and Feagin 1988; Harvey 1973; Molotch 1976; Suttles 1990; Zukin 1980). Cities develop, and neighborhood circumstances are created, in large part because of the decisions made and actions taken by powerful actors—government, developers, corporations, philanthropies—who choose to invest, disinvest, act, or fail to act in any of a range of ways that have major impacts on the ground and that "contribute powerfully to organizing the social space of the ghetto in particular and particularly destabilizing ways" (Wacquant 2007:41). Another focuses on the social organization and dynamics of interaction *within* neighborhoods and their relationship to larger units, including the social construction of space and the ways in which individuals and groups define and negotiate their way through it. Gerald Suttles, for example (working very much in the early Chicago School mode of investigation), describes the ways in which slum neighborhoods are characterized by "ordered segmentation" among component groups defined by space, race, ethnicity, sex, and age that are either reflected in or thrown into opposition by local institutions (such as churches, schools, commercial establishments, recreational facilities, and voluntary organizations). In these contexts (and in contrast to Park's metaphor of a mosaic), the activities of each group within the neighborhood are shaped very much in response to the presence and patterns of activity of other component groups (Suttles 1968).

The first critique is important for our current concerns because, in focusing on issues of agency, it provides alternative "causal stories" (Stone 1989) regarding the emergence of disadvantaged neighborhoods and the concomitant social problems that emerge within them (gangs included) and points the way toward identifying potential policy targets for fostering change. The second clarifies the extent to which "disorganized" neighborhoods and groups within them (gangs included) are in fact organized in different ways (Shaw and McKay 1942; Wacquant 2007; Whyte 1943) and provides insight into the mechanisms and processes through which neighborhood dynamics are shaped, as well as the ways in which neighborhoods can "act" in response to issues such as crime and delinquency.

Of course, the *nature* of social organization matters. For example, neighborhoods rich in local acquaintanceship ties and with high levels of organizational participation tend toward lower crime rates (Sampson and Groves 1989), and those with high levels of "collective efficacy"—the combination of social cohesion, trust, and a willingness on the part of neighbors to intervene—are associated with lower levels of neighborhood violence, partially mediating the effects of neighborhood social composition (e.g., poverty, race and ethnicity, residential stability) on violence (Sampson, Raudenbush, and Earls 1997). Further, the two points are connected, because the ways in which neighborhoods are organized are influenced in part by the broader political economy of place in which they exist: "Neighborhood variations in informal social control and institutional vitality are . . . systematically linked to patterns of resource deprivation and racial segregation, especially the concentration of poverty, joblessness, and family disruption" (Sampson 1999:258). In these ways, although some of the key arguments of the Chicago School remain influential and instructive—for example, the critical importance of space and the relationship among social structure, community process, and social problems—others require revisiting.

Community as a Context for Youth Intervention

The focus on community organization and dynamics propounded by Chicago School researchers has provided a foundation for considering social-intervention responses to social problems concentrated within and, if not *generated* by, particular communities, influenced by the circumstances under which they find themselves operating. Thus the appropriate response to the problem of delinquency and gang formation should look beyond the individual and issues of individual behavior to take account of and address aspects of community resources and community organization that influence such behavior. It should be, in Irving Spergel's words, fundamentally about "how to organize an effective community set or structure of interrelated institutional arrangements that provide social support, control, and especially opportunity for vulnerable gang youths to achieve meaningful social status" (1995:170).

For Thrasher, this meant providing opportunities—activities, groups, and organizations catering to young people's "leisure-time interests as well as all other normal needs"—through the creation of a "comprehensive, systematic, and integrated social program for . . . *all* children in the delinquency area" (1963 [1927]:363, emphasis in the original). It also meant concentrating responsibility for crime prevention in local organizations and agencies working in collaboration (for example, through a local council of social agencies), informed by ongoing data collection on the children in the area and the social problems and influences that affected them. Thus the problem of community organization was largely to be solved through rational planning, organizational provision, and collaborative arrangements among locally sited organizations, agencies, and institutions— schools, police, the juvenile court, social service agencies, youth clubs, and recreational organizations.

For Shaw and McKay, the principal lever for change lay in a process of community organization and self-help spearheaded by *residents* of local communities who, through their own planning activities and the cooperative arrangements they reached with local organizations (churches, schools, clubs), provided a broad set of activities focused on recreation, community improvement (such as through neighborhood cleanups), employment, and mediation. Professionals and social agencies had an important role to play, but in partnership with and in response to the leadership provided by local residents.[6] Similarly, the activities promoted through the planning process and implemented through local organizations, although important, were secondary to the broader process of community organization and capacity building to address crime and delinquency:

> While it [the local community committee] supervised programmatic details and advised on treatment of individual youths, its chief role and goal was to upbuild a new sense of potency among law-abiding residents to transform their neighborhood so it would no longer tolerate conditions that fostered juvenile crime. (Schlossman and Sedlak 1983:419)

At the heart of this approach is an emphasis on indigenous action and informal mechanisms of social control and support akin to (though not framed in quite this way by Shaw and McKay) the idea of collective efficacy: to develop cohesive relationships among neighbors who share a sense of common circumstance, sufficient levels of trust, intergenerational networks, and willingness to intervene.

These ideas were put into play and tested (though never formally evaluated) through Shaw's creation of the Chicago Area Project (CAP), initially set up in three communities in Chicago in the 1930s. In addition to the creation of community committees in each of these areas, CAP made important use of community workers (or "street" workers)—wherever possible recruited and hired from the local neighborhood—who engaged in ongoing, informal, supportive interactions with neighborhood youth, providing advice ("curbstone counseling"), connecting them with opportunities for structured leisure activities and employment, and mediating on their behalf with schools, social agencies, police, and probation officers (Schlossman and Sedlak 1983).[7] At the heart of all this work was an approach to community processes—iterative, relational, responsive—that began with nurturing and shaping informal relations and developed over time through a slow process of hanging out, reaching out, engaging in community discussions, and teasing out community connections (Kobrin 1959; Schlossman and Sedlak 1983). Programmatically, the lion's share of activities that were supported concentrated on recreation—and this has clear limitations—but within this framework concerted efforts were made to connect with the young people most deeply involved with street gangs and engaging in criminal behavior, and to work with them to consider alternatives, provide advice and mediation, and connect them to employment opportunities where possible.

Common to both of these approaches is a focus on internal community dynamics and provision, an emphasis (although somewhat differently defined)[8] on participation and interorganizational collaboration, and an effort to provide opportunities for young people that offer a positive alternative to antisocial behavior and gang affiliation. The stress was on prevention and positive social intervention in the context of community circumstances rather than on individual intervention and a predominant focus on suppression and punishment, which has characterized much of the policy response since the end of the 1960s (Spergel and Grossman 1997; Venkatesh 1999).

It is important to note that significant changes have taken place in communities and in the structure and operation of gang activities since these early studies were conducted and since the early years of CAP activities.[9] Economic opportunity has fundamentally changed in many cities, manifesting in the North and Midwest in particular in a shift from a predominantly manufacturing economy to a service one, bifurcated into low- and high-wage sectors (Jargowsky 1997; Wilson 1987). Urban development schemes and processes—the clearance and reconstruction of slums under urban renewal in the 1950s; the emergence of high-density, highly segregated public housing projects in the 1960s; their demolition and redevelopment today under schemes such as Chicago's "Plan for Transformation" and supported by federal programs like HOPE VI; processes of resettling, redevelopment, and gentrification of selected urban neighborhoods—have generated significant displacement, relocation, and reshaping of neighborhood populations and contexts and the nature and degree of investment in them. And gangs themselves have changed, from the very local, street-corner organizations, described by Thrasher, Whyte, and others, that engaged largely in small-scale delinquency to include now a variety of "types" of gangs that vary by size, membership attributes, structure, and function (Klein and Maxson 2006). In some cases, newer gangs have developed institutionalized structures engaging in a broad range of roles and activities, and may include local groups affiliated with larger gang organizations. Such groups may in combination claim turf in multiple neighborhoods and organize into broader alliances ("supergang" federations or "nations") that support citywide activities and may be more fundamentally oriented toward income generation through criminal activity and protecting their investments through increasingly violent means (Hagedorn 2007; Spergel 1995; Venkatesh 1999). Although gangs organized primarily around drug trafficking are a relatively small proportion of street gangs active today (Klein and Maxson 2006), and although the potential economic benefits of membership in such gangs are significant only for leaders ("foot soldiers" generally earn below minimum wage for their work on the street), such benefits may still be enticing, and for those who attain leadership, remuneration from gang-related criminal activities can far outstrip their likely earnings in the mainstream economy, given their level of education and degree of experience in the workforce (Levitt and Venkatesh 2000).

In the context of these changes, more recent approaches to community-based gang intervention—the Comprehensive Community-Wide Gang Program Model demonstration project (or the Spergel Model) implemented under funding from the Office of Juvenile Justice and Delinquency Prevention (OJJDP) notable among them—combine the community mobilization, resident participation, interorganizational collaboration, and social-intervention strategies that characterized efforts such as the early Chicago Area Project work with suppression and supervision strategies in close collaboration with police and the criminal justice system, and with vigorous efforts to provide opportunities well beyond recreation, especially remedial and enriched educational programs and job training and placement schemes (Spergel 1995, 2007; Spergel and Grossman 1997).

The basic themes of participation, collaboration, and comprehensive planning have been common to community-based efforts of various stripes for decades (Halpern 1995; O'Connor 1999), and there are, of course, enduring challenges to this kind of an approach, reflected in efforts targeting a broad range of social problems, from crime to poverty to child abuse. These include basic implementation issues regarding resident participation and interorganizational collaboration. They also include more fundamental issues about the possibilities and limitations of community-based intervention in light of the broader forces and influences that shape community circumstances and the community's capacity to manage and foster change.

Regarding the former, calls for resident participation are often broadly constructed and may entail a range of different roles, from providing general advice to being part of a resident mobilization campaign to participating as decision-making members of a community governance body to working as program staff. These roles are not equivalent, requiring different capacities and involving different expectations both for and from residents who participate. In addition, participation schemes often become complicated by issues concerning representation, equity, and conflicting interests (Briggs 1998; Chaskin 2005; Day 1997). Who participates, on whose presumed behalf, and with what interests at stake can be contentious. Neighborhoods are, after all, not monolithic, and arguably, as Bursik and Grasmick point out, "those communities most in need of effective crime control programs often are those characterized by a very segmented set of networks that may be difficult to unite in a collective effort" (1993:176–177). In the current context, for example, the inclusion and particular role of gang members in community-based crime prevention efforts can engender significant friction, and the different orientations and prior experiences of, for example, former gang members working as community youth workers and police officers can complicate collaboration among individual participants "at opposite ends of the ideology pole" (Spergel and Grossman 1997:461).

Similar dynamics are in play with regard to crafting collaborative relationships among organizations. Different organizations can contribute different capacities, connections, resources, and substantive expertise that can be brought to bear on community action, and the combination of these contributions provides an opportunity for impact beyond the capacity of any single organization. At the same time, there is invariably an unequal distribution of resources, influence, and power across different organizations within any given community, as well as a history of relationships among them that may have very different valences, from positive prior interactions to limited cooperation to benign avoidance to outright conflict and mistrust (Chaskin 2003b). In the context of working with young people in poor communities, for example, organizations best placed to work with at-risk youth are often what Sudhir Venkatesh describes as "third-tier" or "lower-tier" organizations—grassroots groups with modest resources that operate flexibly and through relatively intimate connections with troubled youth in their communities—but whose ability to maintain operations is often hindered by lack of funding and weak connections with both larger provider organizations and political actors (Venkatesh 1997, 1999).

Regarding the second set of issues, communities exist within and are significantly influenced by the broader systems, processes, and dynamics—social, political, economic, demographic, and cultural—of which they are a part. Community-based efforts to address social problems such as crime and delinquency (or poverty, child abuse, social exclusion, and so forth) are often framed in ways that recognize this influence but may have difficulty responding to macro-level issues that have a bearing on the problem to be addressed locally. Shaw and McKay, for example, suggest that a community-based approach to delinquency is critical, although they recognize that "delinquency-producing communities themselves may be products of more general processes" (1942:443) and, indeed, that without addressing the fundamental economic and social conditions of the neighborhoods in which delinquency is prevalent (much of which is generated exogenously), little significant change should be expected. Recognition of the limitations of CAP's approach to community organization in light of broader dynamics of power, politics, and economy led Saul Alinsky, a street worker in one of the CAP neighborhoods, to leave and work to develop community organizations elsewhere in Chicago that operated through the kind of conflict-oriented political organizing strategies for which he later became famous (Schlossman and Sedlak 1983). Similarly, recognizing the limitations of promoting employment opportunities through local resources alone, Mobilization for Youth, a delinquency-prevention program in New York City informed by the theory of differential opportunity developed by Columbia's Richard Cloward and Lloyd Ohlin (1960)—and designed and implemented with their involvement—soon moved from an exclusive focus on neighborhood-based activities much like those promoted by CAP in Chicago to include mobilizing community actions and demanding change from external actors such as city government, schools, and landlords and focusing more fundamentally on issues of poverty in the neighborhoods targeted for delinquency prevention (Bursik and Grasmick 1993; Helfgot 1981; Moynihan 1969). Community action thus needs to be seen as part of a larger agenda for change that potentially incorporates multilevel alliances and focuses on both local action and broader policy issues, such as national policy targeting education, employment, and income distribution (Ferguson and Stoutland 1999; Spergel 1995).

Research, Intervention, and Knowledge Utilization

The third issue I want to address briefly concerns the role of research in informing policy and social intervention. Just as community and "methods of treatment and prevention" are noted in the quote from Rodney Brandon with which we began, the importance of research in informing and guiding intervention ("These facts indicate . . .") is also clear. Indeed, although Chicago School sociologists from Park on were concerned with establishing sociology as a scientific discipline separate and distinct from reform agendas and advocacy activities (Abbott 1999), belief in the relevance of such inquiry to understanding and responding to social problems was foundational. Thus, for example, Thrasher states: "No adequate program can be formulated or carried on without definite knowledge of facts regarding the children of the area and their problems and the social influences which play upon them" (1963 [1927]:365–366), and Shaw and McKay attempt, through the Chicago Area Project, to create an evidence-based intervention that can provide a model for policy and practice concerned with delinquency prevention. This work has been influential for both subsequent scholarship and approaches to intervention, though the mechanisms through which its influence operated in the broader policy and practice realms are not entirely clear, and there has been no systematic evaluation conducted to demonstrate the effectiveness of the interventions on particular outcomes. With some notable exceptions, as of today the evidence base regarding "what works" in gang intervention more broadly remains fairly weak, and investment in the evaluation and application of research findings to such interventions remains relatively low.

There are a number of challenges to addressing these issues, both in knowledge generation and in knowledge utilization. On the first front, efforts to generate knowledge about effective interventions through evaluation research must confront the complexities of design, measurement, and method inherent in attempting to understand interventions targeting complex, variable, and highly dynamic social phenomena such as gangs. These are further complicated within the context of comprehensive community interventions, for a number of reasons (Chaskin 2002; Kubisch et al. 1995; Rossi 1999). First, such interventions are often highly process-oriented and context-specific. Program models are adapted to different local circumstances, and particular activities and program components evolve through local planning processes, complicating the likelihood of program fidelity across communities and compromising the generalizability of findings. Second, they are highly complex, often working simultaneously across sectors (social, economic, physical) and levels (individual, organizational, community). Such complexity incorporates both multiple points of intervention and a range of outcome goals—some short-term, interim goals; others more distal, ultimate goals—connected to one another by sometimes fairly implicit theories of change. Further, different goals may have more salience for some actors than for others. For which goals do such efforts seek to be held accountable (reducing gang violence, preventing gang involvement, increasing employment, building social capital) and at what levels (individual, organizational, community)? Third, these interventions play out in the context of "open" systems—communities—that are subject to numerous and changing influences that are exogenous to the intervention in question, complicating efforts to attribute causality. Finally, the participation of multiple stakeholders in community interventions can complicate evaluation implementation if there are strong disagreements about the intent, value, or approach to evaluation, or other sources of resistance to stakeholder cooperation and support (Chaskin 2003a; Rossi 1999).

Beyond the challenges of developing knowledge about "what works," there are challenges relating to strategies for knowledge dissemination and utilization that can bridge research and intervention, bringing such knowledge as is developed to bear on policy decisions and front-line practice (Chaskin 2008). The application of research knowledge to policy and practice is neither simple nor linear; as Carol Weiss noted some two decades ago: "Research is not used as a can opener is used" (cited in Huberman 1987). It finds its way into policymaking and practice in various and diffuse ways and often informs decision making, when it does so at all, indirectly and sometimes unintentionally (Weiss 1980). Its use is mediated by a number of factors, including the availability and quality of data and the nature of evidence; the playing out of relationships through multiple interactions and strategic alliances among researchers, policy actors, practitioners, and advocates; the range of different roles and tools that researchers and users may engage; and the influence of context, including the time when and the policy climate in which research questions and findings are brought to the fore. In the context of community interventions, the stakeholders involved—both producers and potential users of knowledge—are often numerous and diverse, operating at different levels (e.g., from the federal program officer overseeing a demonstration grant to a community youth worker engaged in front-line practice), with different priorities and interests, from different bases of understanding, and under different pressures and sources of constraint. Fostering the utilization of research findings by actors within this broad range of stakeholders requires understanding their needs and interests, providing information that is relevant and accessible, tailoring dissemination to the particular requirements of different stakeholders (perhaps requiring multiple products and communication at multiple points in time), and interacting in ways that allow for the concrete engagement of stakeholders (Hutchinson and Huberman 1993).

These challenges regarding knowledge development and utilization, along with refining strategies and programmatic approaches to effectively addressing the youth gang problem in the context of the communities in which it exists, are the subjects of the chapters that follow. Taken together, they provide a picture of contemporary policy and practice regarding youth gang interventions, synthesize what we know about their effectiveness, and point toward future, more effective, evidence-based practice.

Notes

1. There are, of course, several "Chicago Schools" with wide recognition, including the Chicago Schools of sociology, economics, and critical pragmatism.

2. Indeed, as Ruth Kornhauser claims, "Except for strain models, delinquency theory originated at the University of Chicago and was part of the output of the 'Chicago School'" (Kornhauser 1978:21).

3. In his recent volume (published after this chapter was written) that explores the phenomenon of gangs from a global perspective, John Hagedorn (2007) also revisits the Chicago School with an eye toward rethinking how we understand

gangs in contemporary society. Some of the same themes that I will touch on regarding the limitations of urban ecology, as well as the elements that remain relevant, are examined in his opening chapter (and, more critically, in a subsequent chapter by Loïc Wacquant). In chapter 1, Hagedorn seeks to revisit and revise Chicago School orientations to inform our current understanding of gangs in light of the circumstances presented by today's globalized cities, including the need to take into account the impact of globalization on economic opportunity and informal economic activity; the need to understand gangs as institutionalized structures (and the role of institutions—prisons among them—in their genesis), not merely as "interstitial" adaptations; and the need to explicitly acknowledge the dynamics of race and racism. Here, I use Chicago School scholarship, and the kinds of youth gang interventions it has informed, as a foundation for considering contemporary community-based policy and practice with reference to youth gangs in the United States.

4. The relative focus on empirical investigation for purposes of description, classification, and analysis versus direct application differed among those associated with the Chicago School of sociology and those engaged more directly in reform, including those whose work gave rise to social work—what might to a large extent be characterized as the men and women, respectively, of the Chicago School (Deegan 1988). Still, although Chicago School sociologists certainly focused on establishing the scientific foundations of sociological inquiry as objective and distinct from reform agendas and advocacy activities, "reform was consciously close to the surface" (Short 1963:xviii) for most of them, as it clearly was for social workers engaged in empirical research. It is in this light that Deegan (1988) makes the case that the research activities of early social workers and social reformers should be understood as applied sociology, and that it was seminal to—and undervalued by—a sociological profession increasingly focused on establishing its scientific legitimacy. Still, as Abbott points out, the "general relationship between the Chicago School and the social reformers is a larger historical question that has only begun to be explored" (Abbott 1999:14).

5. Examples of the latter include Nels Anderson's (1923) study of the homeless "hobo," Thrasher's (1927) study of gangs, and E. Franklin Frazier's (1932) study of the Negro family. Examples of the former include the kinds of community mapping research conducted by settlement workers associated with Hull House to provide demographic and social needs assessment information that could inform both service provision and advocacy activities (Addams 1895), as well as the kinds of in-depth community studies conducted by sociologists, such as Harvey Zorbaugh's (1929) *The Gold Coast and the Slum* and William F. Whyte's (1943) *Street Corner Society*. This empirical approach was not new; it built on work of earlier

investigators such as Henry Mayhew (1968 [1861]) and Charles Booth (1902) in England, both of whom sought to comprehensively document patterns of poverty and other social ills as they played out geographically and to describe their attributes systematically. Booth's maps of London poverty (initially published in 1889) are quite similar in intent to those produced in *Hull House Maps and Papers* (Addams 1895) and to the mapping of delinquency areas produced by Shaw and McKay (who cite them both). In spite of the similarities, however, the analytic outcomes are quite different. Mayhew and Booth, while acknowledging environmental factors as negative influences fostering a range of antisocial behaviors, characterize the people living in these neighborhoods largely in terms of inherent traits, focusing on the moral degradation of essentially criminal "classes," the conceptualization of which seems nearly racialized. This contrasts significantly with the largely descriptive and inductive approach that Thrasher (1963 [1927]) takes in exploring and categorizing the social dynamics, incentives, and experiences of gang life, or the combined structural and cultural explanations that Shaw and McKay (1942) derive from their analysis.

6. One of the principal limitations of such agencies, in Shaw and McKay's view, has to do with their "outsider" status. Given that such agencies—from settlements to boys' clubs to YMCAs to social service agencies—are funded, governed, and staffed largely from outside the neighborhood, they remain disconnected from neighborhood priorities and definitions of need in fundamental ways. Indeed, "the very fact that these nonindigenous private agencies long have been concentrated in delinquency areas without modifying appreciably the marked disproportion of delinquents concentrated there suggests a limited effectiveness in deterring boys from delinquency and crime" (1942:179).

7. See Spergel (1969) for an extended discussion of the role of the community worker in community problem solving.

8. These approaches could be seen as examples of a social planning approach (Thrasher) versus a locality development approach (Shaw), in Rothman's (1995 [1968]) terms. Saul Alinsky, a street worker in one of the first CAP communities, pushed for a social action approach—Rothman's third "mode" of community intervention—as necessary to get to the root of the problem (Schlossman and Sedlak 1983), and he ultimately left CAP to focus on this approach in other neighborhoods, around other issues (cf. Bursik and Grasmick 1993).

9. CAP, which celebrated its seventy-fifth anniversary in 2009, continues to operate in Chicago and has grown significantly since its inception, operating through more than forty affiliate organizations in different neighborhoods and supporting programs focused on community organizing, community service, educational enrichment, juvenile justice diversion, and other issues (www.chicagoareaproject.org).

References

Abbott, A. 1999. *Department and Discipline: Chicago Sociology at One Hundred*. Chicago: University of Chicago Press.

Addams, J. 1895. *Hull House Maps and Papers*. New York: Thomas Y. Crowell.

Anderson, N. 1923. *The Hobo*. Chicago: University of Chicago Press.

Booth, C. 1902. *Life and Labour of the People in London*. Vol. 1. London: Macmillan.

Briggs, X. 1998. "Doing Democracy Up Close: Culture, Power, and Communication in Community Planning." *Journal of Planning Education and Research* 18:1–13.

Bulmer, M. 1984. *The Chicago School of Sociology: Institutionalization, Diversity, and the Rise of Sociological Research*. Chicago: University of Chicago Press.

Burgess, E. W. 1925. "The Growth of the City." In R. E. Park, E. W. Burgess, and R. D. McKenzie, eds., *The City*, 47–62. Chicago: University of Chicago Press.

Bursik, R. J. and H. G. Grasmick 1993. *Neighborhoods and Crime: The Dimensions of Effective Community Control*. New York: Lexington Books.

Castells, M. 1977. *The Urban Question*. Cambridge, Mass.: MIT Press.

Chaskin, R. J. 2002. "The Evaluation of 'Community Building': Measuring the Social Effects of Community-Based Practice." In A. Maluccio, T. Vechiato, and C. Canali, eds., *Assessing Outcomes in Child and Family Services: Comparative Design and Policy Issues*, 28–47. New York: Aldine de Gruyter.

——. 2003a. "The Challenge of Two-Tiered Evaluation in Community Initiatives." *Journal of Community Practice* 11 (1): 61–83.

——. 2003b. "Fostering Neighborhood Democracy: Legitimacy and Accountability Within Loosely Coupled Systems." *Nonprofit and Voluntary Sector Quarterly* 32 (2): 161–189.

——. 2005. "Democracy and Bureaucracy in a Community Planning Process." *Journal of Planning Education and Research* 24 (4): 408–419.

——. 2008. "Research, Dissemination, and Impact: Issues, Lessons, and Future Directions." In R. J. Chaskin and J. M. Rosenfeld, eds., *Research for Action: Cross-National Perspectives on Connecting Knowledge, Policy, and Practice for Children*, 131–157. New York: Oxford University Press.

Cloward, R. and L. Ohlin. 1960. *Delinquency and Opportunity: Theory of Delinquent Gangs*. New York: Free Press.

Day, D. 1997. "Citizen Participation in the Planning Process: An Essentially Contested Concept." *Journal of Planning Literature* 11 (3): 421.

Deegan, M. J. 1988. *Jane Addams and the Men of the Chicago School*. New Brunswick, N.J.: Transaction Publishers.

Faris, R. E. L. 1967. *Chicago Sociology, 1920–1932*. San Francisco: Chandler.

Ferguson, R. F. and S. E. Stoutland. 1999. "Reconceiving the Community Development System." In R. F. Ferguson and W. T. Dickens, eds., *Urban Problems and Community Development*, 33–76. Washington, D.C.: Brookings.

Firey, W. 1982 [1945]. "Sentiment and Symbolism as Ecological Variables." In G. A. Theodorson, ed., *Urban Patterns: Studies in Human Ecology*, 129–136. University Park: Pennsylvania State University Press.

Frazier, E. F. 1939. *The Negro Family in the United States*. Chicago: University of Chicago Press.

Gottdiener, M. and J. Feagin. 1988. "The Paradigm Shift in Urban Sociology." *Urban Affairs Quarterly* 24 (2): 163–187.

Hagedorn, J. M. 2007. "Gangs, Institutions, Race, and Space: The Chicago School Revisited." In J. M. Hagedorn, ed., *Gangs in the Global City: Alternatives to Traditional Criminology*, 14–33. Urbana and Chicago: University of Illinois Press.

Halpern, R. 1995. *Rebuilding the Inner City: A History of Neighborhood Initiatives to Address Poverty in the United States*. New York: Columbia University Press.

Harvey, D. 1973. *Social Justice and the City*. Baltimore: Johns Hopkins University Press.

Hawthorn, G. 1976. *Enlightenment and Despair: A History of Sociology*. Cambridge, England: Cambridge University Press.

Helfgot, J. H. 1981. *Professional Reforming: Mobilization for Youth and the Failure of Social Science*. Lexington, Mass.: Lexington Books.

Huberman, M. 1987. "Steps Toward an Integrated Model of Research Utilization." *Knowledge: Creation, Diffusion, Utilization* 8 (4): 586–611.

Hutchinson, J. and M. Huberman. 1993. *Knowledge, Dissemination, and Use in Science and Mathematics Education: A Literature Review*. Washington, D.C.: National Science Foundation.

Jargowsky, P. A. 1997. *Poverty and Place: Ghettos, Barrios, and the American City*. New York: Russell Sage Foundation.

Klein, Malcolm W. and Cheryl L. Maxson. 2006. *Street Gang Patterns and Policies*. New York: Oxford University Press.

Kobrin, S. 1959. "The Chicago Area Project—A 25-Year Assessment." *Annals of the American Academy of Political and Social Science* 322:19–29.

Kornhauser, R. R. 1978. *Social Sources of Delinquency*. Chicago: University of Chicago Press.

Kubisch, A. C., C. H. Weiss, L. B. Schorr, and J. P. Connell. 1995. Introduction to J. P. Connell, A. C. Kubisch, L. B. Schorr, and C. H. Weiss, eds., *New Approaches to Evaluating Community Initiatives*, 1–24. Washington, D.C.: Aspen Institute.

Levitt, S. D. and S. A. Venkatesh. 2000. "An Economic Analysis of a Drug-Selling Gang's Finances." *Quarterly Journal of Economics* 115 (3): 755–789.

Mayhew, H. 1968 [1861]. *London Labor and the London Poor*. London: Dover.

McKenzie, R. D. 1925. "The Ecological Approach to the Study of the Human Community." In R. E. Park, E. W. Burgess, and R. D. McKenzie, eds., *The City*, 63–80. Chicago: University of Chicago Press.

Molotch, H. 1976. "The City as a Growth Machine." *American Journal of Sociology* 82 (2): 309–332.

Moynihan, D. P. 1969. *Maximum Feasible Misunderstanding: Community Action in the War on Poverty*. New York: Free Press.

O'Connor, A. 1999. "Swimming Against the Tide: A Brief History of Federal Policy in Poor Communities." In R. F. Ferguson and W. T. Dickens, *Urban Problems and Community Development*, 77–138. Washington, D.C.: Brookings Institution Press.

Park, R. E. 1925. "The City: Suggestions for the Investigation of Human Behavior in the Urban Environment." In R. E. Park, E. W. Burgess, and R. D. McKenzie, eds,. *The City*, 1–46. Chicago: University of Chicago Press.

——. 1982 [1936]. "Human Ecology." In G. A. Theodorson, ed., *Urban Patterns: Studies in Human Ecology*, 20–27. University Park: Pennsylvania State University Press.

Rossi, P. H. 1999. "Evaluating Community Development Programs." In R. F. Ferguson and W. T. Dickens, eds., *Urban Problems and Community Development*, 521–567. Washington, D.C.: Brookings Institution Press.

Rothman, J. 1995. "Approaches to Community Intervention." In J. Rothman, J. L. Erlich, and J. E. Tropman, eds., *Strategies of Community Intervention*, 26–63. Itasca, Ill.: Peacock Publishers.

Sampson, R. J. 1999. "What 'Community' Supplies." In R. F. Ferguson and W. T. Dickens, eds., *Urban Problems and Community Development*, 241–292. Washington, D.C.: Brookings Institution Press.

Sampson, R. J. and W. B. Groves. 1989. "Community Structure and Crime: Testing Social-Disorganization Theory." *American Journal of Sociology* 94:774–802.

Sampson, R. J., D. Raudenbush, and F. Earls. 1997. "Neighborhoods and Violent Crime: A Multilevel Study of Collective Efficacy." *Science* 277:918–924.

Schlossman, S. and M. Sedlak. 1983. "The Chicago Area Project Revisited." *Crime and Delinquency* 29 (3): 398–462.

Shaw, C. R. and H. D. McKay. 1942. *Delinquency and Urban Areas*. Chicago: University of Chicago Press.

Short, J. F., Jr. 1963. Introduction to the abridged edition of F. M. Thrasher, *The Gang*, xv–liii. Chicago: University of Chicago Press.

Small, A. 1916. "Fifty Years of Sociology in the United States (1865–1915)." *American Journal of Sociology* 21 (6): 721–864.

Spergel, I. A. 1969. *Community Problem Solving: The Delinquency Example*. Chicago: University of Chicago Press.

——. 1995. *The Youth Gang Problem: A Community Approach*. New York: Oxford University Press.

——. 2007. *Reducing Gang Violence: The Little Village Gang Project in Chicago*. Lanham, Md.: AltaMira Press.

Spergel, I. A. and S. F. Grossman. 1997. "The Little Village Project: A Community Approach to the Gang Problem." *Social Work* 42 (5): 456–470.

Stone, D. 1989. "Causal Stories and the Formation of Policy Agendas." *Political Science Quarterly* 104 (2): 281–300.

Suttles, G. 1968. *The Social Order of the Slum: Ethnicity and Territory in the Inner City*. Chicago: University of Chicago Press.

——. 1990. *The Man-Made City*. Chicago: University of Chicago Press.

Thrasher, F. M. 1963 [1927]. *The Gang*. Chicago: University of Chicago Press.

Venkatesh, S. A. 1997. "The Three-Tier Model: How Helping Occurs in Poor Communities." *Social Service Review* 71 (4): 574–606.

——. 1999. "Community-Based Interventions Into Street Gang Activity." *Journal of Community Psychology* 27 (5): 551–569.

Wacquant, L. J. D. 2007. "Three Pernicious Premises in the Study of the American Ghetto." In J. M. Hagedorn, ed., *Gangs in the Global City: Alternatives to Traditional Criminology*, 34–53. Urbana and Chicago: University of Illinois Press.

Weiss, C. 1980. "Knowledge Creep and Decision Accretion." *Knowledge: Creation, Diffusion, Utilization* 1 (3): 381–404.

Whyte, W. F. 1943. *Street Corner Society*. Chicago: University of Chicago Press.

Wilson, W. J. 1987. *The Truly Disadvantaged*. Chicago: University of Chicago Press.

Zorbaugh, H. W. 1929. *The Gold Coast and the Slum*. Chicago: University of Chicago Press.

Zukin, S. 1980. "A Decade of the New Urban Sociology." *Theory and Society* 9 (4): 575–601.

The Evolution of Gang Policy

Balancing Intervention and Suppression

GEORGE E. TITA AND ANDREW PAPACHRISTOS

In a 1988 nationwide survey of gang prevention, suppression, and support programs, venerable gang researcher Irving Spergel unearthed an important paradox of youth gang policy: "gang experts" such as police and criminal justice officials simultaneously cite suppression tactics as the most effective *and* the least effective strategies in addressing the gang problem (Spergel and Curry 1990; for discussion, see also Klein 2004:148). This paradox may not come as a great surprise to anyone who has worked with local law enforcement on gang issues. On the one hand, police are vocal about the dangers posed by street gangs, their criminal sophistication, and the general wanton behavior of gang members. Such sentiments can be especially potent among the line officers who spend their shifts gathering intelligence on gang members and investigating gang-related cases. On the other hand, members of the police "brass," typically when addressing community audiences, frequently proclaim that "we can't arrest our way out of this problem." Thus, while the demand for suppression-oriented gang policing is high at many levels of police organizations, at the same time they acknowledge that the "real solution" to the gang problem lies outside the purview of traditional suppression techniques. Often the solution may even be sought in community-based initiatives.

Such a sentiment is not limited to the police, of course. In our own experiences in cities throughout the United States, this paradox is expressed by members of other criminal justice agencies, social service providers, and the community residents who are most directly affected by the presence of gangs. For example, one of the authors witnessed a community meeting in Chicago in which residents called for police to rid the streets of "gang terrorists" but at the same time wanted law enforcement officials to pledge more resources to schools and job training. Similarly, Father Gregory Boyle, a well-known Jesuit priest who has dedicated his life to helping young men and women abandon the gang lifestyle in Los Angeles, strongly believes that a visible and active police presence makes his job easier (Fremon 2005). Father Boyle argues that the threat of being arrested and jailed must be sufficiently high for gang members or they will otherwise lack the incentive to visit his offices and seek to leave the gang. In other words, even though community members desire some suppressive law enforcement tactics in combating gangs, they also explicitly and implicitly believe that "softer" interventions are necessary to curb gang behavior.

Yet just because everyone "knows" that enforcement alone cannot solve the gang problem, this does not necessarily mean that major stakeholders are eager to embrace the broader community approaches, such as those espoused by Spergel and others. But *how* does a community balance suppression-based enforcement efforts with community-based strategies? To answer this question, we draw upon both the extant literature and our own experiences in an attempt to identify the impediments to implementing urban youth gang strategies that extend beyond specialized units and enhanced enforcement and prosecution. We pay particular attention to the deployment of "street worker" programs, focusing on the arguments espoused by proponents and opponents of civilian-based intervention and prevention efforts to address gang participation and violence. We then broaden our focus to include the other elements that define the more balanced approaches that employ a "carrot and stick" ideology, such as cease-fire in Boston and Los Angeles and the more general use of "problem solving" and "working groups" that underpins the Project Safe Neighborhoods model. The role played by the local community in shaping various approaches is a central theme throughout this chapter.

Street Workers and the Community

One of the earliest efforts at utilizing community resources in gang prevention is the use of neighborhood residents and organizations to conduct "street work," a form of grassroots outreach with at-risk youth. This approach entails the use of "street workers"—generally, young men from the community, sometimes gang-involved, sometimes not—whose job consists of engaging in one-on-one interactions or in small-group settings with gangs or gang-involved youth.[1] Broadly, such work encompasses conflict management, job services, ad hoc social and psychological counseling, and general social service provision and referral (such as recreation and education). Despite some geographic and historical variation, the guiding principle of this street-work approach is that any serious efforts at reducing gang behavior at the neighborhood level must consider (1) the group processes at the heart of the gang and (2) how the gang operates within its local community context. For instance, a street-level approach aimed at reducing gang shootings might rely on a worker's intimate local knowledge of gangs and ongoing disputes in order to deter retaliatory violence.

The earliest formalized incarnation of this street-work approach emerged in the 1940s and 1950s when Chicago sociologist and gang researcher Clifford Shaw helped establish the Chicago Area Project (CAP), an organization whose mission entailed reducing crime in impoverished neighborhoods (Kobrin 1959).[2] CAP stressed the structural autonomy of local communities by supporting local neighborhood social organization, where it existed, and mobilizing local residents to conduct formal and informal outreach with delinquent youth. In the CAP street-worker model, adults from the community spent their days and nights on the street trying to steer wayward youth toward nondelinquent opportunities and activities. Frequently the workers themselves were former gang members, con men, and hooligans who managed to age out of crime and turn their lives around. Spergel (2007) describes these CAP workers as some of the first "curbstone counselors," individuals with neighborhood and gang connections whose main goal was to direct youth away from gang activities. This curbstone counselor model spread throughout Chicago and other cities, including New York, El Paso, San Antonio, Seattle, San Francisco, Boston, Philadelphia, and Los Angeles, in part through the adaptation of these programs by national organizations such as the YMCA and the Boys Club (Klein 1995).

The gangs encountered by the early street workers were mainly white, ethnic youth in slum areas who came of age in a wartime industrial economy. These young men were often able to follow the work and social trajectories of other white immigrant groups—they could improve their social position and leave gang life through traditional means, such as factory employment, military service, marriage, and so on. The Great Migration, however, fundamentally changed the dynamics of the street gang and urban neighborhoods. The process of "de-industrialization" altered the organization of work in such a way that the economic ladder that permitted white urban youth to move from working-poor to working-class and middle-class status was removed (Wilson 1987, 1996). Well-paid union jobs in manufacturing were replaced with lower-paying jobs in the service sector. New gangs made up of youth from the burgeoning African American and Hispanic populations began to emerge and integrate into the social fabric of the metropolis, often forming as a means of protection against white ethnic gangs (Perkins 1987; Short and Strodtbeck 1965; Suttles 1968).

Although gang outreach efforts continued, the changing nature of the American city (and the American street gang) challenged earlier notions of what it meant to "help" the community. Spergel (2007) describes a shift in the ethos of gang-community models away from street workers as a source of indigenous social organization—a form of "community capital," as it were—and toward the professionalization of such jobs. That is, rather than hire local, ex-gang members with intimate community knowledge, outreach programs began to recruit workers from local colleges and social work programs.[3] After the Great Migration, paraprofessionals who could (in theory) serve as neutral and "detached" parties replaced the curbstone counselors of the previous generation. In a sense, rather than embrace the nuances of community social organization, the new paradigm evinced an almost judicial interpretation of a street worker: a third party removed from the community social and political structure who, therefore, would be able to provide an unbiased opinion of gang and (by extension) community problems.

The 1960s brought even more changes in gangs and gang control programs. By nearly all accounts, gang violence increased dramatically in most major cities (Klein 1995; Miller 2001). The street-worker programs of the YMCA, Boys Club, and dozens of local organizations across the country continued their gang prevention efforts based largely on the detached-worker approach. More importantly, the 1960s witnessed the scientific evaluation of several street-work programs in Los Angeles (Klein 1971), Chicago (Kobrin 1959), and Boston (Miller 1957). Evaluation results were less than favorable, however. Most evaluations found little or no changes in levels of gang involvement or behavior among those groups who received street-worker attention compared with groups who did not experience such interventions. Moreover, the evaluation of a street-worker program in California by Klein (1971) went so far as to suggest that rather than quell or diminish gang behaviors, the attention given to a gang by an outside worker could in fact have the *opposite effect*. That is, outside recognition of a gang as a legitimate social entity could in fact bolster group identity and increase delinquent behaviors of the group members.[4] After Klein's critique, street work began to wane as a community gang prevention strategy.

The riots, chaos, and civil rights struggles in the late 1960s ushered in a new "community approach" to social practices, policies, and programs aimed at controlling street gangs (Coughlin and Venkatesh 2003; Spergel 2007). The main tenet of this approach was to provide opportunities and resources for communities to "help themselves." This approach would become the rallying cry of several major federal initiatives. At the extreme, it entailed Peace Corps–style community interventions in which an outsider (frequently a white male with experience organizing communities in developing countries) would work within a "disorganized" ghetto with the explicit purpose of improving neighborhood and community mobilization infrastructures. A masterfully narrated depiction of such an approach is provided by the journalistic *A Nation of Lords: The Autobiography of the Vice Lords* (1973), in which David Dawley chronicles his efforts at working with the Conservative Vice Lords gang in Chicago. Even before Dawley's work, the Vice Lords were a rather well-organized gang that was heavily involved in community organizing and civil rights activities throughout the 1960s.[5] Dawley describes the desire of the gang to better its community, and he directed his efforts at formalizing the gang's community activities and organizational capacity. Such efforts included incorporation of the gang as a formal business venture, securing more than $30,000 in grant money, and using local and national press to intentionally change the image of the gang to that of a viable, pro-social community entity.

Although extreme at the individual level, Dawley's efforts mirrored the sentiments toward gangs of other governmental and nongovernmental organizations. Community and governmental organizations began to view street gangs as a potential source of local social organization that might be utilized to funnel federal resources and opportunities into poor urban neighborhoods. In a sense, gangs—along with churches—were some of the most obvious forms of community social organization capable of dealing directly with the growing problem of inner-city violence and poverty. In fact, new programs driven by federal poverty and work grants from the Office of Economic Opportunity, the Department of Health, Education, and Welfare, and the Department of Labor explicitly tried to incorporate gang leaders and structures into programming efforts.[6]

The most widely publicized case of such governmental financial intervention also happens to be a programmatic disaster—the Youth Manpower Demonstration of The Woodlawn Organization (TWO) (see Spergel et al. 1968). Funded with nearly $1 million by the Department of Labor, the Manpower project was specifically designed to utilize the local leadership of two gangs—the Blackstone Rangers and the Devil's Disciples—in the operation of job training and work programs in Chicago's high-crime Woodlawn neighborhood. Local gang leaders were intended to "run" the program with little or no supervision and oversight.[7] To be fair, the origins of this program were not without heated political discourse and debate that tarnished both the image of the organization and its efforts even before the program began (Spergel et al. 1968). As such, it should come as little surprise that the project ended in a highly publicized congressional investigation that uncovered fraud and embezzlement on the part of the gang leaders, who received kickbacks from subordinates and cronies in the program.[8] During the program's short existence, TWO managed to draw national attention to how *not* to work with gangs.

After the damning evaluations of gang street-work efforts and the abysmal failure of TWO's Manpower project, street-work programs and community strategies that dealt with gang structures quickly fell out of favor. At roughly the same time, new "get tough" policing strategies began to gain popularity and ushered in a new criminal-justice approach to gangs, gang research, and gang policy (Coughlin and Venkatesh 2003). The best evidence of this new attitude toward suppression is the birth of the specialized police gang unit in the late 1960s, an organizational practice that spread throughout police agencies in the 1980s and 1990s. Currently, nearly 60 percent of all law enforcement agencies with more than a hundred personnel have a specialized gang unit, with more than 85 percent of this growth occurring in the last ten years (Katz 2001). These specialized gang units, as Klein (1995) notes, represent "hard suppression"—the identification, punishment, control, and separation of gang-involved youth in ways that go above and beyond the usual treatment of youthful offenders. Priority is given to investigations, gathering intelligence, and making arrests. Very little attention is paid to the complex factors underlying gang behavior. Very little attention is paid to the attitudes and concerns of the residents living in gang neighborhoods. This move away from gang intervention and toward gang suppression represents the mainstay of gang policy efforts in the 1980s and 1990s; it is discussed at greater length in the next section.

Even in the context of a predominantly criminal justice approach toward gangs, however, street outreach work continued to a smaller degree through the efforts of local actors such as ministers and community organizations. Efforts by people like Father Greg Boyle in Los Angeles, Brothers Bill Thomes and Jim Fogerty in Chicago, and Reverend Eugene Rivers in Boston continued in the street-worker tradition, but infused it with a quasi-religious flavor.[9] In Chicago, for instance, Brother Bill Thomes provided classic curbstone counseling in Chicago's most notorious housing projects throughout the 1980s and 1990s, when the city's murder rate totals topped nine hundred per year. Meanwhile, Reverend Rivers's efforts to intervene in the lives of gang members gained national attention when, in 1998, he graced the cover of *Newsweek* under the headline "Savior of the Streets: God vs. Gangs."

Following what can be best described as a nearly three-decade hiatus, the street-worker approach has reemerged as a popular strategy—once again with origins in Chicago—and is receiving national attention (see, for example, Kotlowitz 2008). In a strategy reminiscent of the original CAP curbstone counselors, the Chicago Project for Violence Prevention's CeaseFire program utilizes "outreach workers" and "violence interrupters," local workers who possess intimate knowledge of local gang problems (some are themselves formerly gang-involved), who engage in dispute mediation between gangs, with the main goal of reducing shootings.[10] Although this program has only recently undergone its first external evaluation, its model has been touted as a "success" and has already been exported to other cities around the country, including Baltimore, Newark, and Kansas City. Even in Los Angeles, site of Klein's damning evaluation, the street worker is once again being embraced by a variety of entities, including the Los Angeles Police Department (LAPD). Homicides in the city of Los Angeles fell to near a forty-year low in 2007, when there were only 392 incidents, 213 of them gang-related. The police were quick to point to their new partnership with intervention workers as one of the primary reasons for the decrease in homicides. The police believe that the intervention workers have had a dramatic impact on lethal violence because the street workers have been able to intervene and calm things down before a victimized gang launches a retaliatory strike. LAPD's deputy chief says: "For the first time, we're requiring captains to call the gang interventionists, give them the word on the shooting and get out there and avert another homicide We are pretty good at solving homicides, but we are trying to get better at preventing the next homicide" (Los Angeles Times, September 28, 2007).

So, for the moment, it seems that the street-worker approach is once again alive and well, informing gang policy strategies, although the efficacy of such programs is still in question. Many police officers remain skeptical of them, doubting the motives and intentions of the typical street worker. Whether such concerns are unfounded or not, many believe that street workers blur the line between "worker" and "member." That is, members of the criminal justice community believe that being labeled a "worker" simply provides a cover that permits some of the older gang members to continue to hang out and participate in gang activities.

Policing Gangs

As mentioned in the previous section, the genesis of the specialized gang unit dates to the mid-1960s in large cities. The creation and subsequent diffusion of the gang unit as a policing practice result from the complex interplay of (1) moral panic caused by the urban riots of the 1960s and increased levels of gang violence shortly thereafter, (2) the rational bureaucratic response to a growing crime problem by bureaucratic police organizations, and (3) the increased availability of federal grant monies for gang policing efforts (Katz 2001; Katz and Webb 2006). Along with a growing acceptance of conservative crime policies, these three programmatic considerations helped to institutionalize suppression policing tactics as a hallmark of contemporary gang control policy.

Typical hardcore police suppression tactics include hot-spot policing, saturation patrols, enforcement of exclusionary zones, and, perhaps one of the most widely used strategies, gang "sweeps." Briefly, hot-spot policing entails the use of an analysis of geographic patterns of gang crimes and the subsequent designation of certain locations that demonstrate an increased amount of gang activity as "hot." Increased police presence and attention are then directed to the location in the hopes of "cooling" the area. Similarly, saturation patrols involve the massive influx of police resources, often specialized gang officers, into areas of high gang activity to increase arrests during a short period of time. Exclusionary zones require action by local legislatures to designate certain gang activities (for example, recruiting, loitering, and drug dealing) illegal around specified locations, such as schools and public parks. Such policies allow the police to make arrests quickly when illegal behavior occurs in these areas. Finally, gang "sweeps" entail the massive roundup and arrest of a large number of members of a single gang at the same time; the main goal of this tactic is to try to destabilize the gang by locking up its leadership and base members. Typically, such sweeps are the result of long-term, ongoing police investigations that yield intelligence and probable cause on a large number of gang members.

Gang suppression and control efforts now go beyond municipal policing efforts to include specialized prosecutorial units. Many local and federal prosecutors' offices, like police departments, now direct resources toward specialized gang units, which tend to be centralized within prosecutors' offices in order to channel resources and efforts toward gang-specific cases. The basic idea is that gang cases present problems—such as witness intimidation and retaliatory violence—that are unique to the context of gang crimes. Furthermore, centralizing prosecution duties in a smaller unit allows gang cases to be treated more systematically than their nongang counterparts. One common technique in gang prosecution units is "vertical prosecution," a process in which a single prosecutor handles the same case from beginning to end, an important structural change in big departments where often a single case is touched by dozens of individuals before it ends up in court.

In addition to prosecuting cases, specialized prosecution units have also played a role in the development of gang-specific legislation and legal codes. Most of the legal codes involving gang control invoke classic deterrence theory by stressing enhanced criminal sentences and penalties as a means of reducing gang crimes. For example, California's Street Terrorism and Enforcement Prevention (STEP) Act of 1993 makes it a crime to engage in specified gang activities, enhances certain penalties associated with said activities, and even allows for the prosecution of parents who fail to get their children to comply with certain STEP mandates. The STEP Act is modeled on the federal Racketeer Influenced and Corrupt Organizations (RICO)

approaches may seem at odds with each other, they in no way represent an "either-or" ultimatum. On the contrary, gang control strategies that have tried to combine community and law enforcement programs have been in existence for some time. As Klein and Maxson (2006) note in a recent review, two Los Angeles–based initiatives—the L.A. Plan in the 1980s and the L.A. Bridges program in the 1990s—cobbled together enforcement and prevention strategies. School programs, job- and life-skills training, literacy programs, and various other social services were to be delivered to youth at risk of gang membership as well as those already active in gangs. Unfortunately, the delivery of services in these efforts fell far short of the idealized model. The level of "collaboration" was lacking, and the choice about where to initiate the services was driven by political servitude rather than community need. In the end, the programs were grossly watered down, with none of the neighborhoods receiving a meaningful dose of intervention. After these efforts, it took nearly twenty years for the city to finally, and bravely, pull the plug on the second incarnation of L.A. Bridges (Bridges II).

Still, these early collaborative efforts in Los Angeles ushered in a new wave of gang programs that, at least in theory, espoused a more balanced approach to gang control by combining community mobilization, gang prevention strategies, and suppression techniques. The development of such hybrid efforts is the subject of our final section.

The "Spergel Model"

The early collaborative efforts in Los Angeles drummed up political interest in developing a repertoire of "best-practice" programs that might be offered to the growing number of communities experiencing gang problems in the 1990s. Through a series of cooperative agreements and specialized grants, Professor Irving Spergel of the University of Chicago was charged with developing alternative models of gang prevention and control.[12] After considerable research and even the beginning of a pilot test, Professor Spergel devised a complex community-based program, formally titled "The Comprehensive Community-Wide Gang Program Model," but informally known as simply the "Spergel Model" (for complete details, see Spergel 1995, 2007).

The main goal of the Spergel Model is to provide a basic blueprint for a collaborative gang prevention effort that can be tailored to specific locations that have a gang violence problem. The program employs five key strategies: (1) community mobilization, (2) social interventions in the form of street workers, (3) opportunity provision, (4) organizational change, and (5) suppression techniques. *Community mobilization* entails the development and maintenance of a set of working relationships across and between community residents and organizations, the police, other criminal justice agencies, and government officials. *Social intervention* encompasses the use of street workers who counsel gang youth and provide links between youth and schools, social services, community members, and criminal justice agencies. Such mobilization and service efforts are also to be directly linked with *opportunity provision*—i.e., developing means for gang members to gain access to meaningful employment, educational opportunities, and services. These types of programmatic efforts are also to be guided toward *organizational change* designed to bring about new policies and practices of agencies to reduce their tendency to respond negatively to gang youth and, more importantly, to increase their receptivity to working with gang-involved youth. Finally, the Spergel Model also includes *suppression* components, in which police and probation officers (as well as other criminal justice officials) hold youth accountable for their delinquent and criminal behavior; this includes specialized gang policing, prosecution, and so on.

Evaluation results of the model have been promising but mixed (see chapter 3 for a synthesis). The key to programmatic success resided largely in interagency collaboration, community mobilization, and the efficacy of street workers. Given the dynamic and complex nature of the model, it is not surprising that coordination of program efforts was difficult, even in hospitable sociopolitical contexts. Results from the original pilot of the model in the Little Village neighborhood in Chicago highlighted several key programmatic difficulties, including police resistance to street workers, behavioral problems of street workers themselves, the withdrawal of police participation, inconsistent community participation, and the difficulties associated with gang youth more generally (Spergel 2007). In spite of these difficulties, however, the program reported considerable success at the gang-member level; the criminal and delinquent activities of program youth decreased over the program period as compared with such activites among youth not in the program (Spergel 2007). The results of community-level changes in gang behavior were more ambiguous.

Even before the evaluation of the Little Village project was completed, the comprehensive program was expanded to five additional locations in 1995:

Mesa, California; Bloomington, Illinois; Tucson, Arizona; Riverside, California; and San Antonio, Texas. The expansion of the program to other areas brought with it new problems, including difficulties in adhering to the multiple components of the model and program implementation, the continued resistance of police agencies, evaluation issues, and the continued tensions caused by the use of street workers (Klein and Maxson 2006). Furthermore, several of the cities found that the suppression tactics overshadowed the other components of the "comprehensive" program. Impressively, though, some of the same successes found in Little Village are also appearing at some of the additional sites despite programmatic difficulties. Most notably, program youth performed considerably better than non-program youth on measures of serious violent arrests and for certain drug offenses (Parker 2002). However, not even this result is consistent across sites, and at least one city found an increase in certain types of criminal offenses.[13]

Problem-Solving Approach: From Boston to a National Model for Addressing Gang Violence

As the Spergel Model was expanding, another collaborative model that brought together suppression and community efforts was under way in Boston, a city experiencing a growing youth violence problem. The Boston Gun Project, also known as Operation Ceasefire, emerged not only as a programmatic success but also as the impetus for subsequent national policy agendas. Although a complete treatment of the Boston Gun Project is well beyond the scope of this chapter, we would be remiss not to revisit this topic on several fronts.[14]

First, one would be hard pressed to find an example of a project that had as great an impact on anti-gang strategies, both locally and federally. Technically, Operation Ceasefire was not originally designed as a "gang" strategy. However, researchers involved in the design of the intervention quickly realized that the majority of gun violence in Boston was committed by minority youths involved in gangs. Furthermore, given the reality of urban gun violence in many of the mid-sized and large cities in America, any program aimed at reducing gun violence is likely to be a de facto gang strategy. The model developed by the Boston team was replicated in ten cities in the United States under the heading "The Strategic Approach to Community Safety Initiative" (Roehl et al. 2006), as well as in one independent effort conducted by RAND in Los Angeles (Tita et al. 2003). More importantly, Operation Ceasefire provided the master plan for Project Safe Neighborhoods—an anti-gun violence program started under U.S. Attorney General Janet Reno that continued under the Bush administration, which extended key dimensions of the Boston model to all ninety-three federal jurisdictions across the country.[15]

Second, the work in Boston cemented the terms "problem-solving approach" and "working groups" into the collective lexicon of researchers and policy officials interested in reducing gang violence. The key to problem solving is the ongoing production and consumption of data-driven information. Independent researchers survey the data landscape, define the scope and nature of the problem at hand, and then present analysis of the data to working-group members in a timely fashion.[16] In addition to analyzing information gleaned from police data-management systems and other data resources, researchers also conducted interviews with local practitioners (probation and parole officers, service providers, and religious leaders), local community residents, and even youth who were most likely to be affected by or involved in gangs. Boston researchers even pioneered geographic and social mapping techniques that are now commonly used in gang control efforts (Kennedy, Braga, and Piehl 1997; Papachristos, Meares, and Fagan 2007; Tita et al. 2003; Tita et al. 2005).

Third, the Boston Ceasefire project introduced the "pulling levers" strategy to the menu of gang enforcement options. This strategy exploits the structure of the gang by holding the collective "responsible" for the actions of the individual. Members of the participating criminal justice agencies determined the vulnerabilities of individual gang members with respect to outstanding warrants and probation and parole conditions. Recognizing that law enforcement personnel lack sufficient resources to enforce all warrants or conditions of probation (drug testing and search conditions, for example), the law enforcement agencies promised that any individual known to be associated with a gang whose members continued to commit acts of gun violence would be placed at the top of the list for enforcement. When in fact the "ceasefire" was violated, the agencies followed through on their promise in a coordinated and intensified fashion. The group also carefully advertised the "success" of the lever-pulling exercise to the community of potential offenders using word of mouth as well as the public posting of bills identifying the names of individuals prosecuted and the sentencing outcomes. Thus, despite Klein's (1971) caution that such increased attention might increase group cohesion, the evidence from Boston suggests that this was an important component in the lasting deterrent impact of the intervention.

Finally, the Boston model was one of the first to seriously reintroduce the "community" into such coordinated efforts. The local community, especially the faith-based community, played an influential role in the design, implementation, and effectiveness of the program. In addition to employing the classic street-worker model to reach out to local youth, the Boston group also cultivated relationships with important community and faith-based organizations. Community actors were given serious consideration and utilized throughout the project in a variety of ways. For example, community actors actively participated in offender "notification meetings" where gang members were warned about new enforcement efforts, community and religious organizations served as a foundation of gang outreach work, and community members were crucial to spreading the word of the Boston Project's efforts.

Also, unlike many of its predecessors, the Boston Project specifically designed evaluation efforts into its programmatic goals. The Boston team was thus able to demonstrate impressive results in reducing gun violence, especially among gang-involved youth. However, although no one disputes the efficacy of the model in terms of employing problem solving and working groups, replicating the study to the same degree of effectiveness has proved elusive. For example, in Los Angeles, a replication of Boston's Operation Ceasefire demonstrated that the problem-solving approach coupled with working groups led to a tenable and effective pulling-levers strategy (for an overview of results from several problem-solving approaches, see Braga, Kennedy, and Tita 2001). The Los Angeles team demonstrated that the strategy, which mirrored Boston's pulling-levers design, had a short-term impact on gun violence, but that once resources began to drift from the gangs initially targeted, violence slowly crept back to original levels.

We opened this chapter by noting that there is general agreement among law enforcement, other criminal justice agencies, and community members that suppression alone is not the answer to the gang problem. Instead, the consensus is that effective strategies must incorporate aspects of intervention with suppression.[17] Not only are "hybrid models" theoretically sound, but most carefully constructed empirical evaluations have demonstrated at least general support for such an approach. So if "everyone knows" that

At the same time, however, hybrid and collaborative models are now one of the hallmarks of most large-scale gang control programs. Project Safe Neighborhoods (PSN) was recently expanded to include a more gang-specific focus and to require the inclusion of community and faith-based organizations. In addition, those efforts that have seen some success in collaborative strategies have used ongoing programs as a springboard for subsequent programs and funding. For instance, many of the PSN efforts in Chicago have now been adopted by other working groups and agencies as standard procedure. The difficult task still ahead of us entails figuring out how to bring balance to such efforts.

Notes

1. For more on the history and theory behind street gang work and street gang workers, see Spergel (1966) and Klein (1971).

2. A concise history of CAP and its progression over the decades can be found at the organization's Web site (www.chicagoareaproject.org/history.htm).

3. For an example, see the description of "detached workers" offered by Short and Strodtbeck (1965).

4. Jim Short tells a similar story in which gangs in Chicago who did not have a street worker assigned to them were often viewed as less of a gang—i.e., that what it meant to be a gang in Chicago during the mid-1960s was that your actions were serious enough to warrant the assignment of a street worker (personal communication with author).

5. The story of the Vice Lords has been told by several people, including Dawley (1973), Keiser (1969), Knox (2001), and most recently Hagedorn (2008). A wonderful visual tour of the gang during this period can also be found on Hagedorn's Web site (www.gangresearch.net).

6. A detailed account of the federal government's relationship with street gangs during this period can be found in Poston's (1971) *The Gang and the Establishment*.

7. In fact, according to Spergel et al. (1968:9), the program's explicitly stated goals were to utilize "the natural structure of two street youth groups to plan, design, implement, and operate a two-track pre-vocational program linked with on-the-job training and supportive services for 800 youth of Woodlawn."

8. For the government's account, one can consult the several hundred pages of congressional records of the Hearings Before the Permanent Subcommittee on Investigations of the Committee on Government Operations (1968). For a more balanced and academic account of the program's origins, evolution, and ultimate demise, see Spergel et al. (1968).

9. We say "quasi-religious" because although such efforts were supported by religious institutions, they did not include goals such as religious conversion.

10. The organization's first external evaluation was recently completed by Wes Skogan (see www.northwestern.edu/ipr/publications/ceasefire.html). For a journalistic account of the program and its efforts, see Kotlowitz (2008) in the *New York Times*.

11. RICO itself has often been used by the U.S. Attorney's office against highly organized gangs, motorcycle gangs, and other types of organized criminal syndicates. In one of the largest such cases, thirty-eight members of Chicago's Gangster Disciples and one police officer were charged with "operating an on-going criminal organization" (Papachristos 2001). In 1996, RICO was used to great effect in Pittsburgh, Pennsylvania, against a typical urban street gang known as LAW. Though a reasonable person could question whether this gang represented an "organized" entity, the use of federal prosecution had a chilling effect on gangs and gang violence for nearly a decade (see Tita, Cohen, and Engberg 2005.)

12. This is, of course, an extremely abbreviated version of a much longer political and academic process. For more discussion on the etiology of this program, see Spergel (2007) or Klein and Maxson (2006).

13. As a result, Klein and Maxson (2006) suggest that this model may be more aptly described as a "delinquency" prevention model, rather than a gang prevention model.

14. For the formal evaluations of the Boston Project, see Braga, Kennedy, and Tita (2001); Braga, Piehl, and Kennedy (1999); Kennedy (1996); Piehl, Kennedy, and Braga (2000).

15. For more information on the PSN model, see Ludwig (2004); Papachristos, Meares, and Fagan (2007).

16. The nationwide PSN model went so far as to require each federal jurisdiction to have an active "researcher partner" to accomplish such tasks. Unfortunately, this research role was not equally well received in all jurisdictions.

17. Though we have limited our focus to intervention and suppression, prevention is also often incorporated within problem-solving and hybrid models.

References

Barajas, Frank P. 2007. "An Invading Army: A Civil Gang Injunction in a Southern California Chicana/o Community." *Latino Studies* 5:393–417.

Braga, Anthony A., David M. Kennedy, and George Tita. 2001. "New Approaches to the Strategic Prevention of Gang and Group-Involved Violence." In C. Ronald Huff, ed., *Gangs in America*, 271–286. 3rd ed. Newbury Park, Calif.: Sage.

Braga, Anthony A., David M. Kennedy, Elin J. Waring, and Anne Morrison Piehl. 2001. "Problem-Oriented Policing, Deterrence, and Youth Violence: An Evaluation of Boston's Operation Ceasefire." *Journal of Research in Crime and Delinquency* 38:195–225.

Braga, Anthony A., Anne M. Piehl, and David M. Kennedy. 1999. "Youth Homicide in Boston: An Assessment of Supplementary Homicide Report Data." *Homicide Studies* 3:277–299.

Bursik, Robert J. and Harold G. Grasmick. 1993. *Neighborhoods and Crime: The Dimensions of Effective Community Control.* New York: Lexington Books.

Coughlin, Brenda C. and Sudhir Alladi Venkatesh. 2003. "The Urban Street Gang After 1970." *Annual Review of Sociology* 29:41–64.

Dawley, David. 1973. *A Nation of Lords: The Autobiography of the Vice Lords.* Garden City, N.Y.: Anchor.

Decker, Scott H. 2007. "Expand the Use of Police Gang Units." *Criminology and Public Policy* 6:729–734.

Fremon, Celeste. 2005. *G-Dog and Homeboys: Father Greg Boyle and the Gangs of East Los Angeles.* Albuquerque: University of New Mexico Press.

Grogger, Jeffrey. 2002. "The Effects of Civil Gang Injunctions on Reported Violent Crime: Evidence from Los Angeles County." *Journal of Law and Economics* 45:69–90.

Hagedorn, John M. 2008. *A World of Gangs.* Minneapolis: University of Minnesota Press.

Hearings Before the Permanent Subcommittee on Investigations of the Committee on Government Operations. 1968. "Riots, Civil and Criminal Disorders." Washington, D.C.: Government Printing Office.

Katz, Charles. 2001. "The Establishment of a Police Gang Unit: An Examination of Organizational and Environmental Factors." *Criminology* 39:301–337.

Katz, Charles and Vincent J. Webb. 2006. *Policing Gangs in America.* Cambridge, England: Cambridge University Press.

Keiser, R. Lincoln. 1969. *The Vice Lords: Warriors of the Streets.* Chicago: Holt, Rinehart, and Winston.

Kennedy, David M. 1996. "Youth Violence in Boston: Gun Markets, Serious Youth Offenders, and a Use-Reduction Strategy. Boston Gun Project." *Law and Contemporary Problems* 59:147–196.

Kennedy, David M., Anthony A. Braga, and Anne M. Piehl. 1997. "The (Un)Known Universe: Mapping Gangs and Gang Violence in Boston." In David Weisburd and Tom McEwen, eds., *Crime Mapping and Crime Prevention*, 219–262. Monsey, N.Y.: Criminal Justice Press.

Klein, Malcolm W. 1971. *Street Gangs and Street Workers.* Englewood Cliffs, N.J.: Prentice Hall.

——. 1995. *The American Street Gang*. New York: Oxford University Press.

——. 2004. *Gang Cop: The Words and Ways of Officer Paco Domingo*. Lanham, Md.: AltaMira.

Klein, Malcolm W. and Cheryl L. Maxson. 2006. *Street Gang Patterns and Policies*. New York: Oxford University Press.

Knox, George W. 2001. *An Introduction to Gangs*. 5th ed. Peotone, Ill.: New Chicago School Press.

Kobrin, Solomon. 1959. "The Chicago Area Project: A 25-Year Assessment." *Annals of the American Academy of Political and Social Sciences* 322 (1): 19–29.

Kotlowitz, Alex. 2008. "Blocking the Transmission of Violence." *New York Times Magazine*, May 4.

Ludwig, Jens. 2004. "Better Gun Enforcement, Less Crime." Paper presented at the University of Chicago Law School, University of Chicago.

Maxson, Cheryl. 2004. "Civil Gang Injunctions: The Ambiguous Case of the National Migration of a Gang Enforcement Strategy." In F. Esbensen, L. Gaines, and S. Tibbetts, eds., *American Youth Gangs at the Millennium*, 375–389. Long Grove, Ill.: Waveland.

Maxson, Cheryl, Karen Hennigan, and David Sloane. 2003. "For the Sake of the Neighborhood? Civil Gang Injunctions as a Gang Intervention Tool in Southern California." In S. Decker, ed., *Policing Youth Gangs and Violence*, 239–266. Belmont, Calif.: Wadsworth.

——. 2005. "'It's Getting Crazy Out There': Can a Civil Gang Injunction Change a Community?" *Criminology and Public Policy* 4 (3): 503–529.

Meares, Tracey L. 1998. "Social Organization and Drug Law Enforcement." *American Criminal Law Review* 35:191–227.

Meares, Tracey L. and Dan M. Kahn. 1998. "Laws and (Norms of) Order in the Inner City." *Law and Society Review* 32:805–838.

Miller, Walter B. 1957. "The Impact of a Community Work Group Program on Delinquent Crime Gangs." *Social Service Review* 41:390–406. .

——. 2001. *The Growth of Youth Gang Problems in the United States: 1970–98*. Edited by. Office of Juvenile Justice and Delinquency Prevention. Washington, D.C.: U.S. Department of Justice.

Papachristos, Andrew V. 2001. *A.D., After the Disciples: The Neighborhood Impact of Federal Gang Prosecution*. Peotone, Ill.: National Gang Crime Research Center.

——. 2005. "Interpreting Inkblots: Deciphering and Doing Something About Modern Street Gangs." *Criminology and Public Policy* 4:101–110.

Papachristos, Andrew V., Tracey L. Meares, and Jeffrey Fagan. 2007. "Attention Felons: Evaluating Project Safe Neighborhoods in Chicago." *Journal of Empirical Legal Studies* 4:223–272.

Parker, Robert N. 2002. "Project Bridge Local Evaluation, 1994 to 1999." Riverside,

Calif.: Presley Center for Crime and Justice Studies, University of California Riverside.

Perkins, Useni Eugene. 1987. *Explosion of Chicago's Black Street Gangs: 1900 to the Present.* Chicago: Third World Press.

Piehl, Anne M., David M. Kennedy, and Anthony A. Braga. 2000. "Problem Solving and Youth Violence: An Evaluation of the Boston Gun Project." *American Law and Economics Review* 2:58.

Poston, Richard W. 1971. *The Gang and the Establishment: A Story of Conflict Rising Out of the Federal and Private Financing of Urban Street Gangs.* New York: Harper and Row.

Roehl, Jan, Dennis P. Rosenbaum, Sandra K. Costello, James R. Coldren, Jr., Amie M. Schuck, Laura Kunard, and David R. Forde. 2006. "The Strategic Approach to Community Safety Initiative." Unpublished final report available online (see www.ncjrs.gov/pdffiles1/nij/grants/212866.pdf).

Short, James F. and Fred L. Strodtbeck. 1965. *Group Process and Gang Delinquency.* Chicago: University of Chicago Press.

Skogan, Wesley G. and Susan M. Hartnett. 1997. *Community Policing, Chicago Style.* New York: Oxford University Press.

Spergel, Irving A. 1966. *Street Gang Work: Theory and Practice.* Reading, Mass.: Addison-Wesley.

——. 1995. *The Youth Gang Problem: A Community Approach.* New York: Oxford University Press.

——. 2007. *Reducing Youth Gang Violence: The Little Village Gang Project in Chicago.* Lanham, Md.: AltaMira.

Spergel, Irving A., Turner Castellano, John Pleas, and Patricia Brown. 1968. "Evaluation of the Youth Manpower Demonstration of the Woodlawn Organization." Chicago: University of Chicago, School of Social Service Administration.

Spergel, Irving A. and G. David Curry. 1990. "Strategies and Perceived Agency Effectiveness in Dealing with the Youth Gang Problem." In C. R. Huff, ed., *Gangs in America*, 288–309. Newbury Park, Calif.: Sage.

Stewart, Gary. 1998. "Black Codes and Broken Windows: The Legacy of Racial Hegemony in Anti-Gang Civil Injunctions." *Yale Law Journal* 107 (7): 2249–2279.

Suttles, Gerald D. 1968. *The Social Order of the Slum: Ethnicity and Territory in the Inner City.* Chicago: University of Chicago Press.

Tita, George E., Jacqueline Cohen, and John Engberg. 2005. "An Ecological Study of the Location of Gang 'Set Space.'" *Social Problems* 52:272–299.

Tita, George E., K. Jack Riley, Greg Ridgeway, Clifford Grammich, Allan F. Abrahamse, and Peter Greenwood. 2003. *Reducing Gun Violence: Results from an Intervention in East Los Angeles.* Santa Monica, Calif.: RAND Press.

Tita, George E., K. Jack Riley, Greg Ridgeway, and Peter W. Greenwood. 2005. "Reducing Gun Violence: Operation Ceasefire in Los Angeles." *Research in Brief*. Washington, D.C.: National Institute of Justice, U.S. Department of Justice, Office of Juvenile Justice and Delinquency Prevention.

Wilson, William J. 1987. *The Truly Disadvantaged: The Inner City, the Underclass, and Public Policy*. Chicago: University of Chicago Press.

——. 1996. *When Work Disappears: The World of the New Urban Poor*. New York: Knopf (distributed by Random House, Inc.).

Part II

Evidence, Evaluation, and Knowledge Utilization

3

Lessons Learned from Gang Program Evaluations

Prevention, Intervention, Suppression, and Comprehensive Community Approaches

JAMES C. HOWELL

The history of gang intervention is noteworthy for programs that failed outright or were of questionable effectiveness, from the first evaluation in the 1930s (Thrasher 1936) through the 1990s (Howell 1998, 2000). With a few exceptions, the scope of the present review is limited to programs evaluated in the past decade (plus other evaluated programs that were begun earlier and remain operational) that have been rated "effective" in reducing either risk factors for gang involvement or criminal activities of gang members.[1] The exceptions are programs that have not yet been rated but closely resemble others that have been rated effective.

Two cautionary notes are in order. First, this review focuses on gang-related program models. A main drawback to a program model approach is that the replication of program models in everyday practice has proved difficult (Knitzer and Cooper 2006; Lipsey 2005; Littell, Popa, and Forsythe 2006). The highly prescriptive "model" or "exemplary" (dubbed "blueprint" programs in one review, Mihalic et al. 2001) are often difficult to replicate in real-world settings with fidelity to the original program requirements—which must be achieved to reasonably expect similar out-comes. Otherwise, the program could well have the unintended conse-quence of increasing recidivism (Washington State Institute for Public Policy 2004).

Second, three of the programs reviewed below were not designed spe-cifically to have gang impacts. They nonetheless reduced gang involve-ment or gang crime—as a result of addressing precursor delinquency involvement (the Preventive Treatment Program), because the program targeted high-risk offenders (Operation New Hope—see Andrews 2006 on this point), or in taking a general approach to crime reduction (Chi-cago Alternative Policing Strategy). Moreover, gang and non-gang juve-nile offenders share common risk factors (Howell and Egley 2005), and gang involvement overlaps substantially with serious, violent, and chronic offending (Howell 2003:83–84). Hence interventions can reduce multiple problem behaviors.

Review Procedures

Each of the programs discussed below has been rated using scientific cri-teria developed to determine program inclusion in a national database of programs that address child and adolescent problem behaviors.[2] To become eligible for inclusion in this database, each program has been shown to prevent or reduce juvenile delinquency (during the childhood and early- to mid-adolescent period) or criminal activity (in late adolescence or young adulthood) or to reduce risk factors related to delinquency and other anti-social behaviors. In the protocol by which programs described herein were rated, Level 1 programs (L-1) are those evaluated with the most rigorous experimental designs, typically using random assignment. Level 2 pro-grams (L-2) use either an experimental or a quasi-experimental research design with a comparison group. Level 3 programs use less rigorous research designs but have a strong theoretical base and use at least single-group pre- and post-treatment measurements. Using this classification scheme, L-1 programs are considered to be model or exemplary, L-2 pro-grams are also considered effective although the evidence is less robust, and L-3 programs are considered promising (see fig. 3.1 for a summary of reviewed gang-related programs).

FIGURE 3.1 ·
Rated Effective Gang-Related Programs

Prevention Programs
Preventive Treatment Program (L-1)*
Gang Resistance Education and Training (L-2)**
Intervention Programs
Aggression Replacement Training (L-2)*
Operation New Hope (formerly Lifeskills '95) (L-2)*
Little Village Gang Violence Reduction Program**
Building Resources for the Intervention and Deterrence of
    Gang Engagement**
Suppression Programs
Hardcore Gang Investigations Unit (L-2)*
Chicago Alternative Policing Strategy (L-2)*
Tri-Agency Resource Gang Enforcement Team (L-2)*
Comprehensive Programs
Comprehensive Gang Model (L-2)*
Gang Violence Reduction Program (L-2)**
Chicago Project for Violence Prevention***

Legend: L-1: Model or exemplary program; L-2: Effective program
*Source for additional program information (see http://guide.helpingamericasyouth.gov)
** Source for additional program information (see www.iir.com/nygc/tool)
*** See www.ceasefireillinois.org/

Although this rating procedure is very useful for making objective assessments of program effectiveness, it has two important limitations when used to rate gang programs in particular. First, when rating police suppression initiatives, the rater is required to think about punishment as if it were a treatment ingredient. This unusual circumstance is further complicated by the absence of information on the effects of punishment dosages *on individuals* (especially recidivism outcomes) in gang-suppression studies, which typically examine only arrests, successful prosecutions, or convictions.

Second, rating criteria such as these score mainly the scientific strength of the evaluation of *program services* and do not take into account an important prerequisite of gang intervention, the role of *program structures* that may not include therapeutic services. The latter contexts or settings are extremely important for stabilizing gang offenders' behavior sufficiently to give treatment a chance to work. An intervention team is a prime example.

Among other things, intervention teams increase supervision of offenders, but in and of themselves they cannot be expected to have a significant impact unless effective services are provided, because it is the therapeutic services within such structured settings that have the actual power to produce change in offenders (Bonta 1996). Creating a "neutral zone" by the use of "no gang" contracts (Roush, Miesner, and Winslow 2002) in secure juvenile corrections settings is another case. Neither of these settings constitutes a therapeutic service. Gang activity must be restricted before therapeutic interventions have a reasonable opportunity to work.

A review of evaluation findings from research on gang prevention, intervention, and suppression programs follows, together with an assessment of the implications of these findings for informing youth gang strategies. Following this review, I will examine in somewhat greater depth the findings and lessons learned from evaluations of a strategic planning approach to youth gangs—the Comprehensive Community Model—which combines prevention, intervention, suppression, and a focus on community organization and collaborative action.

Gang Prevention

No one has yet discovered any effective strategy for preventing the formation of youth gangs; however, it is possible for programs to prevent some youth from joining gangs by reducing delinquency involvement. It appears that this was accomplished by the Montreal Preventive Treatment Program (L-1), even though it was not a stated goal of the experiment. Rather, the program was designed to prevent antisocial behavior among boys ages 7 to 9 of low socioeconomic status who had previously displayed disruptive problem behavior in kindergarten. This program demonstrated that a combination of parent training and childhood skills development can steer children away from gangs. An evaluation of the program showed both short- and long-term gains, including less delinquency, less substance use, and less gang involvement at age 15 (Tremblay et al. 1996).

The initial evaluated version of the Gang Resistance Education and Training program (GREAT, L-2) aimed to reduce middle school students' involvement in gangs and delinquent behavior through a nine-hour curriculum taught by uniformed law enforcement officers (see chapter 5 for a more detailed description of the GREAT program and evaluation). Students were taught to set positive goals, resist negative pressures, resolve conflicts, and understand how gangs affect the quality of their lives. The program showed a "small but systematic beneficial" effect (Esbensen et al. 2001:102) on participants in terms of reduced victimization, more-negative views about gangs, improved attitudes toward police, more pro-social peers, and less risk seeking—but not on gang involvement, drug use, or delinquency. This outcome is not surprising, given the limitations of program design; it would be quite a feat for social experiments if a nine-week, one hour per week, school-based curriculum prevented gang involvement, especially among high-risk youth.

Gang Intervention

Several gang intervention experiments have produced positive results. Three effective programs have employed interagency intervention teams. These teams typically provide a combination of intensive surveillance of gang-involved offenders under court supervision and a variety of services to them. Another distinctive feature of these programs is the use of gang outreach workers, typically in conjunction with an intervention team.[3] The Little Village intervention team (mainly outreach youth workers, police, and probation officers) convened biweekly and used a case management approach in working with active gang members, supported by the outreach youth workers. Suppression contacts, made mainly by project police, reduced the youths' interest in and attachment to the gang. Services such as job placement reduced the amount of time that gang youths spent with other gang members.

The Building Resources for the Intervention and Deterrence of Gang Engagement (BRIDGE) program in Riverside, California, is another gang program that used an intervention team. BRIDGE was one of the original OJJDP Comprehensive Community Model demonstration sites. It targeted gang-involved youth between the ages of 12 and 22 in two communities. Formation of an intervention team was a key to the success of the program (Spergel, Wa, and Sosa 2006). The team consisted of several core members, including the project coordinator, police, probation officer, parole officer, outreach worker, social service provider, and others. Case management involved development and execution of a treatment plan by the intervention team. This program has not been rated separately because it was included in the research that was reviewed in the course of rating the Comprehensive Community Model. However, the BRIDGE program significantly reduced violent crime arrests among gang members in contrast with a control group (Spergel et al. 2006).

Aggression Replacement Training® (ART, L-2) is a ten-week, thirty-hour cognitive-behavioral program administered to groups of eight to twelve juvenile offenders. During the ten weeks, participating youth typically attend three one-hour sessions per week, one session each of skill-streaming, anger-control training, and training in moral reasoning. ART has produced reduced arrest rates among members of violent gangs in Brooklyn, New York (Goldstein and Glick 1994). An evaluation of ART implementation in the state of Washington (with general court-referred delinquents) found that when it was competently delivered, ART reduced eighteen-month felony recidivism rates among program participants by 24 percent (Washington State Institute for Public Policy 2004).

One correctional aftercare program has produced very positive short-term effects for gang members—the Operation New Hope (formerly Lifeskills '95) program (L-2), which was implemented in California's San Bernardino and Riverside counties (Josi and Sechrest 1999). This program was designed for high-risk, chronic juvenile offenders released from the California Youth Authority. In addition to reintegrating these youth into communities, the program aimed to reduce their need for gang participation and affiliation as a support mechanism. An evaluation of the program's results found that participating youths were far less likely to have frequent associations with former gang associates than were members of the control group. In addition, youth assigned to the control group were about twice as likely as program participants to have been arrested, to be unemployed, and to have abused drugs or alcohol frequently since their release.

Gang Suppression

Suppression strategies, loosely based on deterrence principles, have dominated gang interventions for a quarter century (Klein 1995) and continue to do so. Legislators and policymakers in the United States have a tendency to "declare war" on social problems, and their solutions are often characterized by aggression. The U.S. government has launched "wars" on poverty, crime, drugs, gangs, illegal immigrants, and juvenile offenders (Howell

2003). This curious proclivity, combined with the growth of youth street gangs from the mid-1980s to the mid-1990s, gangs' concomitant increasing use of firearms, and popular myths about gangs and juvenile "superpredators," prompted President Clinton to declare a "war on gangs" in his 1997 State of the Union address.

The first program to demonstrate substantial success in combating gangs, Operation Hardcore (L-2), which targeted habitual gang offenders for prosecution, enhanced vertical prosecution and confinement of gang members (Dahmann 1983). Other outcomes, however, were not measured. Another large-scale suppression initiative, the Los Angeles Police Department's infamous street gang sweeps, was never evaluated, but its "Operation Hammer" street sweeps were shown to be ineffective because gang activity was not reduced (Klein 1995:161–165). A wide variety of gang suppression measures showing little success followed, including forming cul-de-sacs with concrete barriers to alter the flow of gang-driven vehicles, anti-loitering statutes, traffic checkpoints, curfew and truancy enforcement, and cracking down on gun violations (Howell 2000; Weisel 2002). But these strictly enforcement measures could not be expected to eradicate gangs, because gangs are by-products of partially incapacitated communities, and those conditions must be changed for a lasting impact.

Highly targeted gang suppression has shown some success. A three-pronged suppression strategy of (1) selective incarceration of the most violent and repeat older gang offenders in the most violent gangs, (2) enforcement of probation controls (including graduated sanctions and intensive supervision) with younger, less violent gang offenders, and (3) arrests of gang leaders in "hot spots" of gang activity proved somewhat effective in decreasing gang crime in the Tri-Agency Resource Gang Enforcement Team (TARGET, L-2) program in Orange County, California (Kent et al. 2000). Community policing, a gentler form of police suppression, implemented in the Chicago Alternative Policing Strategy (CAPS, L-2), has shown success in reducing adult crimes. In the first phase of CAPS, gang problems were reduced in two of the three experimental police districts (Skogan and Hartnett 1997), but once CAPS was implemented citywide, successes with gang problems were shown only in data on perceptions of African American residents (Skogan and Steiner 2004).

The use of singular suppression tactics in combating gangs and gun crime has earned only "a mixed report card" (Decker 2003:290; see also Bynum and Varano 2003; Fagan 2002; Ludwig 2005). The positive effects of suppression tend to be short-lived (Klein 1995; Papachristos 2001; Sherman 1990). For example, serious gang problems returned after the homicide reductions attributed to the Boston Ceasefire project (Braga et al. 2001), dubbed the "Boston Miracle" (Kennedy 2007), and homicides increased (Braga and Pierce 2005). In addition, the extent of the project's impact specifically on homicide rates has been questioned in other evaluations (Fagan 2002; Ludwig 2005; Rosenfeld, Fornango, and Baumer 2005).

Remarkably, in Chicago, massive federal law enforcement and prosecution succeeded in toppling a major organized criminal gang, the Gangster Disciples, but little difference was observable at the neighborhood level (Papachristos 2001). The main differences locally were that the gang reverted to a collection of loosely organized groups that still dealt drugs and formed associations with other gangs: "They just joined a different gang" (Papachristos 2001:69).

But the Boston Ceasefire project did create a strong individual deterrence model that instituted a zero-tolerance policy for any lawbreaking activity on the part of identified individuals (Kennedy 1999), and this has achieved broad appeal (Kennedy 2007). High-rate violent offenders (identified through a review of police arrest records in a problem analysis) were rounded up and notified in a community meeting that they were subject to long prison sentences for any subsequent law, probation, or parole violations. Successful convictions that drew long federal sentences were widely publicized in the community to deter others.

It is not surprising that the zero-tolerance roundups have not produced consistent noteworthy results. First, the cross-agency "problem analysis" approach used in Boston remains very difficult to implement anywhere else, particularly in larger cities (Duane 2006; Ludwig 2005; Skogan and Steiner 2004; Tita, Riley, and Greenwoood 2003). Second, because only a small subset of high-rate offenders is typically targeted, a large overall impact on citywide crime rates is unrealistic. Third, in cities that have well-established gangs, the groups constantly regenerate themselves. Hence, gang suppression tactics need to be coupled with prevention and intervention measures to reduce the strength of gangs over the long term.

To elaborate on this point, it seems that when suppression strategies are singularly applied to gangs, they are not likely to have a lasting impact without programming that—at the same time—ameliorates the community conditions that give rise to gangs, reduces the number of youth who join gangs, and removes younger members from gangs in order to thwart gang growth. If successful, these initiatives should reduce the scope (if not the severity) of the gang problem and permit suppression tactics to be more effective. These realizations have led to the development of alternative approaches to the youth gang problem that focus more comprehensively on prevention, intervention, and suppression in the context of local communities, and through the coordinated action of a range of community stakeholders. Exemplary in this approach is the Comprehensive Gang Model.

A Review of the Comprehensive Gang Model

In 1987 the OJJDP launched a Juvenile Gang Suppression and Intervention Research and Development Program. In the first phase, the researchers conducted a comprehensive national assessment of organized agency and community group responses to gang problems in the United States (Spergel 1995; Spergel and Curry 1993). It remains the only national assessment of efforts to combat gangs.

In the second phase, the Comprehensive Community-Wide Approach to Gang Prevention, Intervention, and Suppression Program was developed (Spergel 1995; Spergel, Chance et al. 1994; Spergel and Curry 1993) as the final product of the gang research and development program that OJJDP funded. From the information gathered through the multi-method study in phase one (Spergel, Curry et al. 1994), the research team developed twelve technical assistance manuals, one for each type of agency that should be part of a successful local community response to gangs, including organizations that ranged from grassroots child-services agencies to law enforcement, judges, and prosecutors (Spergel et al. 1992).

Although the program used several names, OJJDP adopted the most descriptive title of all, the Comprehensive Gang Prevention, Intervention, and Suppression Model, to emphasize the continuum of community responses to gang problems. Its commonly used title is the Comprehensive Community Model. Notwithstanding the name change, OJJDP made no substantive changes to the model. However, OJJDP embedded the model in a strategic planning and implementation process that recast the model in several respects. First, a comprehensive assessment of local gang problems was strongly recommended prior to implementing any of the components of the model. Second, the "targeting" process called for in the original model was expanded to consist of a strategic planning process, based on the assessment results. Third, just five of the numerous strategies that were recommended in the model were emphasized:

1. *Community mobilization.* Involvement of local citizens, including former gang youth, community groups, and agencies, and the coordination of programs and staff functions within and across agencies.

2. *Opportunities provision.* The development of a variety of specific education, training, and employment programs targeting gang-involved youth.

3. *Social intervention.* Involving youth-serving agencies, schools, grassroots groups, faith-based organizations, police, and other juvenile and criminal justice organizations in reaching out to gang-involved youth and their families, and linking them with the conventional world and needed services.

4. *Suppression.* Formal and informal social control procedures, including close supervision and monitoring of gang-involved youth by agencies of the juvenile and criminal justice system and also by community-based agencies, schools, and grassroots groups.

5. *Organizational change and development.* Development and implementation of policies and procedures that result in the most effective use of available and potential resources, within and across agencies, to better address the gang problem.

To facilitate the implementation process, OJJDP synthesized the critical elements of the Comprehensive Community Model in five steps:

1. The community and community leaders acknowledge the youth gang problem.

2. The community conducts an assessment of the nature and scope of the youth gang problem, leading to the identification of a target community or communities and population(s).

3. Through a steering committee, the community and community leaders set goals and objectives to address the identified problem(s).

4. The steering committee makes available relevant programming, strategies, services, tactics, and procedures consistent with the model's five core strategies.

5. The steering committee, with the assistance of a research partner, evaluates effectiveness, reassesses the problem, and modifies approaches as needed.

Implementation of the Comprehensive Community Model proceeded on two fronts. While Spergel was implementing it in Chicago, OJJDP was repackaging it for widespread dissemination and testing. The Chicago program and its results are described next.

The Little Village Gang Violence Reduction Program

In March 1993 the initial version of the Comprehensive Community Model was implemented in the Little Village neighborhood of Chicago, a low-income and working-class community that is approximately 90 percent Mexican American (Spergel 2007). Called the Gang Violence Reduction Program (GVRP), it lasted five years. It is important to note that the program targeted and provided services to youth involved with two gangs, rather than to the gangs as groups. The program targeted mainly older members (ages 17 to 24) of two of the area's most violent Hispanic gangs, the Latin Kings and the Two Six. Specifically, the Little Village program targeted more than two hundred of the "shooters," the influential persons or leaders, of the two gangs.

The primary goal of the project was to reduce the extremely high level of gang violence among youth who were already involved in the two gangs; drug-related activity was not specifically targeted. This goal was to be accomplished by a combination of outreach work, an intervention team, case management, youth services, and suppression. Outreach youth workers would attempt to prevent and control gang conflicts in specific situations and to persuade gang youth to leave the gang as soon as possible. Virtually all of the outreach youth workers were former members of the two target gangs. Their program-related activities included crisis intervention, brief family and individual counseling and referrals for services, and surveillance and suppression activities. Altogether, a good balance of services was provided (Spergel 2007).

Each of the intervention team members delivered services themselves to project youth and also made referrals for other services. In due course, the team (mainly outreach youth workers, police, and probation officers) convened biweekly and exchanged information on violence that was occurring (or about to occur) in the community. Suppression contacts, made mainly by project police, reduced interest in and attachment to the gang. Services such as job placement reduced the time that target youth spent with other gang members. "The greater the number of contacts and services provided by project team members, the more likely the youth developed realistic income and occupation expectations. Each contact and service, and a combination of these, and other life-course changes predicted a reduction in violence arrests" (Spergel 2007:303).

Police assigned to serve the project area targeted the two gangs and their most violent members. They used standard policing tactics employed elsewhere in the city by Chicago police in controlling gang violence. The outreach youth workers sometimes collaborated with the police officers in the exchange of information vital to the police suppression role, and project police officers often encouraged gang youth to accept services.

A new community advisory group (a steering committee) was established to support the project. This group was made up of representatives from local churches, two Boys and Girls Clubs, a local community organization, a business group, other social agencies, the local alderman, and local citizens.

On another front, the GVRP attempted to mobilize or organize the Little Village community in an organizational change and development strategy to help prevent and control gang activity. This goal was only partially achieved. The Neighbors Against Gang Violence (NAGV) was established for this purpose but was ineffective, partly because the capacity of grassroots groups to mobilize residents was overestimated. Thus, the GVRP's impact at the community level was minimal.

The process evaluation of the GVRP (Spergel, Wa, and Sosa 2006) revealed that it was well implemented, achieving an "excellent" rating on eight of the eighteen program implementation elements: interagency and street (intervention) team coordinators, criminal justice participation, lead agency project management and commitment to the model, social and crisis intervention and outreach work, suppression, targeting—especially of gang members, balance of services, and intensity of services.

In the outcome evaluation, Spergel (2007) examined the effects of the Little Village project on the approximately two hundred targeted hardcore gang youth during the period when they were served by the program. Self-reports of criminal involvement showed that the program reduced serious violent and property crimes, and sharp declines were also seen in the frequencies of various types of offenses. The program was more effective with older, high-rate, violent gang offenders than with younger, less violent offenders. Active gang involvement was also reduced among project youth, but mostly for older members, and this change was associated with less criminal activity. Most youth in both targeted gangs improved their educational and employment status during the program period. Employment was associated with a general reduction in youths' criminal activity, especially drug selling.

In a controlled comparison, Spergel (2007) examined arrests among project youth versus two control groups (one received minimal services, and the other received no services from project workers). Recall that the project specifically targeted violent criminal activity in the gangs. Although the project had no significant effect on total arrests, property arrests, or other minor crime arrests, the program youth had significantly fewer total violent crime and drug arrests. Because the Little Village project specifically targeted the most violent gangsters, and the common presumption is that such youth are typically involved with drugs, Spergel examined program effects on subgroups of offenders (1) with violence and drug involvement and (2) with violence and no drug involvement, using the comparison groups. Program effects were strong for both of these groups but slightly stronger for the violence and no-drug subsample.

Using a similar research design, Spergel compared community-wide effects of the project on arrests between pre-program and program periods in Little Village versus other nearby "high gang crime" communities. The project was less effective in changing the entrenched pattern of gangbanging and gang crime in the two targeted gangs and in the Little Village community as a whole. Gang violence was on the upswing during the project period (1992–1997) in this general area of Chicago—one of the deadliest gang violence areas of the city—but the increase in homicides and other serious violent gang crimes was lower among the Latin Kings and Two Six than among the other Latino and African American gangs in the area. Similarly, the increase in serious violent gang crimes was smaller in Little Village than in all other comparable communities. Notably, residents and representatives of various organizations perceived a significant reduction in overall gang crime and violence in Little Village during the program period.

In sum, although the outcomes for the Little Village project are mixed, the results are consistent for violent crimes across analyses at all three impact levels: (1) the individual, (2) the group (gang), and (3) the community (especially in the views of residents). A similar impact was not seen on gang drug activity (although drug selling was reduced among older gang members when the project facilitated their employment), but the project specifically targeted gang violence, not gang drug activity. The significant reductions in self-reported serious violent crimes and arrests for violent crimes and drug offenses were impressive.

Interestingly, the evaluation suggested that a youth outreach (or social intervention) strategy may be more effective in reducing the violent behavior of younger, less violent gang youth, and that a combined youth outreach and police suppression strategy might be more effective with older, more criminally active and violent gang youth, particularly with respect to drug-related crimes. However, the best indicators of reduced total offenses were older age, associations with probation officers, and spending more time with a wife or steady girlfriend. In contrast, the best predictors of reduced violent offenses were youths' avoidance of gang situations, satisfaction with the community, and more exposure to treatment for various personal problems.

Interactive and collaborative project outreach worker efforts, combining suppression, social support, and provision of social services, were shown to be most effective in changing criminal involvement of gang members. Larger program dosages (multiple providers, frequency, and duration of services) proved to be important, and these were associated with reduced levels of violence arrests. Four types of service or sanctions predicted successful outcomes among program youth: suppression (particularly by police), job referrals by youth workers, school referrals (mainly by youth workers), and program dosage (contacts by all workers together).

In the next phase of its development of a comprehensive program that could address youth gang problems, OJJDP tested the Comprehensive Community Model in several settings.

Demonstration and Testing of the Comprehensive Gang Model

OJJDP implemented and tested the effectiveness of the Comprehensive Community Model in other initiatives, each of which provided varied settings to help gauge the utility of the model. Outcome data are currently available on just one of the subsequent OJJDP initiatives, and those are described here.

In the first of its experiments, OJJDP chose five competitively selected sites that demonstrated strong capacity to implement the Comprehensive Community Model: Mesa, Arizona; Riverside, California; Bloomington-Normal, Illinois; San Antonio, Texas; and Tucson, Arizona. Each of the OJJDP demonstration projects was funded in 1995, and they shared the main goals of the Comprehensive Community Model: (1) to reduce youth gang crime, especially violence, in targeted communities and (2) to improve the capacity of the community—including its institutions and organizations—to prevent, intervene with, and suppress the youth gang problem through the targeted application of interrelated strategies of community mobilization, opportunities provision, social intervention, suppression, and organizational change and development.

In order to develop a composite picture of the implementation process and impact outcomes of the initial Comprehensive Community Model implementations, the evaluators combined the Chicago Little Village evaluation with the studies of the five urban sites (Spergel, Wa, and Sosa 2006).[4] Three of the six communities either made fatal planning mistakes (such as selecting a lead agency that failed to perform) or encountered fundamental implementation difficulties because key agencies in the community simply were unwilling to work together. But when it was well implemented—at three of the sites (Chicago, Mesa, and Riverside)—the Comprehensive Community Model effectively guided the communities in developing services and strategies that contributed to reductions in both gang violence (at three sites) and drug-related offenses (at two sites) (Spergel, Wa, and Sosa 2006). Key factors in implementation success are reflected in the seven lessons outlined below. (For a site-by-site summary of the degree of fidelity to the Comprehensive Community Model, see table 14.1 in Spergel, Wa, and Sosa 2006:216; also in OJJDP 2008:43).

Regarding program impact on clients at the successful sites, a key factor was length of time in the program. When youth were in the program for two or more years, there were fewer arrests for all types of offenses. In general, arrest reductions were greater among older youth and females than among younger youth and males (see table 14.2, Spergel, Wa, and Sosa 2006:219). General deterrence effects (at the project-area level) were not as strong as the program effects for individual youth. Nevertheless, these three sites were somewhat successful in integrating police suppression with service-oriented strategies. In sum, the evaluation indicates that when properly implemented, a combination of prevention, intervention, and suppression strategies was successful in reducing gang-related criminal activity (Spergel, Wa, and Sosa 2006).

Lessons Learned

The evaluations of the Comprehensive Community Model across the six implementation sites suggest that the model's comprehensive approach to gang prevention, intervention, and suppression holds enormous potential for widespread applicability to varying community and citywide gang problems, but implementation of such a strategic planning framework necessarily requires a concerted effort. Gang problems are often complex and intractable, as are the responsible agencies in many communities (Decker and Curry 2002).

To identify best practices for planning and implementing the Comprehensive Community Model, the National Youth Gang Center (NYGC) surveyed representatives in OJJDP-funded sites and others from selected implementation sites in Oklahoma, Utah, Nevada, and North Carolina that used the OJJDP model but that were not funded by OJJDP. Next, NYGC convened a focus group meeting to discuss and record best practices. NYGC then reviewed evaluation reports, got input from its training staff who had been working with the OJJDP sites, and synthesized the lessons learned from all these sources into seven categories (OJJDP 2008:5–32), described in the following section.

CONVENING A STEERING COMMITTEE

In virtually every demonstration of OJJDP's Comprehensive Community Model, the effectiveness of its steering committee has been crucial in determining the success or failure of the community in implementing a strategic planning initiative. Best results have been seen when the steering committee mixes two groups: (1) individuals from upper-level management in key partnering agencies who can effect organizational change within their own agencies and (2) individuals with influence within the community, including residents, and representatives of grassroots community groups, neighborhood associations, religious organizations, and advocacy groups. A commitment to a data-driven, problem-solving approach is also essential.

ADMINISTERING THE PROGRAM

Selecting an appropriate lead agency and program director are crucial steps in ensuring program success. There are advantages and disadvantages to various types of lead agencies (see OJJDP 2008:8, table 1). Selection of a program director who has the professional respect of and is well regarded by all agency leaders and others working on the project, and who has a broad base of skills for performing diverse tasks, is essential for success.

ASSESSING THE GANG PROBLEM

Conducting a comprehensive assessment of the community's gang problem is the foundation for planning and implementing the Comprehensive Community Model. Where assessments were done methodically and comprehensively, efficient and effective targeting usually followed.

PLANNING FOR IMPLEMENTATION

The steering committee serves as the primary decision-making body for implementation planning. It should use the assessment as a guide in formulating a strategic plan to mitigate the community's gang problem. Activities, goals, and objectives for prevention, intervention, and suppression strategies also are predicated on the problems described during the gang assessment.

IMPLEMENTING THE PROGRAM

The implementation process is accelerated when the steering committee agencies, the lead agency, and the program director conduct start-up and capacity-building activities before beginning services. The members of the steering committee should be champions of the program as a vehicle for change within the community.

SELECTING PROGRAM ACTIVITIES

Selecting the appropriate program activities is an important step toward ensuring that program goals are achieved. A balanced combination of prevention, intervention, and suppression produces the best results. (The inclusion of reentry programming for confined gang members is also advisable.) It is best for the intervention team (made up of representatives of key gang-related agencies) and the outreach workers to function as primary service-delivery agents in the Comprehensive Community Model.

SUSTAINING THE PROGRAM

Programs that were sustained long-term had two key practices. First, they standardized and institutionalized data collection to show program outcomes. Access to these data was invaluable for leveraging funds and resources. Second, they benefited from well-organized and engaged steering committees that shared ownership and responsibility for the programs.

Two of these lessons merit special attention. First, a balanced combination of prevention, intervention, and suppression strategies is particularly important for success in any community (Spergel, Wa, and Sosa 2006; see also Wyrick 2006; Wyrick and Howell 2004). To simplify this concept, *prevention programs* are needed to target youth at risk of gang involvement, in order to reduce the number of youths that join gangs. *Intervention programs and strategies* are needed to provide needed sanctions and services for younger youth who are actively involved in gangs in order to separate them from gangs. And law enforcement *suppression strategies* are needed to target the most violent gangs and older, criminally active gang members. Each of these components helps make the others more effective. This continuum sets the Comprehensive Community Model apart from single-dimensional gang suppression models. In addition to Spergel's six-site study, other research shows that the greater the number of strategies a gang program employs, the greater the likelihood of long-term success (OJJDP 2008).

Second, the development of intervention teams with outreach youth worker services is also critical. At each of the successful sites, an interdisciplinary intervention team was utilized as the main case management vehicle. These teams integrate the services of diverse agencies in a manner that the agencies could not accomplish on their own, while targeting a specific subset of gang members—those who are not so entrenched in gang life that they cannot be redirected.

Another example of a comprehensive community anti-gang approach has been tested in Chicago with positive results that suggest lessons for implementing the Comprehensive Community Model in major cities. In this version of the model, under the sponsorship of the Chicago Project for Violence Prevention, the goal was to change community norms about violence, both in the wider community and among its clients, and to enhance the perceived risks of engaging in violence. In addition, Chicago CeaseFire focused on affecting risky activities by a small number of carefully selected members of the community, those with a high chance of either "being shot or being a shooter" in the immediate future (Skogan et al. 2008; see also chapter 4 of this volume). In the CeaseFire intervention, outreach workers called "violence interrupters" (most of whom were former gang members) worked alone or in pairs on the street mediating conflicts between gangs, and in hospital emergency rooms, intervening to stem the cycle of retaliatory violence. "In the gang world, one shooting frequently leads to another, perpetuating a cycle of violence" (Skogan et al. 2008:ES-2). The outreach workers also provided services for gang members. In addition, several CeaseFire host agencies were themselves service providers. Mobilizing two key groups in the community, the clergy and residents who could be stirred to direct action, was another important part of the program strategy. Beginning in the late 1990s, CeaseFire spawned twenty-seven or so sites in Chicago and nearby Illinois cities. An analysis of crime hot spots contrasted shooting patterns before and after the introduction of CeaseFire, with parallel maps detailing changes in shooting patterns in the matched comparison areas (Skogan et al. 2008). Overall, the program areas grew noticeably safer in six of the seven CeaseFire sites, and the researchers found evidence that decreases in the size and intensity of shooting hot spots were linked to the introduction of CeaseFire in four of these areas.

Concluding Observations

This review of youth gang programs indicates that the landscape of gang programming has changed, even though this enterprise is still in its infancy, with relatively few high-quality evaluations. Although only a few gang-related programs have been rated effective, the claim that nothing has been proven to work with gangs or gang members (Klein and Maxson 2006) is no longer supported by the empirical evidence. Despite the fact that the reviews reported here used less-rigid criteria than some other program reviews (cf. Mihalic et al. 2001), there is considerable evidence that programs rated effective by less-restrictive criteria can also produce worthwhile results of practical value. A case in point is Aggression Replacement Training, which, as noted above, scored an effective rating (L-2). Although it is not recognized as a "blueprint" program, it produced reductions in delinquent recidivism comparable to Functional Family Therapy, a well-recognized "blueprint" program, when both models were implemented at multiple sites in the same statewide Washington initiative (Washington State Institute for Public Policy 2004).

If we judge by the rating and classification of gang programs reported here, just one of the programs was rated effective at the highest (L-1) level, comparable to an "exemplary" or "model" classification in other program rating schemes. This suggests that one should not expect supernormal impacts from any of the gang programs tested to date. However, several programs have demonstrated effectiveness at least at a threshold level. As with any research-based program, caution should be exercised in replicating them.

Another cautionary note is in order. It would be unreasonable to expect dramatic success with gang members who are embedded in the gang lifestyle. These youth tend to have multiple risk factors in multiple developmental domains (Howell and Egley 2005; Thornberry et al. 2003). Only small and gradual behavioral improvements are realistic with this typically high-risk, criminally oriented population. Thus a highly structured setting, such as that provided in the Little Village project, may be needed to suppress recalcitrant gangsters' criminal activity while providing high service dosages (see also Schram and Gaines 2005).

The entirety of a community's complement of programs should be considered, as opposed to relying on one program. A noteworthy strength of the Comprehensive Community Model is its emphasis on system-wide strategic planning, a targeted focus, and continuum building (OJJDP 2008).[5] A program continuum is needed that parallels offender careers, beginning with prevention and early intervention in pre-delinquent and delinquent careers, and then juvenile justice system intervention using graduated sanctions, linked with a continuum of rehabilitation interventions (Howell and Egley, 2005; Wyrick 2006; Wyrick and Howell 2004). This continuum can be organized to prevent further development of offender careers toward serious, violent, chronic offending, and gang involvement. Advanced formal decision-making tools are available to assist juvenile justice system professionals in developing a continuum of graduated sanctions that can be linked with a continuum of treatment options, both components of which can be matched with considerable precision to offenders' recidivism risk level and treatment needs (Howell 2003). However, effective program services must be used if the graduated sanctions system and linked interventions are expected to produce worthwhile positive outcomes. This is the next frontier—matching evidence-based programs with offenders' treatment needs.

Notes

1. See Howell (2000):3–4, table 1, or Howell (1998):288–289, table 12.1, for a listing of gang program evaluations, 1936–1999.

2. This database is connected to the *Community Guide to Helping America's Youth* that nine federal agencies worked together to develop in 2005. The program rating criteria were agreed upon by the participating agencies, which included the U.S. Department of Health and Human Services, the U.S. Department of Justice, the U.S. Department of Education, the U.S. Department of Labor, the U.S. Department of Agriculture, the U.S. Department of Housing and Urban Development, the Office for National Drug Control Policy, and the Corporation for National and Community Service. The overall rating is derived from four summary dimensions of program effectiveness: the conceptual framework of the program, program fidelity, strength of the evaluation design, and the empirical evidence demonstrating the prevention or reduction of problem behaviors.

3. Outreach workers in these modern-day gang programs perform a different role from that of their counterparts in gang programs in the 1950s and 1960s (Howell 1998, 2000). Whereas the outreach workers of the mid-1900s attempted to transform entire gangs into law-abiding groups, their modern-day counterparts work directly with individual gang members and at-risk youth rather than with the gang as a whole.

4. OJJDP chose to disseminate only one gang program model from its multi-site research and development initiative, the Comprehensive Gang Model, instead of the separately tested versions of this model.

5. The National Youth Gang Center (NYGC) has developed the Strategic Planning Tool, an operating system that communities can use to assess their gang problem and then use the Comprehensive Gang Model to develop a prevention,

intervention, and suppression continuum (www.iir.com/nygc/tool). This tool includes research-based risk factors and indicators, and information on promising and effective juvenile delinquency and gang programs and strategies that address specific risk factors among various age groups. It incorporates a problem-solving approach to gang-related crime, for example, in engaging participating sites in an analysis of crime trends involving gang members, identification of hot spots, and the targeting of high-rate gang offenders and violent gangs. To complement use of the Strategic Planning Tool, an assessment protocol is available that any community can use to assess its gang problem and to promote the development of a data-driven continuum of gang prevention, intervention, and suppression programs and strategies (National Youth Gang Center 2002a). Resource materials that assist communities in developing an action plan to implement the Comprehensive Gang Model are also available (National Youth Gang Center 2002b). Both of these resources are available online at www.iir.com/nygc/acgp/default.htm. This operating system contains user-friendly tools that empower communities to assess their gang problem, inventory existing program resources, identify gaps, and select preferred solutions from a menu of research-based programs and strategy options. Gang programs should be integrated with a community's continuum of delinquency programs. An abundance of such programs is available online (http://guide.helpingamericasyouth.gov).

References

Andrews, D. A. 2006. "Enhancing Adherence to Risk-Need Responsivity." *Criminology and Public Policy* 5 (3): 595–602.

Bonta, J. 1996. "Risk-Needs Assessment and Treatment." In A. T. Harland, ed., *Choosing Correctional Options That Work*, 18–32. Thousand Oaks, Calif.: Sage.

Braga, A. A., D. M. Kennedy, E. J. Waring, and A.M. Piehl. 2001. "Problem-Oriented Policing, Deterrence, and Youth Violence: An Evaluation of Boston's Operation Ceasefire." *Journal of Research in Crime and Delinquency* 38:195–225.

Braga, A. A. and G. L. Pierce. 2005. "Disrupting Illegal Firearms Markets in Boston: The Effects of Operation Ceasefire on the Supply of New Handguns to Criminals." *Criminology and Public Policy* 4 (4): 717–748.

Bynum, T. S. and S. P. Varano. 2003. "The Anti-Gang Initiative in Detroit: An Aggressive Enforcement Approach to Gangs." In S. H. Decker, *Policing Gangs and Youth Violence*, 214–238. Belmont, Calif.: Wadsworth/Thompson Learning.

Dahmann, J. 1983. *Prosecutorial Response to Violent Gang Criminality: An Evaluation of Operation Hardcore*. Washington, D.C.: National Institute of Justice.

Decker, S. H. 2003. "Policing Gangs and Youth Violence: Where Do We Stand, Where Do We Go from Here?" In S. H. Decker, *Policing Gangs and Youth Violence*, 287–293. Belmont, Calif.: Wadsworth/Thompson Learning.

Decker, S. and G. D. Curry. 2002. "'I'm Down for My Organization': The Rationality of Responses to Delinquency, Youth Crime, and Gangs." In A. R. Piquero and S. G. Tibbits, eds., *Rational Choice and Criminal Behavior*, 197–218. New York: Routledge.

Duane, D. 2006. "Straight Outta Boston." *Mother Jones*, January–February, 61–80.

Esbensen, F.-A., D. W. Osgood, T. J. Taylor, D. Peterson, and A. Freng. 2001. "How Great Is G.R.E.A.T.? Results from a Longitudinal Quasi-Experimental Design." *Criminology and Public Policy* 1 (1): 87–118.

Fagan, J. 2002. "Policing Guns and Youth Violence." *Future of Children* 12 (2): 133–151.

Goldstein, A. P. and B. Glick. 1994. *The Prosocial Gang: Implementing Aggression Replacement Training*. Thousand Oaks, Calif.: Sage.

Howell, J. C. 1998 "Promising Programs for Youth Gang Violence Prevention and Intervention." In R. Loeber and D. P. Farrington, eds., *Serious and Violent Juvenile Offenders: Risk Factors and Successful Interventions*, 284–312. Thousand Oaks, Calif.: Sage.

——. 2000. *Youth Gang Programs and Strategies*. Washington, D.C.: U.S. Department of Justice, Office of Juvenile Justice and Delinquency Prevention.

——. 2003. *Preventing and Reducing Juvenile Delinquency: A Comprehensive Framework*. Thousand Oaks, Calif.: Sage.

Howell, J. C. and A. Egley, Jr. 2005. "Moving Risk Factors Into Developmental Theories of Gang Membership." *Youth Violence and Juvenile Justice* 3 (4): 334–354.

Josi, D. and D. K. Sechrest. 1999. "A Pragmatic Approach to Parole Aftercare: Evaluation of a Community Reintegration Program for High-Risk Youthful Offenders." *Justice Quarterly* 16 (1): 51–80.

Kennedy, D. M. 1999. "Pulling Levers: Getting Deterrence Right." *National Institute of Justice Journal* 236 (July): 2–8.

——. 2007. *Going to Scale: A National Structure for Building on Proved Approaches to Preventing Gang Violence. A Discussion Document*. New York: Center for Crime Prevention and Control, John Jay College of Criminal Justice.

Kent, D. R., S. I. Donaldson, P. A. Wyrick, and P. J. Smith. 2000. "Evaluating Criminal Justice Programs Designed to Reduce Crime by Targeting Repeat Gang Offenders." *Evaluation and Program Planning* 23:115–124.

Klein, M. W. 1995. *The American Street Gang*. New York: Oxford University Press.

Klein, M. W. and C. L. Maxson. 2006. *Street Gang Patterns and Policies*. New York: Oxford University Press.

Knitzer, J. and J. Cooper. 2006. "Beyond Integration: Challenges for Children's Mental Health." *Health Affairs* 25 (3): 670–679.

Lipsey, M. W. 2005. "The Challenges of Interpreting Research for Use by Practitioners: Comments on the Latest Products from the Task Force on Community Preventive Services." *American Journal of Preventive Medicine* 28 (2S1): 1–3.

Littell, J. H., M. Popa, and B. Forsythe. 2006. "Multisystemic Therapy for Social, Emotional, and Behavioral Problems in Youth Aged 10–17." *Cochrane Database of Systematic Reviews* 2005, Issue 3. Art. No.: CD004797. DOI: 10.1002/14651858. CD004797.Pub3.

Ludwig, J. 2005. "Better Gun Enforcement, Less Crime." *Criminology and Public Policy* 4 (4): 677–716.

Mihalic, S., K. Irwin, D. Elliott, A. Fagan, and D. Hansen. 2001. "Blueprints for Violence Prevention." *Juvenile Justice Bulletin.* Washington, D.C.: U.S. Department of Justice, Office of Juvenile Justice and Delinquency Prevention.

National Youth Gang Center. 2002a. *OJJDP Comprehensive Gang Model: Assessing Your Community's Youth Gang Problem.* Washington, D.C.: Office of Juvenile Justice and Delinquency Prevention.

——. 2002b. *OJJDP Comprehensive Gang Model: Planning for Implementation.* Washington, D.C.: Office of Juvenile Justice and Delinquency Prevention.

Office of Juvenile Justice and Delinquency Prevention. 2008. *Best Practices to Address Community Gang Problems: OJJDP's Comprehensive Gang Model.* Washington, D.C.: Author (www.ncjrs.gov/pdffiles1/ojjdp/222799.pdf).

Papachristos, A. V. 2001. *A.D., After the Disciples: The Neighborhood Impact of Federal Gang Prosecution.* Peotone, Ill.: New Chicago School Press.

Rosenfeld, R., R. Fornango, and E. Baumer. 2005. "Did Ceasefire, Compstat, and Exile Reduce Homicide?" *Criminology and Public Policy* 4 (3): 419–449.

Roush, D. W., L. D. Miesner, and C. M. Winslow. 2002. *Managing Youth Gang Members in Juvenile Detention Facilities.* East Lansing: Center for Research and Professional Development, National Juvenile Detention Association, School of Criminal Justice, Michigan State University.

Schram, P. J. and L. K. Gaines. 2005. "Examining Delinquent Nongang Members and Delinquent Gang Members: A Comparison of Juvenile Probationers at Intake and Outcomes." *Youth Violence and Juvenile Justice* 3 (2): 99–115.

Sherman, L. 1990. "Police Crackdowns." *NIJ Reports* 219:2–6.

Skogan, W. G. and S. M. Hartnett. 1997. *Community Policing, Chicago Style.* New York: Oxford University Press.

Skogan, W. G., S. M. Hartnett, N. Bump, and J. Dubois. 2008. *Evaluation of Cease-Fire-Chicago: Executive Summary.* Chicago: Northwestern University.

Skogan, W. G. and L. Steiner. 2004. *CAPS at Ten: Community Policing in Chicago.* Chicago: Illinois Criminal Justice Information Authority.

Spergel, I. A. 1995. *The Youth Gang Problem.* New York: Oxford University Press.

——. 2007. *Reducing Youth Gang Violence: The Little Village Gang Project in Chicago.* Lanham, Md.: AltaMira.

Spergel, I. A., R. Chance, C. Ehrensaft, T. Regulus, C. Kane, and R. Laseter. 1992. *Technical Assistance Manuals: National Gang Suppression and Intervention Program.* Chicago: University of Chicago, School of Social Service Administration.

Spergel, I. A., R. Chance, C. Ehrensaft, T. Regulus, C. Kane, R. Laseter, A. Alexander, and S. Oh. 1993. "The National Youth Gang Survey: A Research and Development Process." In A. Goldstein and C. R. Huff, eds., *The Gang Intervention Handbook*, 359–400. Champaign, Ill.: Research Press.

——. 1994. *Gang Suppression and Intervention: Community Models*. Washington, D.C.: U.S. Department of Justice, Office of Juvenile Justice and Delinquency Prevention.

Spergel, I. A., G. D. Curry, R. Chance, C. Kane, R. Ross, A. Alexander, E. Simmons, and S. Oh. 1994. *Gang Suppression and Intervention: Problem and Response*. Washington, D.C.: U.S. Department of Justice, Office of Juvenile Justice and Delinquency Prevention.

Spergel, I. A., K. M. Wa, and R. V. Sosa. 2006. "The Comprehensive, Community-Wide, Gang Program Model: Success and Failure." In J. F. Short and L. A. Hughes, eds., *Studying Youth Gangs*, 203–224. Lanham, Md.: AltaMira.

Thornberry, T. P., M. D. Krohn, A. J. Lizotte, C. A. Smith, and K. Tobin. 2003. *Gangs and Delinquency in Developmental Perspective*. New York: Cambridge University Press.

Thrasher, F. M. 1936. "The Boys' Club and Juvenile Delinquency." *American Journal of Sociology* 41:66–80.

Tita, G., K. J. Riley, and P. Greenwood. 2003. "From Boston to Boyle Heights: The Process and Prospects of a 'Pulling Levers' Strategy in a Los Angeles Barrio." In S. H. Decker, ed., *Policing Gangs and Youth Violence*, 102–130. Belmont, Calif.: Wadsworth/Thompson Learning.

Tremblay, R. E., L. Masse, L. Pagani, and F. Vitaro.1996. "From Childhood Physical Aggression to Adolescent Maladjustment: The Montreal Prevention Experiment." In R. De, V. Peters, and R. J. McMahon, eds., *Preventing Childhood Disorders, Substance Abuse, and Delinquency*, 268–298. Thousand Oaks, Calif.: Sage.

Washington State Institute for Public Policy. 2004. *Outcome Evaluation of Washington State's Research-Based Programs for Juvenile Offenders*. Oympia: Author.

Weisel, D. L. 2002. "The Evolution of Street Gangs: An Examination of Form and Variation." In W. S. Reed and S. H. Decker, eds., *Responding to Gangs: Evaluation and Research*, 25–65. Washington, D.C.: U.S. Department of Justice, National Institute of Justice.

Wyrick, P. A. 2006. "Gang Prevention: How to Make the 'Front End' of Your Anti-Gang Effort Work." *United States Attorneys' Bulletin* 54 (3): 52–60.

Wyrick, P. A. and J. C. Howell. 2004. "Strategic Risk-Based Response to Youth Gangs." *Juvenile Justice* 10 (1): 20–29.

4

An Examination of the Role of CeaseFire, the Chicago Police, Project Safe Neighborhoods, and Displacement in the Reduction in Homicide in Chicago in 2004

CHARLIE RANSFORD, CANDICE KANE, TIM METZGER,
ELENA QUINTANA, AND GARY SLUTKIN

Violent crime and homicide rates have historically been much higher in the United States than in most other developed nations. The homicide rate reached a peak in 1991 at 9.8 homicides per 100,000 people and thereafter began to decrease slowly throughout most of the United States. By 2004 it was down in many areas to the lowest level since the 1960s, at a rate of 5.5 homicides per 100,000 people (FBI 2004), followed by a slight increase to 5.7 homicides per 100,000 in 2006 (FBI 2006).

The reason for the decline in the homicide rate has been hotly debated, with many possible explanations suggested: increased police activity, increased incarceration rates, stricter sentencing, easing of the crack market, reduction in segregation, increased opportunities for minorities, reduced use of guns, decreasing domestic violence, the aging of the population, improvement in the economy, and even the delayed effects of the legalization of abortion (Blumstein and Wallman 2000). The extent to which any of these explanations accounts for the decline is difficult to determine and has not been established (Maltz 1998).

Although an understanding of the cause of the reduction in homicides across the United States may be elusive, it may be better ascertained by minimizing the number of variables that need to be considered as possibly affecting the homicide rate. In this chapter, we examine the reduction in homicides in one specific geographic location, over one short time period, thus systematically eliminating other variables from consideration.

In 2003, Chicago had 598 homicides, giving it a rate of 20.7 homicides per 100,000 residents. To put that rate in context, in 2003 New York had a homicide rate of 7.4 per 100,000 residents and Los Angeles had a rate of 13.4 (FBI 2004). Most European cities had even lower rates, around 1 to 3 homicides per 100,000 residents.

One year later, in 2004, homicides declined in Chicago by 25 percent, to a total of 448, a rate of 15.5 homicides per 100,000 residents and the lowest number in Chicago since 1965. Similarly, shooting rates in Chicago declined by 40 percent from 2003 to 2004,[1] and public violence with a firearm declined by 13 percent (Rosenbaum and Stephens 2005).

Although Chicago still has a relatively high homicide rate, the 25 percent reduction was an unusually large decline. In fact, 38 percent of the 2.4 percent reduction in homicides nationally in 2004 occurred in Chicago. As shown in figure 4.1, other major cities in the United States did not have similar reductions in homicides.[2] Something unique occurred in Chicago in 2004 that did not occur in other cities, something that caused a sharp reduction in homicides.

This large drop was also, notably, unique to homicides. As shown in table 4.1, although all categories of crime decreased, only homicides and arson had large declines.[3] No other category of crime had more than an 8.1 percent reduction. These data suggest that something unique happened in Chicago specifically with regard to homicides.

The reduction of homicides in Chicago in 2004 offers a unique opportunity to analyze homicide reduction in a less complex situation.[4] It is notably less complex because it allows us to focus on a limited time frame of one year and the limited geography of Chicago, rather than seeking to understand common causes of changes across a region or the entire nation. The short time period in which this reduction occurred allows us to exclude variables that occur over long periods of time, such as the aging of the population. Though the aging of a population could affect homicide rates, the distribution of ages in the population of Chicago did not change drastically enough in one year to affect them substantially. The single geographic

FIGURE 4.1

Trends in Homicide Rates per 100,000 in Major Cities in the United States

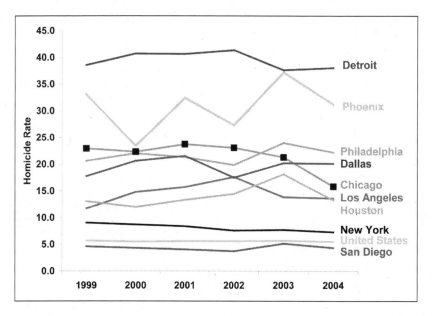

location permits the exclusion of factors that did not occur specifically in Chicago in this time period. For example, gun laws could have an effect on homicides, but Chicago did not have any significant changes in its gun laws during this time period.

Our research has identified four primary reasons for the decline in homicides in 2004 in Chicago. Three of these are connected to different policies and programs that were intentionally focused on reducing homicides and violent crime—particularly focused on gang violence—through violence prevention, suppression, and aggressive prosecution strategies. These are the CeaseFire violence prevention program, more-effective police strategies, and the introduction of Project Safe Neighborhoods. A fourth factor, the relocation of key violent offenders out of the city, may also have had an impact and may have been partially attributable to the influences of some of these programs and partially the result of other factors. Each of these factors, we argue, played an important role in reducing homicides in Chicago in 2004. Table 4.2 summarizes these factors, which we discuss below. Before exploring them in greater depth and examining their impact on the reduction in homicides in Chicago in 2004, however, it is important to

TABLE 4.1

Percent Change in Categories of Crime in Chicago (Compared with Previous Year)

TYPES OF CRIME		1995	1996	1997	1998	1999	2000	2001	2002	2003	2004
VIOLENT CRIME	Homicide	-11.1%	-3.9%	-4.4%	-7.5%	-8.8%	-1.7%	5.5%	-1.8%	-8.6%	-25.1%
	Criminal Sexual Assault	-9.5%	-3.0%	-9.5%	-5.3%	-8.7%	-5.2%	-2.6%	2.0%	-8.4%	-7.0%
	Robbery	-11.2%	-10.8%	-5.6%	-9.0%	-13.4%	-3.3%	-4.6%	0.6%	-6.6%	-8.1%
	Aggravated Battery/Assault	-19.1%	-5.2%	-1.1%	-0.1%	-9.3%	-4.5%	-3.8%	-2.1%	-20.8%	-5.3%
	Total Violent	-15.2%	-7.6%	-3.5%	-4.2%	-11.0%	-4.0%	-3.9%	-0.9%	-14.4%	-6.9%
PROPERTY CRIME	Arson	10.6%	6.4%	-1.3%	-17.1%	-7.0%	-10.6%	-5.5%	1.8%	-7.5%	-17.2%
	Burglary	-8.3%	0.6%	0.6%	-11.7%	-16.9%	-5.2%	-8.2%	-2.3%	-1.2%	-2.7%
	Theft	0.4%	-1.9%	0.3%	1.5%	-8.1%	-5.1%	-7.6%	-1.5%	0.7%	-4.0%
	Auto Theft	-9.1%	-6.1%	-1.7%	-5.0%	-4.2%	-2.3%	-6.9%	-8.9%	-9.7%	0.1%
	Total Property	-3.2%	-2.1%	0.0%	-2.5%	-9.1%	-4.6%	-7.6%	-3.0%	-1.5%	-3.2%
Total Crime		-6.5%	-3.5%	-0.8%	-2.9%	-9.5%	-4.5%	-6.7%	-2.5%	-4.5%	-4.0%

TABLE 4.2

Summary of Major Programs and Factors that Affected the Decrease in Homicides in Chicago in 2004

PROGRAM OR FACTOR	GEOGRAPHIC COVERAGE OF CHICAGO	POPULATION SERVED	QUANTITATIVE DATA	QUALITATIVE DATA	OTHER
CeaseFire	• Active in 11 of the most violent communities in Chicago	• Serves those who are at highest risk for committing violent crimes • Works with 40 of the most violent gangs in Chicago • Works during days and times when violence is most likely to occur • External evaluation confirms program works with highest risk	• Decreases in homicides and shootings in target communities that are greater than neighboring and comparison communities and twice the percentage reduction in the city as a whole • 152 documented conflicts mediated • External evaluation confirms large reductions in shootings	• Increased number of outreach workers by 300% in 2004 • Tripled the number of communities in 2004	• Also showed positive results in the suburb of Maywood
Project Safe Neighborhoods	• Active in two of Chicago's 25 police districts	• Serves parolees who have been convicted of a gun crime	• Decreased homicides in its two districts • Reached over 50% of gun offenders in its two districts	• Began program in late 2003	• Collaborated with CeaseFire for its forums • CeaseFire tripled its efforts in one of PSN's districts

continued

TABLE 4.2 (continued)

Summary of Major Programs and Factors that Affected the Decrease in Homicides in Chicago in 2004

PROGRAM OR FACTOR	GEOGRAPHIC COVERAGE OF CHICAGO	POPULATION SERVED	QUANTITATIVE DATA	QUALITATIVE DATA	OTHER
Chicago Police	• Active throughout Chicago	• Serve the whole city	• 25% decrease in homicides in 2004 across whole city	• New strategies in 2004 (cameras, DOC, gang unit)	• Similar strategies have worked in other cities
Displacement	• Occurred throughout Chicago	• Affects a large variety of people	• Increase in gangs migrating to collar communities	• Increase in crime in collar communities	• Increased police activity and prosecution influence displacement

understand why many of the typical explanations for the decline of violent crime and homicide do not apply to Chicago in 2004.

Factors That Likely Did *Not* Play a Role in the 2004 Reduction in Homicides in Chicago

Several possible explanations that are frequently offered for the dramatic reduction in violent crime and homicide in Chicago in 2004 can be excluded from consideration. Among them are the idea of a reduction in the "supply side" of criminal youth because of abortion policy, changes in the distribution of ages in the population, changes in the drug market (particularly the diminished popularity of crack cocaine), the advent of community-oriented policing, broader economic changes, changes in the availability of guns, increasing incarceration of violent offenders, increasing police resources, and the reduced lethality of violence when it does occur. We briefly consider each of these possible explanations in turn.

Abortion

Abortion has been advanced as a factor in the decline of crime and specifically the decline in homicides in the United States, primarily because of the popular book *Freakonomics* (Levitt and Dubner 2005), in which Steven Levitt reiterates the analysis from his paper "The Impact of Legalized Abortion on Crime" (Donohue and Levitt 2001). The theory states that the legalization of abortion in the mid-1970s resulted in a reduction in crime in the 1990s, twenty years after abortions started occurring at a higher rate. This conclusion rests on three assumptions: (1) legalization led to fewer "unwanted" babies' being born, (2) unwanted babies are more likely to suffer abuse and neglect and are therefore more likely to exhibit criminal behavior, and (3) violent crime begins to be exhibited by those older than 20.

The legalization of abortion in Chicago occurred thirty years before the 2004 decline in homicides. Because more than 70 percent of homicides were committed by people under the age of 30, the legalization of abortion happened too long ago to have had a drastic effect on homicides in 2004. In addition, crime rates for the first generation after the legalization of abortion did not decrease, as claimed by Donohue and Levitt. In 1993, those 14 to 17 years old—who were part of the first generation after the legalization of abortion—were actually 3.6 times more likely to commit murder than 14- to 17-year-olds in 1984 (Sailer 1999).

Aging

Homicides are predominantly committed by and perpetrated on males between the ages of 15 and 25 (Pridemore 2003). Research has shown that the probability of violence for males of all races peaks at ages 17 to 18 and falls back almost to the starting point by age 25 (Earls 2005). Therefore, the age composition of the population could have an effect on the homicide rate if the number of males aged 15 to 25 declines relative to the population as a whole.

This theory makes intuitive sense but fails to explain the rise in homicides in the late 1980s, when the proportion of individuals aged 18 to 24 was declining and violent crime was increasing (Fox 2000). More specifically, in Chicago the population of 15- to 24-year-olds has increased slightly in the past decade, by about 4,000, and represents only a slightly smaller percentage of the overall population (down by 0.5 percent). This small decline does not seem to be a logical explanation for the dramatic drop in homicides in Chicago in 2004.

Change in the Drug Market

The large increase in homicides in the late 1980s and the subsequent decline between 1991 and 2004 coincided with the rise and fall in the use of crack cocaine (Blumstein and Wallman 2000). When crack appeared on the drug market, it proved to be a highly lucrative product that took over much of the drug trade for a time and was strongly tied to the violent use of handguns, largely in regard to disputes over drug territory. The crack market eventually subsided and has been largely replaced by other drugs, such as marijuana and heroin, a transition that may have had an effect on the level of violence. The reason the crack market subsided is not clear, but possible explanations include a strong police response and the negative effects of crack, which a new generation of drug dealers and users recognized (Grogger 2000).

Although Chicago did experience a decline in homicides since the early 1990s that may be linked to the crack epidemic, no major changes have occurred more recently; therefore the large reduction in 2004 did not likely have any connection to a change in the drug market.

Community-Oriented Policing

Community policing is a method employed to help build relations between police and community residents with the intention of increasing residents' confidence in police, encouraging resident assistance for police, and decreasing fear of crime, which ultimately could increase the effectiveness of police. Typical elements include holding community meetings to hear resident input and feedback and having officers stay in one community to increase residents' familiarity with individual officers and officers' familiarity with the community.

Results of community policing have been mixed. In terms of satisfaction with police, of seventeen studies identified, eight showed a positive effect, eight found no change, and one showed negative effects (Zhao, Scheider, and Thurman 2002). Studies have found that community policing does not decrease fear of crime (Scheider, Rowell, and Bezdikian 2003; Zhao, Scheider, and Thurman 2002), nor have its effects on crime been demonstrated.

The Chicago Alternative Policing Strategy (CAPS), Chicago's community policing program, was started in 1993. It encourages police officers' turf orientation by maintaining long assignments in police beats, training in problem solving, and monthly beat meetings and district advisory committees. Although some studies have claimed that CAPS has been successful, no clear link to a reduction in crime has been demonstrated (Skogan 2004). Indeed, though an extensive evaluation performed on the Chicago CAPS program covering ten years of its implementation provided strong evidence of the effectiveness of community policing on neighborhood dynamics and fear of crime, no clear link was established between the program and a *reduction* in crime (Skogan 2004). Furthermore, because no changes were made in the program in 2004 or in the years preceding 2004, CAPS is not a good explanation for the significant reduction in homicides that occurred in 2004.

Economic Changes

Economic changes are not directly related to crime but do act as an indirect influence through employment. Put simply, when more jobs are available, there is less incentive to turn to crime. However, this fails to explain the dramatic drop in homicides in Chicago in 2004. The economy in Illinois did not experience any dramatic improvement during 2004 or in the period preceding 2004. Indeed, the overall employment rate of working-age Illinois residents fell by 4 percent between 2000 and 2004 (Sum et al. 2005). The employment rate for teens fell by almost 10 percent (Olszewski 2005), making Illinois one of the five worst states for teen employment (Sum et al. 2005). This same trend also occurred in the Chicago metropolitan area, as well as in the city of Chicago, where the employment/population ratio had double-digit reductions for teens from 2000 to 2003 (Sum et al. 2005). The Chicago metropolitan area employment rate fell overall from January 2003 to June 2004 (Bureau of Labor Statistics 2008).

Gun Availability

Most homicides in the United States are committed with a firearm. In 2004, 66 percent of homicides in the United States and 75 percent of homicides in Chicago were committed with a firearm (FBI 2004). Therefore, the availability of guns, which is influenced most notably by gun laws, could have a significant effect on homicides. Research has indicated that the rate of household gun ownership is correlated with the homicide rate (Kellerman et al. 1993; Killias 1993; Sloan et al. 1988) and that the reduction in homicides in the 1990s can be traced to a reduced use of handguns (Surgeon General 2001), but there is mixed evidence regarding the effect of local gun laws on gun violence (Kleck 1991; Loftin et al. 1991). In Chicago, handguns have been illegal for more than twenty years, but guns are still prevalent due to prolific gun trafficking. Chicago police seized just over 10,000 guns per year between 2002 and 2008, with 10,509 seized in 2004 (Chicago Police Department 2004). Because there was no major change in gun laws and because gun seizures were at typical levels, gun availability is an unlikely factor in the 2004 drop in homicides in Chicago.

The type of guns used is also important, because most gun violence could be less lethal if the guns or ammunition used was less lethal. Handguns, semiautomatic guns, and higher-caliber ammunition were cheaply available and increasingly used in the late 1980s and early 1990s and were partly responsible for the increase in homicides (Wintemute 2000). It is not clear if there was any change in the cost of more-lethal weapons or the general availability in the past several years, but it is unlikely that a major change occurred specifically in 2004 in Chicago.

Incarceration

The prison population in the United States has been increasing at a rate of between 2 percent and 4 percent each year for the past decade and reached 2,135,901 prisoners in federal, state, and local facilities in 2004. With the number of people incarcerated increasing every year, some analysts have offered the hypothesis that crime is decreasing because the individuals that are most likely to commit crimes are safely out of society and in prison (Spelman 2000) or because a purported increased threat of incarceration deters individuals from committing crimes (Levitt 1996). Although incarceration may have played a part in the gradual decline in homicides in Chicago over the past two decades, there is no evidence that it was a factor in the sudden 25 percent drop in homicides in 2004. Indeed, the number of incarcerated adults remained constant in Illinois, with less than 1 percent difference from 1999 to 2005 (Illinois Department of Corrections 2005).

Increased Police Force and Budget

In the past decade, police departments across the nation have increased in size to attempt to address the crime problem. Operating budgets increased 20 percent from 1990 to 2000 (controlling for inflation). The number of full-time law enforcement employees increased 20 percent from 1990 to 2000—a 9 percent increase in police per capita. In addition, advancements in technology were achieved, with increased computer use for police in large cities (Reaves 2002). However, increases in the number of police and the size of the budget do not necessarily result in better outcomes.

Some studies have claimed that the level of law enforcement may not matter at all (Philipson and Posner 1996).

In Chicago, the number of police officers and the size of the budget played no role in the 2004 reduction. Chicago had the second-largest police department in the United States, at 13,466 officers in 2000, fourth in officers per capita (Reaves 2002). However, in 2004, when the large reduction in homicides occurred, there was not a substantial increase in police personnel or budget. In fact, the number of police *decreased* from 2003 to 2004 by 3.5 percent, and the budget decreased minimally from 2003 to 2004 (Chicago Police Department 2004).

Lethality of Violence

A decrease in homicides could be a result of gun violence being less lethal, which would occur if response times for emergency calls improved. When a person suffers a life-threatening wound, the length of time that it takes to receive medical attention is extremely important to the likelihood of survival, and slight improvements can potentially increase the survival rate and therefore decrease the number of homicides. Although data on response times are not immediately available, what is known is that the number of shootings, which would not be affected by response times, declined in 2004 by 40 percent[5] and aggravated assaults and batteries with a firearm declined by 18 percent, suggesting that response times did not have a substantial effect on the homicide rate. Whatever played a major role affected people *before* a shooting occurred.

Factors That Likely *Did* Play a Role in the 2004 Reduction in Homicides in Chicago

Having provided an analysis of a set of factors that are often offered as possible explanations for the reduction of violent crime and homicide in the United States and shown how they are unlikely explanations for Chicago's dramatic reduction in homicides in 2004, we now turn to an examination of three factors that, we argue, *were* important contributors to this phenomenon: new police activities (including directed patrols, surveillance cameras, and specialized gang units); aggressive prosecution strategies (especially Project Safe Neighborhoods); and violence prevention programs (specifically, the CeaseFire program). A fourth factor, population displacement, whose effects are more speculative, is also discussed.

New Police Activity

In general, police suppress criminal activity by making crime costly to individuals through the enforcement of laws. Police are the intermediary between the criminal and the criminal justice system, which punishes criminal offenses.

The evidence is mixed with regard to the effectiveness of suppression in general (see chapters 2 and 3 of this volume for brief reviews). Some studies have claimed that the effectiveness of suppression is dependent on its being part of a multi-agency, community-based approach rather than a stand-alone strategy (Spergel and Wa 2000).

Although the use of police is obviously pervasive throughout the United States, in Chicago the police began using some new methods in 2003 that may have increased their effectiveness and that likely contributed to reducing the homicide rate. The Chicago Police Department had several new initiatives that were active in 2004, including directed patrols, the use of cameras, and increased gang task force activity.

DIRECTED PATROLS

A popular method of addressing crime is the concentration of police resources in the areas where crime is most likely to occur, such as near bars, street corners, parks, parking lots, crack houses, and other places that have a history of crime (Washington 1996). Increasing police resources in those areas can address crime in general and thus address the homicide problem.

Directed patrols saturate high-crime areas and therefore increase the risk of an individual's being caught if he or she commits a crime in these areas. Often this strategy is accompanied by traffic stops, which are used to check for any other criminal activity, such as possession of guns or drugs. Because criminals can respond to police activity by moving their operations, particularly those related to drugs and the violence that often accompanies drugs, crime-incidence data are used on a regular basis to reallocate resources to the areas where crime is occurring. This method also employs the important element of accountability. With up-to-date data for each area of the city, police chiefs are able to determine whether area commanders are successfully addressing crime in their areas and can hold them accountable if the data suggest they are not.

One example of this data-driven response is the CompStat program in New York City. With CompStat, commanders of the New York City Police Department meet on a weekly basis and use current crime statistics to target their officers for patrols exactly where the crime is occurring. Many cities have increased their use of this method, and many articles have been written in support of it (Cordner 1981; Marvel and Moody 1996; Sampson and Cohen 1988; Sherman et al. 1997; Tita et al. 2004). Specific evidence of success has been offered for programs in Kansas City (Sherman, Shaw, and Rogan 1995), San Diego (Boydstun 1975), Indianapolis (McGarrell, Chermak, and Weiss 2002), and Boston (Kennedy 1998).[6]

The Chicago Police Department employed a data-driven, targeted response in the summer of 2003 with its Deployment Operations Center (DOC) meetings, which are very similar to New York City's CompStat meetings. Chicago's program had the commanders of all the police districts in Chicago meet once a week, discuss the trends and patterns of gun violence in the city, and plan strategies for deploying units to combat the problems.

Few data are available on the outcomes associated specifically with the DOC meetings, and it would be difficult to determine what is actually attributable to this program. That the communities targeted are areas that have experienced major reductions in homicide and that the use of these meetings began in the summer of 2003 suggest that the meetings could have had an effect on the homicide rate in 2004.

CAMERAS

Police cannot be everywhere at every moment to suppress criminal activity. In response, police departments in cities such as New York, Chicago, London, and Washington, D.C., have begun using cameras to monitor activity in public places. Mounted in bulletproof cases on tall poles, these color video cameras are capable of monitoring street activity for several blocks.

The cameras are usually mobile, so they can be taken down and moved to a new location relatively easily.

Although there is anecdotal evidence of individual arrests and of individual streets being cleaned up because of the cameras, it is not clear if overall crime is affected or if cameras only displace crime to another street, to the alleys, inside buildings, or otherwise out of view of the cameras. It is also not clear if the cameras have any specific effect, positive or negative, on violent crimes. Although it might be intuitive to assume that having the ability to monitor streets and having the effect of moving criminal activity away from areas would decrease violence, homicide, and crime overall, those capabilities could also, in theory, have the opposite effect. Disrupting drug territory could increase violence by creating turf conflicts or moving individuals to areas not as visible to the public.

The installation of cameras in Chicago began in 2003, and by the end of 2005 a total of approximately eighty cameras were in place. Cameras are usually left in a location for at least a month and up to two years. Most of the cameras were put in locations on the west side of Chicago, in neighborhoods with high levels of criminal activity, such as Garfield Park, Humboldt Park, Lawndale, and Austin. Information on the location of the cameras and the duration of the cameras at particular locations is not currently available, thus making it difficult to determine whether the cameras had any effect.

GANG UNITS

For decades, police have deployed teams of officers that specialize in particular types of crime in order to utilize the benefits of specialization. Officers specialize in areas such as homicide, drugs, organized crime, and traffic control. This approach is worthy of mention here because of the development of specialized officers to address urban street gangs. As the problems posed by urban street gangs reached a peak in the 1990s, the need grew for specialized officers who would know the intricacies of gang organization, relationships, and culture. By 2002, special units to address gangs were used in 84 percent of cities, and special units to address the similar issue of juvenile crime were active in 68 percent of cities (Reaves 2002).

Chicago has a significant gang problem, with about 70 gangs, more than 600 factions, and about 70,000 members. In 2003 Chicago police began to target gang shootings by utilizing a new Gang Intelligence Unit, resurrecting the old Gang Crimes Unit that was disbanded in 2000. Through this unit and other police activities, the police targeted specific gangs and made many arrests of gang members. This targeting of violent gangs was successful in incarcerating many violent individuals, but it also created violent situations. When gang leaders are locked up, younger gang members compete for control, and when old leaders return from prison, they compete to reclaim leadership. Because the location, size, and duration of Gang Intelligence Unit assignments have not been made public by the Chicago Police Department, the overall effect of the strategy, positive or negative, is not known.

Aggressive Prosecution

The theory behind increasing the aggressiveness of prosecution for crimes is much the same as that for improving police activity. With more vigorous prosecution, criminals face a higher cost for committing crimes, which should, if criminals are rational decision makers, prevent some individuals from choosing to commit crimes. In addition, more vigorous prosecution leads to more criminals being locked up in prison and therefore being unable to commit crimes in society.

Project Safe Neighborhoods (PSN), a program run by the U.S. Department of Justice, began operating in two of Chicago's most violent police districts in 2002 and by 2004 had reached more than half of the individuals convicted of a gun crime in those districts. Since 2002, PSN has been the national program to increase the aggressiveness of prosecutions. Funded with $1 billion from 2001 to 2004 and modeled on existing programs, such as Project Exile (Richmond, Virginia) and Operation Ceasefire (Boston), PSN is active in some capacity in all ninety-four United States court districts. PSN's mission is to reduce gun crimes across the country. It addresses this mission by targeting those who have at least one prior gun offense and are living in targeted districts, prosecuting criminals federally, and holding forums to warn felons of the consequences that they face if they continue to commit crimes. In addition, PSN establishes and utilizes a partnership between the U.S. Attorney's Office, state's attorney's offices, local police, local prosecutors, and the Bureau of Alcohol, Tobacco, Firearms and Explosives (ATF) to use all available resources to target gun crimes.

Another important element involves developing a strategic plan for each district so that the intricacies of each district's problems are addressed. These strategies are consistently reviewed to provide accountability for outcomes achieved. The U.S. Attorney provides reports that describe the status of its plan and any emerging trends in the district.

Through the U.S. Department of Justice, PSN has also implemented an advertising campaign aimed at gun violence. The campaign, geared toward warning criminals that there are tough consequences for committing gun crimes, includes such messages as "hard time for gun crime" and "when you commit a gun crime, your family pays the price." All messages are designed to make would-be criminals aware of the costs of crime.

In Chicago, PSN started in 2002 in two of Chicago's twenty-five police districts, with forums starting in 2003. The districts chosen are home to the Garfield Park and Austin neighborhoods, two of the most violent neighborhoods in the city. At the end of 2004, two more police districts were added. In Chicago, 70 percent of the individuals targeted by PSN had a prior offense and 40 percent had a prior gun offense. All of the individuals resided in the designated districts. The forums also reached every individual who was paroled to a PSN district by requiring participation as a condition of their parole.

Because it was implemented in 2002–2003 and specifically addresses gun violence, PSN could have played a significant role in the decline in 2004. An evaluation of the Chicago PSN program reported successful results (Papachristos, Meares, and Fagan 2007), but the study failed to control for other interventions, such as CeaseFire or the operations of the Chicago Police Department, and therefore a much more rigorous evaluation would be required to determine the actual effect of PSN. Evaluations of Project Exile, on which PSN was modeled, have been mixed, with initial evaluations claiming reductions in homicides due to the program, but subsequent reviews claiming no effect on homicides (Raphael and Ludwig 2003).

In addition, because this program was implemented nationwide and because similarly large decreases in homicides have not occurred in most other communities, it seems unlikely that PSN by itself played a large role in the reduction in Chicago. Because PSN has worked closely with the Chicago Police Department and with CeaseFire,[7] and because the program targets the same individuals with another intervention, PSN could have an effect as it interacts with these other efforts.

Violence Prevention Programs: CeaseFire Chicago

CeaseFire is a violence prevention program whose sole mission is to reduce homicides and shootings.[8] In 2004, it was active in Chicago and three smaller Illinois cities, and through an influx of funding, it tripled its efforts during 2004. The only program with that single focus in Chicago, CeaseFire targets specific communities that have violence problems and implements a program with a public health strategy, an approach that is supported by the World Health Assembly (Pridemore 2003) and the U.S. Surgeon General (Department of Health and Human Services 2001). The appropriateness of taking a public health approach is also supported by the prevalence of homicide, making that a leading cause of death in the United States; as a leading cause of death, it is a threat to the health of a community and is therefore a public health concern (Kellerman et al. 1998; Philipson and Posner 1996). As a public health strategy, CeaseFire takes a preventive approach and includes outreach to high-risk individuals, public education to promote the message of violence prevention, involvement of faith leaders to influence the thinking and behavior of the community, involvement of law enforcement to share information and coordinate efforts, and community mobilization. Central to all its work is the desire to change the norms and thinking of individuals and communities so that they reject violence as an acceptable form of behavior.

Other violence prevention efforts that preceded CeaseFire demonstrated some success. One example was the Little Village Gang Violence Reduction Project (GVRP), which operated between 1992 and 1997 and involved a set of interrelated strategies similar to those of CeaseFire, involving community mobilization, provision of social opportunities, violence suppression, and organizational change and development. Also like CeaseFire, GVRP used outreach workers to target high-risk youth. An evaluation of GVRP found significant reductions in crime, particularly violence and drug crimes (Spergel 2007; Spergel and Wa 2000; see also chapter 3 of this volume).

The success of CeaseFire, like that of all community interventions, is difficult to ascertain, precisely because of the number of other variables present in the communities in which the program operates. All of the communities in which CeaseFire operated experienced a drop in both homicides and shootings, but given the presence of other interventions, such as police activity and Project Safe Neighborhoods, in many of these communities, it is difficult to determine the relative impact of each individual program in reducing shootings and homicides. There are data available, however, that offer strong evidence that CeaseFire reduced homicides in 2004. Three types of evidence support this conclusion: programmatic, statistical, and circumstantial.

The programmatic evidence lies in the where, when, and with whom CeaseFire operated. For a violence prevention program to be effective, it must locate where the problem is. In 2004 CeaseFire operated in eleven of the most violent communities in Chicago. The level of violence in these communities was highly variable, but several of the communities experienced homicide rates in excess of 50 per 100,000 residents in 2003. The magnitude of violence in these neighborhoods is further supported by an outside evaluation of the program that found that the neighborhoods where CeaseFire worked were "plagued by high rates of violence" as well as having high rates of poverty, gang activity, and low levels of community activism (Skogan et al. 2008).

A violence prevention program must also operate when the problem is occurring in order to be effective. CeaseFire outreach staff members work during the evening hours on Tuesday through Sunday, when violence is most likely to occur.

And finally, in order to affect the rate of violence, a program needs to work with the population that is most likely to commit violent acts. Many studies have identified several key indicators to target individuals likely to commit violent acts. They include membership in a gang, having previously committed a violent act, and being between the ages of 15 and 25. These three indicators (with some variation) were also used in identifying high-risk youth for the Little Village GVRP mentioned previously (Spergel 2007; Spergel and Wa 2000). Using these and similar indicators, in 2004 CeaseFire worked with more than 1,300 clients who were deemed to be at high risk of committing a violent act. An independent survey of CeaseFire clients confirmed that most were high-risk individuals: 82 percent had been arrested (45 percent had been arrested more than five times), more than 90 percent were involved in gangs, 76 percent were in need of employment, and almost 60 percent had only a grade school education (Skogan et al. 2008). In addition, CeaseFire worked to decrease violence with forty of the most violent gangs in Chicago, both with outreach clients and in conflict mediations. For example, the program documented 152 conflicts mediated in 2004; in each instance the outreach worker thought the situation could likely have resulted in a violent crime. Although the

Table 4.3 Reductions in Shootings in CeaseFire Zones 2000–2005 (Versus Neighboring Beats, Comparison Beats, and the City)

CeaseFire Community	Beat	'99	'00	'01	'02	'03[1]	'04	'05	First Implementation Year	Since Implementation	Neighboring Beats (based on first implementation year)	Comparison Beats[2] (based on first implementation year)	City (based on first implementation year)	Ratio Between CeaseFire and Comparison[3]
W. Garfield Park	1115	44 →14		15	21	15	9	8	-68%	-82%	-25%*	-20%**	0%**	3.4
W. Garfield Park 2	1114	13	10 →12		17	16	7	6	20%	-40%	+53%	-17%	0%	<0.0
Auburn Gresham	611													
	612	42	54 →42		45	33	20	11	-22%	-80%	-24%	+32%*	0%‐	>5.0
W. Humboldt Park	1111													
	1112	85	61	75 →52		43	22	44	-31%	-41%	-5%	-20%	-6%	1.6
Southwest Chicago	823													
	825	30	42	55	72 →24		23	16	-67%	-78%	-34%**	-38%*	-24%**	1.8
Logan Square	1413													
	2525	30	52	47	50 →33		12	8	-34%	-84%	-34%	-7%	-24%	4.9
Rogers Park	2422													
	2424													
	2431													
	2432	48	37	37	38	26 →14		10	-46%	-62%	-50%	-23%	-40%	2.0
Average % change									-42%	-69%	-14%**	-15%**	-12%**	2.8

*p<.05   **p<.01   →Full CeaseFire implementation with 4 or more workers

[1] Comparison beats are police beats with shooting rates similar to CeaseFire zones the year before CeaseFire was implemented in that zone. All comparisons are with the first year of implementation

[2] The ratio is a comparison of percentages for CeaseFire versus comparison communities for its first year implementation. For Auburn Gresham, the ratio was arbitrarily assigned >5.0 because the comparison communities had a positive increase (ratio is larger).

outreach workers may have been biased reporters, the fact that a weapon was present in 60 percent of these conflicts lent credence to their assessment that the conflicts could have resulted in a shooting or a homicide.

The statistical evidence demonstrates specific reductions in homicides in CeaseFire communities. The data on where the reductions in homicides and shootings in 2004 occurred show that areas where CeaseFire was operating experienced greater reductions than other areas. As table 4.3 shows, reductions in shootings were greater in CeaseFire zones than on neighboring beats, comparison beats, and in the city as a whole. These data are consistent with results observed in CeaseFire zones between 2000 and 2003. CeaseFire zones experienced an average decline of 42 percent in shootings after the first year of implementation (Chicago Project for Violence Prevention 2005). The external evaluation of CeaseFire confirmed these findings using a variety of types of statistical analysis at seven program sites. The evaluation found that the CeaseFire program decreased shootings (including attempted shootings) by 17 to 24 percent at six sites, decreased actual shootings and homicides by 16 to 34 percent at four sites, decreased the size and density of shooting hot spots at four sites, decreased gang homicides at five sites, and decreased retaliatory homicides at four sites (Skogan et al. 2008). These are among the most significant and comprehensive findings for a violence prevention program to date.

Additional evidence of CeaseFire's effect lies in the timing of the large drop in homicides and shootings in 2004, which coincides with a substantial increase in CeaseFire efforts. In February 2004 CeaseFire received additional funding from the State of Illinois that it used for an immediate expansion from five to fifteen communities and from twenty to eighty outreach workers. Thus, although CeaseFire had been in operation since 2000, this large expansion could account for why there was such a significant reduction in homicides and shootings in 2004 and not previously. The new communities to which CeaseFire expanded had a 51 percent reduction in shootings, with neighboring beats, comparison beats, and the city having smaller reductions. In 2004, overall reductions in shootings in CeaseFire zones were 45 percent, which was significantly and substantially higher (twice as high) than the change experienced outside CeaseFire zones.

As a result, there were several significant "firsts" in CeaseFire zones in 2004. The 11th District, formerly the most violent district in Chicago and an area where CeaseFire tripled its efforts, had its first month without a homicide in many years. Police Beat 1413 in Logan Square, which had the most homicides in Chicago in 2003 and where CeaseFire tripled its efforts in 2004, had no homicides in 2004.

CeaseFire also worked in areas outside of Chicago, in places such as Maywood, Illinois, offering a chance to look at CeaseFire's effects without many of the other confounding factors. Maywood is a western suburb of Chicago that has a substantial violence problem. The community has its own police department and is therefore not affected by the new initiatives of the Chicago Police Department. It is also not affected by Project Safe Neighborhoods because it is not one of the areas in which that program operates. CeaseFire began operating in Maywood at the end of 2003. In 2004 Maywood had a 50 percent drop in homicides and a 62 percent drop in shootings. And for the first time in years, Maywood had no homicides in 2004 from April to mid-June.

Displacement

A decrease in crime in one geographic area may occur simply because the perpetrators of crime move out of that area and into another area, thereby displacing crime rather than actually diminishing it. To analyze whether such displacement occurred, the potential causes of the displacement and the expected outcomes can be examined to determine to what degree they existed in Chicago around 2004.

CAUSES OF DISPLACEMENT

Many factors strongly influence people's decision to move; two that are relevant to our discussion here will be discussed. Gentrification, or the upgrading of deteriorated urban property by middle-class or affluent people, often results in displacement of lower-income people as well as of certain criminal populations. Another possible cause of displacement is an increase in aggressive police activity and prosecutions, which increases the risk and cost of committing crime in one area and may therefore cause criminals to move to areas with a lower risk and cost.

The level to which gentrification has occurred in impoverished neighborhoods in Chicago recently is not completely understood without detailed economic and housing information. In Chicago, this type of information from 2000 showed gentrification occurring in some communities, including Garfield Park, Logan Square, and the Near West Side, while other areas, such as Englewood, Roseland, and Auburn Gresham, showed weak gains (Taylor and Puente 2004). In addition, many of Chicago's public housing projects have been torn down, forcing residents to relocate, either in the city or out of the city. In 2001 the number of units rebuilt was only 40 percent of the number of units torn down (Berdik 2003). So to some degree, gentrification is occurring in some Chicago neighborhoods, leading to resident relocation.

Increased police activity and prosecution can also cause migration of criminals. For example, if police in one area initiate a program to enforce drug laws more rigorously, a drug dealer may be motivated to move to an area where he has less risk of being caught, which may also offer less competition from other dealers. Federal officials have cited stronger police activity and prosecution in cities as a cause of dealers' fleeing to rural areas (Butterfield 2002). In many areas of Chicago, police activity has increased in high-risk neighborhoods and therefore could be a potential cause of displacement.

If crime is being displaced into other communities because people are moving out of the city, one indication would be shifts in population. In Chicago, general population shifts did occur. From 2000 to 2004, 260,000 people moved out of Chicago.[9] Counties outside Chicago but in the Chicago area grew by 344,000 (U.S. Census Bureau 2004). Population figures from 2000 also show population losses for African Americans and Hispanics in Chicago and gains for non-Hispanic whites, a statistic that suggests gentrification based on income disparities between races. However, the data do not provide detail on which specific neighborhoods experienced changes, making it impossible to definitively tie the population losses to the high-crime neighborhoods. Similarly, more-recent data show the trend reversing for Hispanics and non-Hispanic whites. From 2000 to 2005, the Hispanic population in the city of Chicago increased 10 percent, while that of African Americans and non-Hispanic whites decreased (Metro Chicago Information Center 2005).

OUTCOMES OF DISPLACEMENT

Although population shifts indicate the possibility of displacement of crime, such displacement does not require large numbers of people fleeing the city. If a few key individuals leave an area, it could have a large effect on crime, particularly if those people are gang members and drug dealers. Many studies have looked into evidence of gang migration, with mixed results. Some have found little evidence of gangs' branching out to new communities (Decker and Van Winkle 1996; Hagedorn 1998; Zevitz and Takata 1992). On the other hand, a survey of law enforcement officials reported a substantial perceived connection (Knox et al. 1996), with 69 percent of responding law enforcement jurisdictions citing gang migration as a cause for their gang problem. According to the National Youth Gang Center (2007), 37 percent of cities reported their gang problem was getting worse, up from 25 percent in 1999.

It is not clear, however, if this is a result of migration from larger cities such as Chicago, individuals who are native to the community, or simply a law enforcement perspective based on types of crimes. Some officials, such as the DuPage County assistant state's attorney, claim that the majority of the gang members in their counties come from Chicago. Michael Smith, from the Cook County State's Attorney's Office, stated:

> We are seeing a gang migration out of Chicago. The vast majority of it is heading south, some west. Black gangs, Hispanic gangs, some whites. It started three years ago when a number of big gang leaders wanted to get out from the watchful eye of the Chicago Police. So they moved out to places where nobody knew who they were and the police departments were small and ill-equipped. They figured they could get away with more out there without being caught. (Keegan 2004)

Note that these officials reported increased gang migration but that this migration is also said to have been occurring for years. Though that would seem to argue against displacement being a factor specifically in 2004, there could be a delayed effect of the displacement, or key members who have greater effects on homicides could have moved later.

One way to gauge whether this migration of gang activity is occurring is to look at crime trends in surrounding areas. Nationwide, according to FBI data, arrests fell in cities by 11.2 percent and rose in rural areas by 10.5 percent. From 1990 to 1999, the percentage of drug-related homicides tripled in rural areas but fell by nearly half in large urban areas. Specifically, in the Chicago area in 2004 homicides increased in suburban Cook County by 9 percent and by 6 percent in the collar counties (Illinois State Police 2004).

Although it could be argued that rural communities are more cohesive and therefore likely to report crimes at a higher rate, it is also true that rural police departments have fewer officers to investigate crimes, which could lead to lower levels of reporting. Furthermore, because rural areas probably have fewer conflicts over turf since they are more geographically spread out, certain crimes such as homicide and aggravated assault and battery might not increase in rural areas even if gang members are moving into the area.

Overall, although there is not specific evidence to claim that displacement played a role in the reduction in homicides in Chicago in 2004, there is also not sufficient evidence to rule it out.

Conclusion

Homicides have been decreasing in the United States for the past decade. A large decline in crimes occurred in the 1990s, as shown by FBI reports of crime, the National Crime Victimization Survey, and health statistics on homicides. The homicide rate among adults has been in decline since 1980 (Rosenfeld 2004). Nationally, homicides have declined, with rates ranging from 10.5 per 100,000 in 1991 to 5.0 per 100,000 in 2004. There has also been a steady decline in violent crimes since 1994 (Bureau of Justice Statistics 2006). In 2004 the reduction in the United States continued, with the homicide rate declining by 3.3 percent, to the lowest rate in forty years. Although the homicide rate in the United States is declining, it is still much higher than in other countries with established market economies (Pridemore 2003), and there is evidence that it is stabilizing at this high level (Catalano 2004).

Despite the many theories about why homicides have been decreasing, the exact cause has been elusive. Discovering the cause for this reduction is of great importance, because homicide is among the top five causes of death for individuals under 34 years of age in the United States (CDC 2004). In Chicago, homicide is the leading cause of death for individuals under 34 and accounts for 48 percent of deaths of individuals under the age of 24 (Harper-Jemison, Bocskay, and Thomas 2008). In addition, homicides affect the community and the residents who live in areas with homicides by creating fear, uncertainty, and stress and adversely affecting businesses (Lehrer 2000), economic conditions of the area (Lehrer 2000), and mental health (Fleming et al. 1992; Reich, Culross, and Behrman 2002).

The reduction in homicides in Chicago in 2004 offers a unique opportunity to examine the variables that affect homicides.[10] In looking at all of the crimes in Chicago in 2004, the one statistic that jumps out is that only homicides and shootings dropped substantially. Although there were modest reductions in other crimes, crimes involving a gun—and gun homicides in particular—were where significant declines occurred.

It is true that homicide is often the fatal outcome of many other, different crimes, such as domestic abuse, armed robbery, unlawful use of weapons, and the selling of drugs (Maltz 1998). However, when looking at the factors that likely contributed to the substantial reduction in homicide in Chicago in 2004, the ones that are most important are those that focused on shootings and homicides, particularly those concentrating on reducing gang-related violence. CeaseFire, new police initiatives, and Project Safe Neighborhoods emerge as the only strategies that specifically addressed shootings and homicides in Chicago in 2004. A fourth factor, the relocation of key violent offenders out of the city, may also have had an impact and may have resulted, in part, from the influences of some of these programs.

Determining how much of an effect each of the four identified factors had is difficult because all or most of the factors were present in the neighborhoods that experienced the greatest reductions. For example, the 11th Police District has had the largest absolute and relative drop in killings of any district in Chicago since 2001 (from 72 to 25 killings). This is the district where CeaseFire has been most active for the longest period of time, with the largest continuous effort and with a tripling of activity in 2004, including the addition of eighteen outreach workers; it is where PSN has been most active and has had a high percentage of gun felons attending forums; and it is where police have been highly active, locating cameras in the district and targeting efforts on high crime areas. Which factor was responsible? What combination was responsible?

We have identified three factors in the reduction in homicides in Chicago in 2004, with a fourth possible factor needing more research. If a complete analysis of these programs were to be undertaken, variables such as education, employment, social service resources, and housing—just to name a few—would need to be quantified. In addition, more-precise measures for these factors would be needed in order to provide more-precise levels of program activity and location.

With CeaseFire, much of this work has been accomplished. The external evaluation of CeaseFire, funded by the U.S. Department of Justice, was extensive and was able to quantify the effects of the program, showing its large and significant effect on shootings as well as its effect on high-risk clients. With regard to new police initiatives, Project Safe Neighborhoods, and displacement, without more data all that can be said is that these factors may have played a role in the reduction. There were more substantial reductions in Project Safe Neighborhoods target districts, and increases in targeted efforts by the Chicago Police coincided with the large reduction in homicides. Whether these efforts produced those results has not been established, but they may have contributed to the overall effect.

It is our hope that looking at the specific causes behind the decline in homicides in Chicago in 2004 can tell us much about how to reduce crime in other cities. The evidence presented here suggests that large urban areas in the United States would benefit from implementing a program similar to the CeaseFire intervention to reduce shootings and homicides. Also, more directed police patrols, police cameras, gang units, and more aggressive prosecution of gun crimes could be considered as approaches that might reduce shootings and homicides. With the notoriety of programs such as CompStat in New York City and a nationwide rollout of Project Safe Neighborhoods in all court districts, some of these efforts have already spread to many urban areas. What is lacking in most cities is the specific public health outreach and community mobilization components that have recently proved effective and that offer alternatives both to potential offenders and to communities plagued by violence.

Notes

1. Statistics are derived from data provided by the Chicago Police Department. Shooting rates, technically termed "aggravated batteries with a firearm," are affected by a change in definition of a shooting by the Chicago Police Department in June 2003. This change decreased the number of incidents reported as shootings, and thus part of the 40 percent reduction in shootings is strictly a result of the definition change. Levels of aggravated assaults and batteries with a firearm, which collectively are not affected by the definition change, give us a more unadulterated statistic. Aggravated assaults and batteries decreased by 18 percent.

2. Houston and Phoenix also experienced large reductions in homicides; however, the reduction in Chicago remains unique because neither the reduction in Houston nor that in Phoenix was sustained in 2005. Homicides in Chicago in 2005 were at approximately the same level as in 2004, while Houston

had a large increase in crime, partly the result of the effects of Hurricane Katrina, and Phoenix was highly variable from 1999 to 2005, with a 10 percent increase in 2005.

3. Though arson decreased considerably in 2004, it is a highly unstable statistic, fluctuating frequently, and is very unlikely to have any connection to the reduction in homicides, because of its relatively low frequency.

4. The interventions that address homicides that we discuss in this chapter for the most part involve homicides that are committed with guns and that occur with street gangs or within the context of the street culture. Although these types of homicides constitute a large proportion of the homicides in the United States, particularly in cities such as Chicago, we acknowledge that there are many other types of homicides that we do not address here, such as those resulting from domestic violence.

5. As previously mentioned, this reduction in shootings is affected by the change in the definition of a shooting.

6. Although CompStat is widely held up as an example because of New York's large decrease in homicides, there is little evidence to support this conclusion. The homicide reduction in New York City started happening long before CompStat was initiated, and there is little evidence that the program accelerated the existing declines (Eck and Maguire 2000).

7. CeaseFire played a role in some of the offender forums that PSN held in Chicago. The forums were designed to warn past gun offenders of the harsh new consequences they would face if they were arrested for another gun crime. CeaseFire's role was to talk to the offenders about the services the CeaseFire program offered to help them change their way of life, such as outreach, job training, job placement, drug treatment, and education.

8. This chapter is intended to address the reduction in homicides; however, shooting reductions are also discussed. Although shootings do not always result in homicides, shootings are highly related to homicides and fluctuate directly in relation to homicides. Furthermore, with some programs operating in small neighborhoods, analysis of homicides can present problems because of the relatively small number of homicides. In these instances, analysis of shootings will be used to determine program success, with the assumption that a reduction in shootings is directly related to a reduction in homicides.

9. The city population overall declined by 34,000 after immigration and births were accounted for.

10. As stated previously, the interventions described in this chapter address homicides that are gang-related or involve street activity. Other classifications of homicides are not addressed.

References

Berdik, Chris. 2003. "Housing Complex." *Boston Globe*, March 9.

Blumstein, Alfred and Joel Wallman. 2000. *The Crime Drop in America*. Cambridge, England: Cambridge University Press.

Boydstun, John. 1975. *San Diego Field Interrogation*. San Diego: Police Foundation.

Bureau of Justice Statistics. 2006. Available online (www.ojp.usdoj.gov/bjs/glance/viort.htm).

Bureau of Labor Statistics. 2008. "Chicago Metropolitan Area Job Count in February 2008 Rose by 28,600 Over Year." Press release, April 15.

Butterfield, Fox. "As Drug Use Drops in Big Cities, Small Towns Confront Upsurge." *New York Times*, February 11, 2002.

Catalano, Shannan. 2004. *Criminal Victimization, 2003*. Washington, D.C.: Bureau of Justice Statistics.

Centers for Disease Control. *10 Leading Causes of Death by Age Group, United States—2004*. Available online at ftp://ftp.cdc.gov/pub/ncipc/10LC-2004/JPEG/10lC-byAgeGrp.jpg.

Chicago Police Department. *2004 Annual Report*. Available online (www.cityofchicago.org/police).

Chicago Project for Violence Prevention. 2005. "CeaseFire: The Campaign to Stop the Shooting." *10th Anniversary Report*. Chicago: University of Illinois at Chicago.

Decker, Scott and Barrik Van Winkle. 1996. *Life in the Gang: Family Friends and Violence*. Cambridge, England: Cambridge University Press.

Department of Health and Human Services. 2001. "Youth Violence: A Report of the Surgeon General."

Donahue, John J. and Steven D. Levitt 2001. "The Impact of Legalized Abortion on Crime." *Quarterly Journal of Economics* 116:379-420.

Earls, Felton. 2005. "Selected Findings on the Project for Human Development in Chicago Neighborhoods." Unpublished report.

Eck, John and Edward Maguire. 2000. "Have Changes in Policing Reduced Violent Crime?" In Alfred Blumstein and Joel Wallman, eds., *The Crime Drop in America*, 207–265. Cambridge, England: Cambridge University Press.

Federal Bureau of Investigation. 2004. *Crime in the United States 2004: Uniform Crime Report*. Washington, D.C.: U.S. Department of Justice, Federal Bureau of Investigation.

———. 2006. *Crime in the United States 2006: Uniform Crime Report*. Washington, D.C.: U.S. Department of Justice, Federal Bureau of Investigation.

Fleming, A. W., R. P. Sterling-Scott, G. Carabello, I. Imari-Williams, B. Allmond, F. Kennedy, and W. C. Shoemaker. 1992. "Injury and Violence in Los Angeles:

Impact on Access to Health Care and Surgical Education." *Archives of Surgery* 127 (6): 671–676.

Fox, James. 2000. "Demographics and U.S. Homicide." In Alfred Blumstein and Joel Wallman, eds., *The Crime Drop in America*, 288–318. New York: Cambridge University Press.

Grogger, Jeff. 2000. "An Economic Model of Recent Trends in Violence." In Alfred Blumstein and Joel Wallman, eds., *The Crime Drop in America*, 266–287. New York: Cambridge University Press.

Hagedorn, John 1988. *People and Folks: Gangs, Crime, and the Underclass in a Rustbelt City*. Chicago: Lake View Press.

Harper-Jemison, D. M., K. A. Bocskay, and S. D. Thomas. 2008. *Leading Causes of Death in Chicago*. Health Status Index Series. Vol. 17, no. 2. Chicago: Chicago Department of Public Health, Office of Epidemiology.

Illinois Department of Corrections. 2005. Available online (www.idoc.state.il.us/subsections/reports/default.shtml).

Illinois State Police. 2004. *Crime in Illinois 2004*. Available online (www.isp.state.il.us/docs/cii/ciio4/CII04_Sect_I_9to26.pdf).

Keegan, Anne. 2004. "Deadly Migration." *Illinois Issues* (April). Available online (http://illinoisissues.uis.edu/features/2004apr/gangs.html).

Kellerman, A. L., D. S. Fuqua-Whitley, F. P. Rivara, and J. A. Mercy. 1998. "Preventing Youth Violence: What Works?" *Annual Review of Public Health* 19:271–292.

Kellerman, A. L., F. P. Rivara, N. B. Rushforth, J. G. Banton, D. T. Reay, J. T. Francisco, A. B. Locci, J. Prodzinski, B. B. Hackman, and G. Somes. 1993. "Gun Ownership as a Risk Factor for Homicide in the Home." *New England Journal of Medicine* 329 (15): 1084–1091.

Kennedy, David. 1998. "Pulling Levers: Getting Deterrence Right." *National Institute of Justice*, no. 236, 2–8.

Killias, M. 1993. "Gun Ownership, Suicide, and Homicide: An International Perspective." In Anna del Frate, Uglijesa Zvekic, and Jan J. M. van Dijk, eds., *Understanding Crime: Experiences of Crime and Crime Control*, 289–303. Rome: UNICRI.

Kleck, Gary. 1991. *Point Blank: Guns and Violence in America*. New York: Aldine de Guyter.

Knox, G. W., J. G. Houston, E. D. Tromanhauser, T. F. McCurrie, and J. Laskey. 1996. "Addressing and Testing the Gang Migration Issue." In J. M. Miller and J. P. Rush, eds., *Gangs: A Criminal Justice Approach*, 77–81. Cincinnati: Anderson Publishing.

Lehrer, Eli. 2000. "Crime Fighting and Urban Renewal." *Public Interest* 141:91–103.

Levitt, Steven. 1996. "The Effect of Prison Population Size on Crime Rates: Evidence from Prison Overcrowding Litigation." *Quarterly Journal of Economics* 111 (2): 319–351.

Levitt, Steven and Stephen J. Dubner. 2005. *Freakonomics: A Rogue Economist Explores the Hidden Side of Everything*. New York: Harper Collins.

Loftin, Colin, David McDowall, Brian Wiersema, and Talbert Cottey. 1991. "Effects of Restrictive Licensing of Handguns on Homicide and Suicide in the District of Columbia." *New England Journal of Medicine* 325:1625–1630.

Maltz, Michael. 1998. "Which Homicides Decreased? Why?" *Journal of Criminal Law and Criminology* 88 (4): 1489–1496.

Marvel, T. B. and C. E. Moody. 1996. "Specification Problems, Police Levels, and Crime Rates." *Criminology* 34 (4): 609–646.

McGarrell, Edmund, Steven Chermak, and Alexander Weiss. 2002. *Reducing Gun Violence: Evaluation of the Indianapolis Police Department's Directed Patrol Project*. Washington, D.C.: U.S. Department of Justice, National Institute of Justice, November 2002 (NCJ 188740).

Metro Chicago Information Center. 2005. Available online (http://info.mcfol.org/www/index.aspx).

National Youth Gang Center. 2007. National Youth Gang Survey Analysis. Retrieved April 18, 2008 (from www.iir.com/nygc/nygsa).

Olszewski, Lori. 2005. "Teens Shut Out of Jobs." *Chicago Tribune*, April 29.

Papachristos, Andrew, Tracey Meares, and Jeffrey Fagan. 2007. "Attention Felons: Evaluating Project Safe Neighborhoods in Chicago." *Journal of Empirical Legal Studies* 4 (2): 223–272.

Philipson, Tomas and Richard Posner. 1996. "The Economic Epidemiology of Crime." *Journal of Law and Economics* 39 (2): 405–433.

Pridemore, William. 2003. "Recognizing Homicide as a Public Health Threat." *Homicide Studies* 7 (2): 182–205.

Raphael, Steven and Jens Ludwig. 2003. "Prison Sentence Enhancements: The Case of Project Exile." In J. Ludwig and P. J. Cook, eds., *Evaluating Gun Policy: Effects on Crime and Violence*, 251–286. Washington, D.C.: Brookings Institution Press.

Reaves, Brian. 2002. *Police Departments in Large Cities, 1990–2000*. Washington, D.C.: U.S. Department of Justice, Office of Justice Programs, Bureau of Justice Statistics.

Reich, Kathleen, Patti Culross, and Richard Behrman. 2002. "Children, Youth, and Gun Violence: Analysis and Recommendations." *Future of Children* 12 (2): 4–23.

Rosenbaum, Dennis and Cody Stephens. 2005. *Reducing Public Violence and Homicide in Chicago: Strategies and Tactics of the Chicago Police Department*. Chicago: Center for Research in Law and Justice, University of Illinois at Chicago.

Rosenfeld, Richard. 2004. "The Case of the Unsolved Crime Decline." *Scientific American* 290 (2): 82–89.

Sailer, Steven. 1999. "Does Abortion Prevent Crime." *Slate*, August 24. Available online (http://slate.msn.com/id/33569/entry/33575).

Sampson, Robert and Jacqueline Cohen. 1988. "Deterrent Effects of the Police on Crime." *Law and Society Review* 22 (1): 163–190.

Scheider, Matthew, Twanda Rowell, and Veh Bezdikian. 2003. "The Impact of Citizen Perceptions of Community Policing on Fear of Crime: Findings from Twelve Cities." *Police Quarterly* 6 (4): 363–386.

Sherman, Lawrence, Denise Gottfredson, Doris MacKenzie, John Eck, Peter Reuter, and Shawn Bushway. 1997. *Preventing Crime*. Washington, D.C.: U.S. Department of Justice, National Institute of Justice.

Sherman, Lawrence, James Shaw, and Dennis Rogan. 1995. *The Kansas City Gun Experiment: Research in Brief.* Washington, D.C.: U.S. Department of Justice, National Institute of Justice.

Skogan, Wesley. 2004. *Community Policing in Chicago, Year Ten*. Chicago: Illinois Criminal Justice Information Authority.

Skogan, Wesley, Susan Hartnett, Natalie Bump, and Jill Dubois. 2008. *Evaluation of CeaseFire—Chicago*. Washington, D.C.: U.S. Department of Justice, National Institute of Justice. Available online (www.northwestern.edu/publications/ceasefire.html).

Sloan, J. H., A. L. Kellerman, D. T. Reay, J.A. Ferris, T. Koepsell, F. P. Rivara, C. Rice, and J. LoGerfo. 1988. "Handgun Regulations, Crime, Assaults, and Homicide: A Tale of Two Cities." *New England Journal of Medicine* 319:1256–1262.

Spelman, William. 2000. "The Limited Importance of Prison Expansion." In Alfred Blumstein and Joel Wallman, eds., *The Crime Drop in America*, 97–129. Cambridge, England: Cambridge University Press.

Spergel, Irving A. 2007. *Reducing Youth Gang Violence: The Little Village Gang Project in Chicago*. Lanham, Md.: AltaMira.

Spergel, Irving A. and Kwai Ming Wa. 2000. "Combating Gang Violence in Chicago's Little Village Neighborhood." Illinois Criminal Justice Information Authority. *On Good Authority* 4 (2): 1–4.

Sum, Andrew, Ishwar Khatiwada, Sheila Palma, and Paulo Tobar. 2005. "Lost in the Wilderness: The Deteriorating Labor Market for Teens and Young Adults in Illinois, 2000–2004." Boston: Center for Labor Market Studies, Northeastern University.

Surgeon General. 2001. *Youth Violence: A Report of the Surgeon General*. Rockville, Md.: U.S. Department of Health and Human Services.

Taylor, Garth and Sylvia Puente. 2004. "Immigration, Gentrification, and Chicago Race/Ethnic Relations in the New Global Era." Paper presented at the 2004 Conference on Chicago Research and Public Policy, May 12–13, Chicago.

Tita, George, Scott Hiromoto, Jeremy Wilson, John Christian, and Clifford Gram-mich. 2004. *Gun Violence in the LAPD 77th Street Area*. Working Paper, Rand Public Safety and Justice.

U.S. Census Bureau. 2004. Available online (www.census.gov).

Washington, Earl. 1996. "A Survey of the Literature on Theories and Prevention of Black Male Youth Involvement in Violence." *Journal of Negro Education* 65:403–407.

Wintemute, Garn. 2000. "Guns and Gun Violence." In Alfred Blumstein and Joel Wallman, eds., *The Crime Drop in America*, 45–96. Cambridge, England: Cambridge University Press.

Zevitz, R.G. and S. R. Takata. 1992. "Metropolitan Gang Influence and the Emergence of Group Delinquency in a Regional Community." *Journal of Criminal Justice* 20:93–106.

Zhao, Jihong, Matthew Scheider, and Q. Thurman. 2002. "The Effect of Police Presence on Public's Fear Reduction and Satisfaction: A Review of Literature." *Justice Professional* 15:273–299.

5

From Knowledge to Response
and Back Again

Theory and Evaluation in Responding to Gangs

G. DAVID CURRY

There are three factors that make a crime prevention program successful (Bursik and Grasmick 1993:153). First, the program must be based on a valid theoretical explanation of the causes of the crime to be prevented. Second, the program must be implemented in a way that conforms to the demands of the theory that is its basis. Finally, a method of evaluation must be conceived that will effectively measure the impact of the program and test the underlying theory. Achieving all three of these goals has, in Bursik and Grasmick's view, been "notoriously difficult." Here I examine the integration of theory and evaluation using gang prevention and intervention programs as a primary focus.

The standard approach to social science fundamentally connects theory and research. In the classic deductive model, theory is formulated and then empirically tested with quantitative analysis. Qualitative research provides an alternative, inductive approach in which the collection of empirical evidence can inform theory building and the development of hypotheses that can be later tested systematically. Either approach can be conceptualized as a cyclical process with theory generating research findings and research findings generating new theory (Taylor 1993). In selected disciplines, such as social work and criminal justice, policy development and program implementation are an integral part of the process, with (in ideal circumstances) policy responses and programmatic approaches based on particular theoretical arguments, tested through implementation, and evaluated through research. Historically, youth gang research and theory have almost invariably been associated with programs. Often referred to as "action research" (Klein 1971:226), this process explicitly links theory, program, and evaluation in order to foster the use of evaluation evidence to refine, reshape, and rethink intervention as needed. It is generally agreed that evaluations that do not take advantage of prior research and existing literature—specifically theory—are comparatively useless, resulting in an intellectually isolated exercise with little hope of adjusting program or policy toward more effective future efforts to address a social problem (Nagel 1990). Indeed, in spite of the presumed links between theory, program design and implementation, and evaluation, research on gangs and policies and programs designed to address gangs have too often been disconnected.

In this chapter, I provide a review of some of the most important examples of work in this field, focusing on three kinds of cases. First, I briefly examine two seminal programs—the Chicago Area Project and Mobilization for Youth—that were both reputedly well grounded in social science theory and were highly influential in shaping subsequent policies and programs concerned with youth gangs, yet had no evaluations conducted to test their effectiveness. Second, I review a more recent, highly influential program—Gang Resistance Education and Training (GREAT)—that began with neither theory nor evaluation but that ultimately engaged both to more rigorously understand and assess the underpinnings of the effort and its effectiveness. Finally, I look briefly at two programs—the Ladino Hills Project and the Comprehensive Community Model—both efforts to explicitly design and test a theory-based response to youth gang violence through demonstration and evaluation projects. My purpose here is less to review our knowledge base with regard to the effectiveness of particular programs than to explore the critical relationships among theory, program, and implementation. In doing so, I argue for the essential role that evaluation can play not only in testing interventions but also in testing theory, informing the creation of new programs, and generating new theory that can be fruitfully applied in future efforts.

Theoretically Based Programs Without Evaluations

The history of gang research is a series of theories and programs. Outcome evaluation has most often been a neglected part of this process. In two of the most famous gang prevention and intervention programs in the history of the United States, there was a lot of theory and effective implementation, but no effective evaluation. These primary examples are the Chicago Area Project (CAP) and New York City's Mobilization for Youth (MFY).

The Chicago Area Project (CAP) has survived from 1939 to the present, though its focus has changed over the years (Schlossman and Sedlak 1983; http://www.chicagoareaproject.org). The project was originally based on social disorganization theory as developed by Clifford Shaw and Henry McKay (1943). Social disorganization theory tied the prevalence of delinquency to the failure of residents to exercise social control over their communities. Shaw served as director of the program, and McKay, Ernest Burgess, Solomon Kobrin, and other University of Chicago intellectuals contributed guidance. The goal of CAP was to establish organized delinquency prevention and intervention programs in communities where social control was weak (Bursik and Grasmick 1993). It was important to Shaw to make CAP endeavors part of the "natural order" of the targeted neighborhoods. To do this, Shaw attempted to involve existing community organizations in CAP. The second step in CAP was to employ "indigenous workers" as CAP representatives in each community. It was the indigenous worker's job to organize local residents into formal associations dedicated to the welfare of community children, always with a particular focus on youth avoidance of delinquency as an important part of any child's welfare. The result was a set of autonomous, community-based, youth-serving organizations in several Chicago neighborhoods.

From a process evaluation perspective, CAP was implemented as planned (Finestone 1976:136–145). According to Shaw, delinquency was a community problem and could not be brought under control except by local community efforts. These were established, and some remain autonomous neighborhood components of CAP today. A key to accomplishing this rested with autonomous community-level organizations that were well grounded in the community and could plan for and provide programs for youth. Many of the CAP organizations were able to obtain external funding from philanthropic and governmental sources. Given the conditions of autonomy and the community-based nature of these organizations, there was no uniform program of delinquency prevention or record keeping of service delivery across sites, let alone any effort to address issues of outcome attribution by identifying appropriate comparison communities or control groups. Despite CAP's being well grounded in theory that had been developed from careful analysis of empirical evidence, the experience provided no basis for a systematic outcome evaluation of the program at either the individual or the community level in terms of gang involvement or delinquency. Indeed, a number of the intellectuals who contributed to the organization of the project model, including Solomon Kobrin (cited in Finestone 1976:138) doubted that social disorganization theory or social research was well developed enough to test the impact of a community-level program on delinquency or gang involvement.

A similar notable example of a theory-based program is provided by Mobilization for Youth (MFY). In 1957 a meeting in a settlement house in New York City generated a planning and proposal-writing effort for what was to become MFY. Five years passed, from 1957 to 1962, before funding for the project was obtained and the program was finally initiated (Helfgot 1981; Moynihan 1969). During the time of proposal submission and revision, the project responded to reviewers by incorporating theory, a program plan, a research plan, and an evaluation component. In order to accomplish these modifications, MFY planners relied increasingly on input from faculty at the Columbia University School of Social Work. By the time funding was secured, members of the School of Social Work dominated MFY's board of directors. Funding came in the form of a three-year, $12.5 million grant jointly supported by the Ford Foundation, the City of New York, the National Institute of Mental Health, and the President's Commission on Juvenile Delinquency and Youth Crime. MFY had three major problems: the program directors and planners did not understand opportunity theory, the program was not executed as proposed, and although there was a little research associated with the program, there was no evaluation.

In its funded form, MFY (1961–1967) was based on differential opportunity theory, developed from the work of Richard Cloward and Lloyd Ohlin (1960). On the surface, Cloward and Ohlin's theory sounds very simple: provide legitimate opportunities to inner-city youth that offer greater promise than available illegitimate opportunities. In fact, the theory contained a number of complex assumptions. First, Cloward and Ohlin focused not on delinquent acts but on delinquent norms. They stated that theirs was "an attempt to explore two questions: (1) Why do delinquent 'norms' or rules of conduct develop? (2) What are the conditions that account for the distinctive content of various systems of delinquent norms—such as those prescribing violence or theft or drug use?" (Cloward and Ohlin 1960:ix). Although the word "gang" is seldom used by Cloward and Ohlin, when it is used, it is almost always casually substituted for the word "subculture." An important example is in the subtitle of their book: *Delinquency and Opportunity: A Theory of Delinquent Gangs*. For Cloward and Ohlin, delinquent acts did not occur without the existence of subcultures of norms and values that were associated with the legitimate or illegitimate opportunities in the community setting. Differences in values between delinquent youth, including gang members, and nondelinquent youth have never been empirically documented, despite several efforts to do so (Klein 1971; Matza 1964; Short and Strodtbeck 1965).

Despite the fact that MFY's proposals repeatedly invoked opportunity theory as the theoretical basis, there were statements to the contrary in MFY practice. Helfgot, for example, quotes an MFY document: "The tendency of social workers is to explore the motivation underlying the individual's membership in a delinquent group. . . . [They] explain the existence of the gang on the basis of maladjustment of its individual members, without acknowledging the influence of the social order" (1981:62). In the proposed program, an urban youth services unit would create thousands of temporary job positions for youth for training purposes, and a youth employment center would find jobs for trained youth. "In each case, new positions were not created, institutions were not altered" (Helfgot 1981:53).

In 1961, MFY included a research unit. According to Helfgot (1981), three kinds of research were planned: basic research on juvenile delinquency, evaluation of the net impact of the program on the community, and evaluation of specific services. In the end, a survey of community youth and community organizations was conducted in 1961, after which no further research was recorded.

A similarity of the MFY plan to the CAP strategy was the mobilization of local neighborhood resources in the targeted community area, in this case Manhattan's Lower East Side. Unfortunately, opportunity resources in the targeted neighborhoods were controlled by "forces outside of the community" (Bursik and Grasmick 1993:168). MFY activities thus became more focused on structural issues of poverty and power and became confrontational, including rent strikes, school boycotts, and demands for the resignation of metropolitan officials. Indeed, the Legal Services Unit of MFY began increasingly to see the City of New York—one of the funding sources for the program—as the enemy of the people of the Lower East Side.[1]

The response of New York City's established institutions to MYF's confrontational tactics was well organized and sudden (Helfgot 1971; Moynihan 1969). On August 16, 1964, the *New York Daily News* published its belief that MYF was infested with subversives. In a continuing series, the *News* explicitly identified MYF staff as communists. These accusations by the press were followed by special government investigations by the city, the state, and the federal government. A check of MYF staff by the Department of Justice revealed no officially recognized communists. Professional employees of MFY either ended their confrontational activities or left the organization. Eventually, MFY was absorbed by the New York City government, and no evaluation of its efforts was conducted. Thus, although both MYF and CAP were explicitly built on theory and served as models for numerous future projects, neither of these programs received adequate evaluation.

A Program Without Theory

A program not based on theory is not uncommon among crime prevention efforts to reduce gang activity and other forms of delinquency. As Malcolm Klein (1971:51) has noted, "Most gang prevention programs have been either totally atheoretical or blandly eclectic." Primary examples of such programs in other efforts at delinquency prevention include "Scared Straight" (Finkenauer 1982) and Drug Abuse Resistance Education (DARE). Both were founded with much hope and public acceptance, yet neither was explicitly based on theoretical arguments about delinquency or able to generate evidence of effectiveness through impact evaluation. Gang Resistance Education and Training (GREAT) has been the counterpart of these good-faith endeavors in responding to gang problems.

In 1991, GREAT was developed by law enforcement officers in the Phoenix, Arizona, police department, drawing upon their experiences in dealing with gang youth on the streets and officers' perceptions of how gang involvement occurred as they had observed it on the street. The stated goals of GREAT were to reduce gang activity and to educate a population of young people to the negative consequences of gang involvement. GREAT did not have an explicit theoretical basis. The response to GREAT from parents, participants, teachers, and participating law enforcement officers was universally positive. GREAT's adoption by the Bureau of Alcohol, Tobacco, Firearms and Explosives (ATF) made it the most promising program in gang prevention. The program was widely adopted by police departments. Although other programs to prevent gang involvement had been proposed, none had at that time obtained the sponsorship of a federal agency. But GREAT was seen as a promising program essentially based on common sense and the perceptions of law enforcement officers—without theory and with no evaluation.

In order to remedy the absence of an evaluation, ATF turned to the National Institute of Justice (NIJ) to select an evaluator to investigate the effectiveness of GREAT. In 1995, NIJ awarded a contract to evaluate GREAT to Finn-Aage Esbensen and a research team assembled by him. The selection of Esbensen for the award stemmed in part from his stated goal of constructing a theoretical model of how GREAT should work. From the outset, Esbensen was uncomfortable with the atheoretical nature of GREAT. He and his colleagues believed that "a thorough evaluation of GREAT is possible only if we can clarify linkages between the program and particular theories" (Winfree et al. 1996:183). Tom Winfree, Esbensen, and D. Wayne Osgood analyzed the GREAT program content and determined that the GREAT program, as practiced, represented a combination of self-control theory and social learning theory.

Self-control theory, or the General Theory of Crime, was developed by Michael Gottfredson and Travis Hirschi (1990) as a response to other disciplines' (such as psychology, sociology, and economics) "staking out" explanations of crime when, they argue, any accurate theory of crime should be produced by criminologists. Gottfredson and Hirschi distinguish between criminals and crime. Criminals, they argue, are not malevolent actors but selfish, unrestrained individuals taking advantage of opportunities that are necessary for a criminal incident to occur. This opportunity element fits perfectly with Klein's (1971:124) oft-repeated characterization of gang offending as "cafeteria style" delinquency. A product of weak social control is a willingness to take risks to reach hedonistic objectives. According to Winfree, Esbensen, and Osgood (1996:186), "several linkages between self-control theory and the gang literature seem apparent."

Winfree, Esbensen, and Osgood (1996:193–195) specifically tie elements of the GREAT curriculum to elements of self-control theory. Lesson 4 of the curriculum ("Conflict Resolution") suggests alternatives to aggression through self-control and nonviolent problem solving. Strategies for meeting social and emotional needs without gangs or drugs are covered in Lesson 5 ("Meeting Basic Needs") and Lesson 6 ("Drugs and Neighborhoods"). Self-control theory attributes delinquent behavior to self-centeredness. Lesson 7 ("Responsibility") emphasizes the social dependence of humans on one another for peaceful and productive social life. "Goal-setting and how to develop short and long-term goals," including personal and career goals, is offered as a way of avoiding impulsive behavior and is the objective of Lesson 9. Gottfredson and Hirschi attribute poor self-control to ineffective parenting. This fits well with the uneasy relationships between gang members and their families, and their reliance on peers. Low self-control opens the door for delinquent peer influences but also serves as a door opener for peers with similarly weak self-control.

Social learning theory is a combination by Ronald Akers of differential association theory and instrumental conditioning theory from psychology (Akers 1998; Winfree et al. 1996). The major premise of Edwin Sutherland's (1947) differential association theory is that delinquent behavior and values are learned. Sutherland attributes delinquent behavior to the child's exposure to an excess of definitions supporting law violation instead of definitions opposed to law violation. Akers's (1998) addition of operant conditioning specifies the mechanisms involved in the learning process. Winfree et al. (1996:193–195) point out that Lesson 1 of the GREAT curriculum ("Introduction") reinforces the basic values that underlie legitimate society, and Lesson 2 examines the costs of crime to victims, neighborhoods, and schools. From Lesson 3 ("Culture and Prejudice") forward, gangs are presented in what Sutherland would characterize as unfavorable definitions. A central component of the GREAT curriculum is the acronym FADE, which stands for fighting (associated with gangs), avoidance, discrimination (gangs discriminate against those outside the gang), and extermination (gangs try to exterminate their opposition). Specific reference is made to Hitler's use of extermination. "The instructor is told to say the following: 'We need gangs to FADE from our society, community, and neighborhood'" (Winfree, Esbensen, and Osgood 1996:194). Similarly, Winfree and his colleagues conclude: "Clearly, the police officer instructor's materials, student workbook, and classroom teacher materials all contain implicit and explicit linkages both to Gottfredson and Hirschi's general theory of crime (self-control theory) and Akers's social learning theory" (Winfree, Esbensen, and Osgood 1996:195). Although these theoretical connections appear to have been "incidental and accidental"—they did not explicitly guide program development or implementation—"for the purposes of evaluation [it is] very fortuitous" (Winfree, Esbensen, and Osgood 1996:195). In constructing a theoretical model for the evaluation that incorporates the two theories, it became possible to test which components of each theory are associated with the effectiveness of the GREAT curriculum in producing positive or negative outcomes.

The evaluation was conducted in a way that did not pose the two theoretical models as competing explanations. By including theoretical constructs in their evaluation of the program, the research team hoped to "be able to assess why it failed or succeeded." In addition to self-control and social learning theories, Esbensen included preexisting and tested scales measuring social control, social strain, labeling, and self-concept theories of delinquency. Esbensen was following a technique employed by Short and Strodtbeck (1965), who used a whole battery of gang-theoretical measures in a single survey. Whatever the result of the evaluation, the collection of comprehensive data on gang involvement and delinquency would be a valuable by-product of the research.

The GREAT evaluation consisted of two stages: a cross-sectional evaluation and a longitudinal evaluation. The cross-sectional evaluation occurred one year after the treatment group had received the GREAT program in eleven cities (Esbensen et al. 2001). The survey included 5,935 eighth graders from 315 classrooms in 42 different schools. Excluding nonrespondents on a question about receiving the GREAT program one year earlier, 45 percent reported that they had received the program and 55 percent that they had not. Those who reported receiving the GREAT program were the treatment group and those not reporting participation were designated the control group. This was clearly a nonrandomized experimental design (Esbensen et al. 2001). Results from the cross-sectional study revealed that GREAT was fulfilling its goals. A statistically significant number of the treatment group reported not being involved in gangs or delinquency.

Until the longitudinal analysis results came in, all appeared well with the GREAT program as an effective intervention in reducing gang involvement and delinquency. The longitudinal design included a number of features (such as random assignment of classrooms) that made it much more rigorous than the cross-sectional analysis. The results of the longitudinal analysis, however, were far more disappointing than those of the cross-sectional design for all involved. There were no significant differences between the treatment and control groups for gang involvement or delinquency from the longitudinal analysis (Esbensen et al. 2001).

ATF set out immediately to preserve its infrastructure of training and instructors by developing a revised GREAT curriculum. The major tools for the revision were the results from Esbensen and his colleagues on the relationship between gang involvement and delinquency and the "attitudinal" variables representing theories of delinquency and gang involvement. The new GREAT curriculum is published and deployed, and the new evaluation has been launched with the value of theory in evaluations facing another test. The evaluation of GREAT is a model of integrating extant theories into a program evaluation that facilitates redevelopment of the program with clear theoretical foundations. The reevaluation of GREAT will test the theoretical models as well as the effectiveness of the program.

Integrating Theory, Program, and Evaluation

A model of how evaluation and theory can work to better each other is found in Malcolm Klein's (1969, 1971) study of two Los Angeles–area gang intervention programs. The first of the two programs chronologically was the Group Guidance Project (GGP). In GGP, detached street workers provided services for individual gang members but also worked with gang members as a group. A "cornerstone" goal of the GGP was to "transform gang organization into a prosocial club orientation" (Klein 1971:164). The detached street workers used the weekly club meetings to teach "democratic values, procedural mechanisms, [and] activity planning." Club meetings were seen as a time for a show of group strength and an opportunity to "reinforce togetherness" (Klein 1971:165). When Klein conducted the outcome evaluation of GGP, he found that the program had failed to produce declines in gang delinquency. In fact, the effort had resulted in a statistically significant *increase* in delinquency for gangs who were targets of the program (Klein 1971:50). Klein hypothesized that the problem could be attributed to the group nature of programming. By organizing gang meetings and activities, workers increased recruitment and thereby gang size. Participation in gang activities improved cohesion in the gang. Ironically, Klein found that GGP group programming resulted in larger gangs and more delinquency. Klein constructed a theoretical model of group programming, group cohesion, and higher levels of delinquency.

As Klein noted at the end of chapter 7, "the book might well stop right here" (Klein 1971:225). But he would get a chance, in his words, "to quest for new experience and new knowledge" (Klein 1971:225) in a subsequent gang intervention effort, the Ladino Hills Project. From the empirical findings in his evaluation of GGP, Klein had developed a theoretical model upon which to design the Ladino Hills Project. "The new project was to be a test of a major hypothesis concerning the relationship between gang cohesiveness and delinquent behavior" (Klein 1971:225). Klein concluded that some of the few aspects of gangs that could be affected by the action of detached workers were their structure and their cohesion. Whereas GGP had tried to build up these aspects, Ladino Hills would work to break them down. The Ladino Hills Project would take advantage of existing gang structure and typologies of gang membership. The project would manipulate sources of cohesiveness and utilize alternative community resources to pull members away from gang activity.

The Ladino Hills Project had no group programming; it concentrated on employment and educational counseling with individual gang members. The result was a smaller gang. With fewer members and reduced retention, targeted gangs grew smaller. The level of criminality of remaining gang members stayed the same, but the reduction in gang members resulted in an overall reduction in delinquency. As the size of a gang shrank, so did the community's level of delinquency. From his research, Klein had developed a theoretical explanation of why GGP failed. Then he developed a program to test his theoretical model that an effective gang intervention program should reduce rather than improve group cohesion within the gang. The result was a gain for gang theory and programs. Klein used an evaluation of one unsuccessful program to derive a change in program goals based on a theory of gang cohesion and delinquent behavior.

The Comprehensive Community Model provides another example of using existing program experience to develop theory and new programs. In 1987, the Office of Juvenile Justice and Delinquency Prevention (OJJDP) entered into a cooperative agreement with the School of Social Service Administration of the University of Chicago to shape a research and development project to create "a model" gang response program. Professor Irving A. Spergel was designated the principal investigator of the project. Spergel had been described as the individual "who has most successfully bridged the gap between research and action involvements with juvenile gangs" (Klein 1971:55), and he was not shrinking from that role. Rather than basing his theory and program development on an evaluation of a single program, as had Klein, Spergel determined to move deliberately forward with an extensive review of all available literature on gang theory and research, examining hundreds of programs in a diversity of settings. The official title of the research and development project was the National Youth Gang Suppression and Intervention Program.

The literature review (eventually published as Spergel [1990] and Spergel [1995]) represented Spergel's determination from the outset to make theory an integral part of building his prevention, intervention, and suppression model. Spergel had always integrated theory into his research and programs. In his earliest work (1964), he had tested differential opportunity theory (Cloward and Ohlin 1960), discussed above. Spergel's research on three very different New York City communities did not reveal "gangs" that were different in values or behavior, as would have been predicted by differential opportunity theory. He also only found conflict gangs. As he would eventually write, "We do not believe that lower-class culture or subculture theory is sufficient to explain the development of youth gangs, let alone its inception" (Spergel 1995:149).

On the basis of different community contexts that determined the structure of conflict gangs in two of the neighborhoods he had observed in New York, Spergel (1964) focused on the structural features of communities for understanding and addressing gang problems. Although two of his New York communities produced conflict gangs, the conflict gangs in Racketville were very different from those in Slumtown. Racketville was a community with a highly organized legitimate structure and a highly organized crime structure. In Racketville, the conflict gangs had strong ties to the legitimate and criminal elements of the community, and gangs were very stable, rarely engaging in conflict with other gangs in the same neighborhood. Slumtown had practically no community organizations, either legitimate or criminal, and there were only weak ties, if any, between gang members and other members of the community. Slumtown gangs were unstable and perpetually engaged in conflict with one another. (This distinction would guide the development of Spergel's eventual theoretical focus on gang activity for criminal gain and gang activity for status through violence.)

Spergel was not the only researcher and theorist to move in the direction of linking neighborhood structural variables to gang emergence and development. Ironically, Lloyd Ohlin—one of the proponents of subculture theory involved in MFY—would in 1985 write in his book coauthored with

Aldon Miller: "Delinquency is a community problem. In the final analysis, the means for its prevention and control must be built into the fabric of community life" (Miller and Ohlin 1985:11). Bursik and Grasmick conclude in a chapter on defining and measuring gangs: "Certain patterns have emerged in a sufficient number of studies and locations to provide at least a minimal degree of confidence in those empirical regularities. This is especially the case in gang research that has emphasized the neighborhood dynamics related to such behavior" (Bursik and Grasmick 2006:11). Spergel came to cluster his theories of gang emergence into two categories: poverty theory and social disorganization theory (Curry and Spergel 1988; Spergel 1984, 1995, 2007).

In the cluster of theories that he labels "poverty theory," Spergel cites William Julius Wilson's theory of the "underclass" as "the most popular and influential theory" in his analysis of poverty's role in the development and persistence of youth gangs (1995:149). Although Spergel considers structural aspects of poverty to be important in explaining gangs, he does not think poverty is a sufficient theoretical explanation of gangs. He writes, "I believe that social disorganization better and more specifically explains the origin of youth gangs at different levels of analysis" (Spergel 1995:152). For Spergel, social disorganization theories emanate from population movements, whether associated with migration or immigration. He associates social disorganization on the neighborhood level with family disorganization and personal disorganization at the individual level, both of which play a part in the individual behavior of gang members.

The dual theories of poverty and social disorganization lead Spergel (1984) to attribute to Chicago gangs two different kinds of gang crime: gain-motivated crime, which is more heavily associated with poverty, and violent crime, which is more heavily associated with social disorganization. Spergel (2007) considers the distinction between the two kinds of theory and the two kinds of crime important to understanding any gang problem. He does allow the two sets of structural causes and the two types of gang crime to interact and overlap, especially since gain-motivated crime may lead to violence between gangs (1995, 2007).

Spergel organized a team to survey every "promising" gang program in the United States. Identifying promising programs involved conducting surveys of spokespersons for 254 agencies and organizations, including 45 multi-agency jurisdictions. The level of promise was assessed in two ways. First, Spergel eliminated jurisdictions that had no reported gang problem or no "organized response" to their gang problem. Usually this conclusion was based on law enforcement information (spokespeople from police departments, state police agencies, and sheriff's departments). Law enforcement assessments are still used for national-level estimates of gang problems. The best-known national survey is OJJDP's National Youth Gang Survey (Egley 2002). From those surveys, we know that law enforcement assessments may be based on a range of empirical sources, from detailed computerized incident records to a police administrator's "informed" opinion of a problem. Spergel and Curry (1993:280–282) constructed a scale based on three survey items of perceived effectiveness. These consisted of perceived change in the gang problem since 1980 by all agencies for the total jurisdiction, perceived effectiveness of the individual agency in dealing with the gang problem in 1987, and perceived effectiveness of any collective interagency group in dealing with the gang problem in 1987. From these three items on the survey, self-reported effectiveness for each agency and for each jurisdiction was computed.

These quantitative analyses were coupled with qualitative analysis of strategies, agencies, and community networks. Data were added from site visits to the most promising jurisdictions and face-to-face interviews. Through the process of grounded theory development, Spergel and his research team developed prototype models for each of ten potential kinds of program partners (Spergel et al. 1992): police, prosecutors, judges, probation, corrections, parole, schools, youth employment, community-based youth agencies, and grassroots organizations. In addition, there were two cross-cutting prototypes on general community design and community mobilization. For each prototype, a technical assistance manual (Spergel et al. 1992) was developed for each different practitioner. Each manual contained common introductory materials, allowing the manuals to stand alone for each partner, specific guidelines for assessing local gang problems, and specific guidance for the type of agency. The guidelines were action-oriented theories for effective community implementation depending on the nature and context of local gang problems and each type of agency or organization. Behind each guideline were the theoretical strategies that Spergel had made the elements of his proposed model. For each guideline action, there was a theoretical tie to each outcome variable at the micro and macro levels. To deal with poverty, the social service and opportunity provision strategies were to be implemented. To deal with social disorganization, suppression (getting the most violent gang members off the streets) and community mobilization strategies were to be implemented. The organization of the other four strategies depended on the development of new or revised community institutions.

From the extensive review of the literature and his own earlier research, Spergel developed the theoretical structure (Spergel 1995:146, 2007:28) for what became a complex but flexible model for community action. An assessment of local gang problems was always a first step, because response to a community's gang problem required an understanding of the social context and nature of the problem. The National Youth Gang Center developed assessment packages and training (http://www.iir.com/nygc/acgp/assessment.htm) for pilot sites for the model. The implementation prototypes and manuals were available for conducting process evaluations that would assess fidelity to the model as implemented at each site. Measures of the impact of the programs were made at the community level and the individual level (see Spergel, Wa, and Sosa 2006 and chapter 3 in this volume).

Throughout this chapter, I have reviewed a number of ways that programs, theory, and evaluation have been integrated or have failed to be integrated in gang response programs. Two of the programs, the Chicago Area Project and Mobilization for Youth, were designed to incorporate specific theories of gang involvement and delinquency. Both programs had plans for evaluations, but in neither case did the proposals for evaluation reach fruition. Both theories of gangs involved in these large-scale gang intervention experiments, social disorganization and differential opportunity, did not fare well in academic circles in the decades that followed each experiment (Kornhauser 1978). Social disorganization was modified in the early 1990s and has maintained a central role in gang theory, including Spergel's, since then (Bursik and Grasmick 1993).

Next I examined a gang prevention program that had been developed without theory, Gang Reduction and Education Training (GREAT). The program developers were practitioners who dealt with gangs—police officers from Phoenix, Arizona. Based initially on the officers' experiences with gang members and a sizable measure of common sense, GREAT was provided an explicit theoretical perspective by a team of evaluators. From the interpretation of the GREAT program in theoretical terms, the program became a theoretically based program, and evaluations, program revisions, and future evaluations of GREAT represent instructive examples of the benefits of integrating theory and evaluation into program design and implementation.

Finally, two programs that were based on the results of earlier programs were examined. When Malcolm Klein evaluated the Group Guidance Project, he could not have imagined a program that had gone more wrong. GGP had attempted to build cohesion in delinquent gangs to help them become pro-social groups, but GGP participants were significantly more delinquent than control youths. The more active that gang members were in the program, the greater was their delinquency. On the basis of these findings, Klein developed a theoretical model of group programming and group cohesion and their relationship to delinquency and designed the Ladino Hills Project to avoid group-focused activities. Here, counselors worked with gang members as individuals, helping them to move forward in educational and occupational directions. The overall levels of gang delinquency dropped because the project enabled gang members, especially new members, to leave the gang.

A more ambitious effort at learning from existing programs was the National Youth Gang Suppression and Intervention Project. Through an extensive review of gang research literature, surveys, and site visits to gang programs around the United States, Spergel and his team of researchers developed a comprehensive community model for reducing gang crime and delinquency. Both theory and empirical evidence were harnessed to inform program design, and program evaluation was built into program implementation to determine effectiveness and inform practice.

The examination of these cases makes clear the essential role of evaluation in both developing knowledge and contributing to knowledge utilization. Properly conceived and well implemented, evaluation can play a critical role in testing theory, testing interventions, refining implementation of existing programs and informing the creation of new ones, and generating new theory to inform future knowledge building, knowledge utilization, and policy and program development.

Note

1. There are different views on the nature of the advocacy that MFY represents. Daniel Moynihan (1969) identified it as a historically new avenue of reform, which he labeled "professional reform," because reform was coming not from the community or from institutions but from a group of professionals who were part of

neither. Helfgot (1981:107) labeled MFY a "professional reform organization" that took upon itself the symbolic representation of the poor.

References

Akers, Ronald L. 1998. *Social Learning and Social Structure: A General Theory of Crime and Deviance.* Boston: Northeastern University Press.

Bursik, Robert J., Jr., and Harold G. Grasmick. 1993. *Neighborhoods and Crime: Dimensions of Effective Community Control.* New York: Lexington Books.

——. 2006. "Defining and Researching Gangs." In Egley Arlen, Cheryl L. Maxson, Jody Miller, and Malcolm W. Klein, *The Modern Gang Reader.* 3rd. ed., 2–13. Los Angeles: Roxbury.

Cloward, Richard A. and Lloyd E. Ohlin. 1960. *Delinquency and Opportunity: A Theory of Delinquent Gangs.* Glencoe, Ill.: Free Press.

Curry, G. David and Irving A. Spergel. 1988. "Gang Homicide, Delinquency, and Community." *Criminology* 26 (3): 381–405.

Egley, Arlen, Jr. 2002. National Youth Gang Survey Trends from 1996 to 2000. Washington, D.C.: U.S. Department of Justice, Office of Justice Programs, Office of Juvenile Delinquency Prevention.

Esbensen, Finn-Aage, D. Wayne Osgood, Terrance J. Taylor, Dana Peterson, and Adrienne Freng. 2001. "How Great Is G.R.E.A.T.? Results from a Quasi-Experimental Design." *Criminology and Public Policy* 1:87–118.

Finestone, Harold. 1976. *Victims of Change: Juvenile Delinquents in American Society.* Westport, Conn.: Greenwood.

Finkenauer, James O. 1982. *Scared Straight and the Panacea Phenomenon.* Englewood Cliffs, N.J.: Prentice Hall.

Gottfredson, Michael R. and Travis Hirschi. 1990. *A General Theory of Crime.* Stanford, Calif.: Stanford University Press.

Helfgot, J. H. 1981. *Professional Reforming: Mobilization for Youth and the Failure of Social Science.* Lexington, Mass.: Lexington Books.

Klein, Malcolm W. 1971. *Street Gangs and Street Workers.* Englewood Cliffs, N.J.: Prentice Hall.

Kornhauser, Ruth Rosner. 1978. *Social Sources of Delinquency: An Appraisal of Analytic Models.* Chicago: University of Chicago Press.

Matza, D. 1964. *Delinquency and Drift.* New York: John Wiley.

Miller, Alden D. and Lloyd E. Ohlin. 1985. Delinquency and Community: Creating Opportunities and Controls. Beverly Hills, Calif.: Sage.

Moynihan, Daniel P. 1969. *Maximum Feasible Misunderstanding: Community Action in the War on Poverty.* New York: Free Press.

Nagel, Stuart S., ed. 1990. *Policy Theory and Policy Evaluation: Concepts, Knowledge, Causes, and Norms.* New York: Greenwood.

Schlossman, Steven L. and Michael Sedlak. 1983. *The Chicago Area Project Revisited.* Santa Monica, Calif.: RAND.

Shaw, Clifford R. and Henry D. McKay. 1943. *Juvenile Delinquency and Urban Areas: A Study of Rates of Delinquency in Relation to Differential Characteristics of Local Communities in American Cities.* Chicago: University of Chicago Press.

Short, James F., Jr. and Fred L. Strodtbeck. 1965. *Group Process and Gang Delinquency.* Chicago: University of Chicago Press.

Spergel, Irving A. 1964. *Racketville, Slumtown, Haulburg.* Chicago: University of Chicago Press.

——. 1984. "Violent Gangs in Chicago: In Search of Social Policy." *Social Service Review* 59:541–559.

——. 1990. "Youth Gangs: Continuity and Change." In Michael Tonry and Norval Morris, eds., *Crime and Justice: A Review of Research,* 171–275. Chicago: University of Chicago Press.

——. 1995. *The Youth Gang Problem: A Community Approach.* New York: Oxford University Press.

——. 2007. *Reducing Youth Gang Violence: The Little Village Gang Project in Chicago.* Lanham, Md.: AltaMira.

Spergel, Irving A., Ronald L. Chance, K. Ehrensaft, T. Regulus, Candace Kane, and Alba Alexander. 1992. *Prototype/Models for Gang Suppression and Intervention.* Washington, D.C.: U.S. Department of Justice, Office of Justice Programs, Office of Juvenile Delinquency Prevention.

Spergel, Irving A. and G. David Curry. 1993. "The National Youth Gang Survey: A Research and Development Process." In Arnold Goldstein and Ronald Huff, eds., *The Gang Intervention Handbook,* 361–402. Champaign-Urbana, Ill.: Research Press.

Spergel, I. A., K. M. Wa, and R. V. Sosa. 2006. "The Comprehensive, Community-Wide Gang Program Model: Success and Failure." In J. F. Short and L. A. Hughes, eds., *Studying Youth Gangs,* 203–224. Lanham, Md.: AltaMira.

Sutherland, E. H. 1947. *Principles of Criminology.* Philadelphia: Lippincott.

Taylor, Ralph. B. 1993. *Research Methods in Criminal Justice.* New York: McGraw-Hill.

Winfree, L. Thomas, Jr., Finn-Aage Esbensen, and D. Wayne Osgood. 1996. "A School-Based Gang Prevention Program and Evaluation: From a Theoretical Perspective." *Evaluation Review* 20:181–203.

6

Promoting Research Integrity
in Community-Based Intervention Research

JAMES F. SHORT, JR. AND LORINE A. HUGHES

The nature of gangs was, is, and always will be problematic. This is so primarily because of the nature of phenomena so loosely grouped under the label "gang."[1] Debate concerning gang definitions aside, progress has been made—at least empirically—largely as a result of the arguments generated by comparative research, especially the ambitious international effort that has become known as the Eurogang Program of Research (Decker and Weerman 2005; Klein 1995; Klein et al. 2001).[2] Although the Eurogang consensus definition—"any durable, street-oriented youth group whose involvement in illegal activity is part of their group identity"—is excellent as a starting point for gang control programs, it leaves unanswered the critical question of how illegal activity became part of group identity in the first place. Fortunately, the Eurogang researchers are sensitive to this question, and by virtue of the relatively undeveloped nature of youth gangs in some European countries, important insights into the processes that lead to such identity are emerging.

Although gangs are not concerned with semantic differences among scholars, gang members' talk about their behavior and its meaning must be viewed with skepticism, absent careful observation. As Andrew Papachristos observes, "Form is fluid and externally attributed, often detached from reality" (2005:644). We must listen carefully to what gang members have to say, of course, because it can tell us a lot about how they view the world and their place in it.

Constructing as accurate and precise a picture of the gang problem as possible is fundamental to research integrity, whether the goal is basic science, informing public policy, or evaluating program performance.[3] As we explain in the following section, we believe that research integrity requires recognition of the problematic nature of gangs, and that relational processes and network interactions must be studied as a means of evaluating intervention policies and practices. Research on street gangs is offered in support of our proposal that measures of *social capital* and *collective efficacy* be employed, independent of customary measures of offending, in evaluating street gang programs. Following discussion of cultural influences on research design and the importance of comparative research, the chapter closes with a note on legitimating the disciplines and practices of the social and behavioral sciences.

The Problematic Nature of Gangs

The nature of gangs will always be problematic for at least three reasons, two of which are familiar to everyone who has studied or worked with gangs. First, no two gangs are ever exactly the same, and they vary along many dimensions, in defiance of even the best-informed typologies. Second, gangs change in many ways—for example, in membership over time, often with considerable fluidity, and they do not sit still to be examined under a microscope (or by any method yet devised by social scientists). When we study them, whether by observation, interviews, administration of questionnaires and other research instruments, or arrest rates, the best we can hope for is "snapshots" at a given time or over a period of time.

The third reason that the nature of gangs will always be problematic follows from the second: that is to say, in the process of taking those snapshots, whether simply by observing, as participants or nonparticipants, in the process of studying them with whatever instruments, or in whatever capacity as change agents, we *influence* the groups and the individuals who are the objects of study or change efforts. This, of course, is the purpose of change agents and programs, but it greatly complicates research under-standing of gangs and the task of untangling the effects of program efforts. Determining what those changes are and precisely what influences account for them is a major challenge for all of us.

This third problem is the social science counterpart of the physicist's problem of measurement. All physicists know that any measurement pro-cess influences the outcome of an experiment to some degree. Ideally, such influences can be reduced to the point that the numbers that result are certain to some critical degree of precision. Physicists are very good at this, although most physicists will admit that a few of their own experi-ments have been flawed by failure to exercise sufficient care in this respect. Additionally, physicists are confronted with a second type of influence, derived from quantum mechanics.[4] This "uncertainty principle" is specific to particle physics in that it has to do with particle position and movement (energy). It holds that higher measurement precision regarding a particle's position comes at a cost to certainty of its momentum (energy).[5]

Physicists regard the first of these problems as most analogous to those faced by social scientists. Perhaps, but our problems are a good deal more complex and difficult than those of the physicist—more so than we like to admit. The social sciences have problems analogous to the uncertainty principle as well, however, in such common practices as studying gangs by means of interviewing and administering "tests" (sociometric or psycho-metric) to individual gang members. At the very least, the idea of uncer-tainty suggests that it is an illusion to think that we can understand or control gang behavior by means of ever more precise study of individual gang members, because doing so removes the individual from relational processes and interactions that influence behavior.

Social science measurement problems are conventionally viewed in terms of *reliability* on the one hand and *validity* on the other. We are, most would agree, better at the former than the latter. Sophisticated research designs in the armamentarium of the social sciences—e.g., direct observa-tion, interviews, testing of various sorts, sorting out, the inevitable sifting that official actions and records entail—at least improve the reliability of our data. No study meets all of these criteria with equal rigor. Although we can never completely eliminate observer bias, question and instrument effects, or the discretionary decisions and sometimes hidden agendas of law enforcement and other official agents and agencies that make and record arrests and other official actions, we can, and increasingly we do, achieve greater reliability by triangulating sources and subjecting them to careful scrutiny.

Validity, however, is the greater problem, no matter what the source of data, and it is here that the uncertainty principle of physics is most analogous. Triangulation and rigorous scrutiny of data sources help, certainly, but capturing the reality of moving targets, such as street gangs, will always remain elusive. In their book, *Street Gang Patterns and Policies*, Malcolm Klein and Cheryl Maxson (2006)—two of the most knowledgeable and careful gang researchers in the business—repeatedly urge gang program workers and administrators to *evaluate!* Good advice, but what to evaluate, and how? More importantly, how can we know that our evaluations provide valid measures of what it is that we wish to know? Klein and Maxson provide excellent advice here, too, and they cite Irving Spergel's work as exemplary of what should be done, even though they disagree with Spergel concerning the success of the Little Village and related projects (cf. Klein and Maxson 2006; Spergel 2007; Spergel, Wa, and Sosa 2006). Evaluation problems arise in the *details of execution*—of research designs, instruments, and observations, as well as program initiatives—and in how we *interpret* the data they yield.

Research Integrity as Validity: A Proposal

Revisiting the observational data from the Short and Strodtbeck (1965) Chicago gang study provides an illustrative case in point. For her dissertation, Lorine Hughes read the more than 16,000 pages of transcribed detached-worker interviews and graduate student field observations that had been compiled over a three-year period (Hughes 2005). In order to get a better handle on the nature of gang violence, she identified nearly 2,500 disputes involving members of the several gangs we had studied. We began with hypotheses drawn by Short and Strodtbeck concerning processes of "status threats" and "status management" based on previous but unsystematic examination of these qualitative data, hypotheses that we could not, at the time, document systematically. The basis for these hypotheses was the observation that gang leaders often behaved aggressively when their status was threatened. Incidents in which other members, individually or collectively, did so as well were also discovered. These theoretical ideas held up pretty well under more systematic analysis of the full set of dispute-related incidents, but important qualifications were noted (Hughes and Short 2005).

Perhaps surprisingly, in view of the image of these gangs as highly violent, nearly two-thirds (62 percent) of the dispute-related incidents were resolved nonviolently (Hughes and Short 2005). There was significant variation in the outcome of disputes that developed from different *pretexts*, but of three broad pretext categories (normative or order violations, identity attacks, and retaliation), only for disputes involving *retaliation* did a majority—and then only 55 percent—end in violence.[6] Importantly, *mediation*—usually by detached workers—accounted for a large proportion of nonviolently resolved disputes.[7] Spergel also emphasizes the importance of Little Village field workers (the counterpart of the YMCA detached workers) in violence reduction among targeted youth. In contrast, Klein's early research found that the efforts of workers in his Los Angeles studies were associated with *increased* offending. Clearly, field workers alone cannot prevent offending by gang members, and their strengths and limitations are the subject of much debate. Detached-worker approaches differ from one another, within as well as between programs, and we know little of the effects of such variation. Moreover, workers can be on the street for only a limited time and they are unable to "supervise" all gang members all of the time, even with the most intense efforts.[8] This is essentially a "weak stimulus" argument.

Klein attributes increased offending to increased *cohesion* among gang members that resulted from the workers' efforts. Leon Jansyn's (1966) carefully documented observations of the Chicago gang he was studying, however, suggested that both delinquent and nondelinquent gang activities increased following *low periods* of gang cohesion; and Sanchez-Jankowski found that "fear of organizational decline" sometimes motivated gang leaders to "launch an attack on a rival gang . . . to deter internal conflict, encourage group cohesion, and create more control over members" (1991:163).[9]

Theoretical as well as empirical issues are at stake here, issues concerning fundamental knowledge of individual and group behavior as well as strategies of intervention. Parties to this controversy can probably agree that group cohesion may have both positive and negative effects (see below) that differ among gangs, and that workers bear some responsibility for being aware of such variations and their consequences. Moreover, group cohesion clearly is not the only—and, we argue, not the most important—variable or process related to the behavior of gang members for either intervention or the advancement of knowledge. Our proposal, rather, is that the extent to which detached workers—and others—act to develop *social capital* for gang members and *collective efficacy* within communities is a vital missing ingredient in arguments concerning their effectiveness.[10]

Social capital has yet to come into clear focus for gang intervention programs. Although its roots lie in classical sociological and economic texts, its contemporary revival is relatively recent (Portes 1998).[11] The essence of social capital is the quality of a person's relationships with other people and with organizations and institutions—relationships that take place within such networks as family, friends, and neighbors, within local organizational and institutional contexts, and within public networks that "connect local residents to noncommunity-based persons or agencies that control political, economic, and social resources" (Bursik 2002:74).[12] Detached workers typically attempt to smooth gang members' relationships with adults in each of these important institutional settings (their families, schools, local business establishments, and the police), and they try to facilitate job placement and career planning. A critical point, however, is the distinction between individual counseling (about school, jobs, etc.) and actions (including counseling) that explicitly *promote effective networks of relationships* between young people and institutional representatives in order that they may be better prepared to negotiate the often difficult transition to adulthood.[13]

James Coleman's theorizing emphasized the importance of *intergenerational closure, normative content*, and the *social control* functions of social capital (for example, making it possible for people to walk the streets at night or to permit their children to play outside the home without fear) (Coleman 1988; Coleman and Hoffer 1987). Robert Sampson and his colleagues extended this notion by focusing on specific dimensions of social capital at the level of local (neighborhood) social organization: *intergenerational closure, reciprocated exchange*, and *informal social control and mutual support of children* (Sampson, Morenoff, and Earls 1999; Sampson, Raudenbush, and Earls 1997). In combination, these dimensions make up what they term *collective efficacy*, a property of neighborhoods and communities. The focus of collective efficacy is on shared expectations that neighborhood residents will take responsibility for each other's children.[14] Emphasis is on "the *process* of activating or converting social ties" in ways that facilitate actions toward the goal of effective child rearing (Sampson, Morenoff, and

Earls 1999:635). Thus although both social capital and collective efficacy hypothesize the importance of intergenerational closure, the latter concept includes a shared-action component. Sampson (2002; see also Granovetter 1973) emphasizes that strong personal (primary) ties such as those found in families and among close friends are not necessary for collective efficacy. Detached workers, for example, may not wish to develop close personal ties to gang members (although many do so) in order to be effective as change agents, e.g., by means of helping gang members to develop social capital that bridges gaps in adolescent-adult relationships.[15]

Sampson, Raudenbush, and Earls (1997) found that violent crime rates were lower in Chicago neighborhoods for which measures of collective efficacy were high. Importantly, similar findings are reported by Papachristos and David Kirk when the dependent variable is gang homicides in Chicago (Papachristos and Kirk 2006).[16] Other research suggests that collective efficacy has broad implications for understanding behavior (Browning, Leventhal, and Brooks-Gunn 2005) and for effective parenting (Simons et al. 2005).

The extent to which detached workers—and other therapeutic or change agents and programs—develop social capital and collective efficacy among gang members and communities is, we believe, an important missing ingredient in arguments concerning their effectiveness. Research integrity requires new tools that can be justified theoretically and empirically. Social capital and collective efficacy can be justified on both counts. Although much work remains to be done before that claim can be demonstrated, we argue that social capital and collective efficacy are of critical importance to such tasks as enhancing legitimate opportunities, controlling violence, and facilitating positive conventional socialization.

Early research by Short, Rivera, and Marshall (1964) provided tantalizing clues regarding social capital and collective efficacy in the context of youth gangs and gang intervention. Detached workers appeared to "compensate for 'deficits' in gang boys' relations with other adult roles," especially adults occupying "caretaker" and high-status positions, suggesting a lack of social capital development among them (Short, Rivera, and Marshall 1964:61).[17] Other data suggested that the significant adults in the lives of gang members, compared with those of their non-gang counterparts, lacked a sense of responsibility for the welfare of young people—in the aggregate, they lacked collective efficacy (Rivera and Short 1967).[18] Interviews with a sample of the significant adults named by the boys revealed that much higher percentages of contacts with the boys occurred "around the neighborhood," compared to contacts with adults among four non-gang categories (white and black, lower class and middle class). "Things you're likely to talk about" with the boys were reported by "gang" adult nominees to involve neighborhood matters more often than was the case for those named by the comparison adult samples, who more often focused on how the boys were getting along in school and in other problematic institutional relationships. Far fewer of the gang-nominated adults indicated school as a topic of conversation with the boys, for example, while somewhat higher percentages of the former than the latter concerned work-related matters. When questioned specifically about whether any boy on the list of those from whom adult respondents were selected had "ever spoken to you about how he should go about finding a job," however, only about half of the gang-nominated adults responded positively, compared with three-quarters of those who had been named by non-gang boys in the same neighborhood. The contrast between gang and lower-class, non-gang adult respondents was even greater with respect to "problems at school": when presented with a list of twenty-two specific school-related problems, in every case fewer of the gang-nominated adults responded positively (Rivera and Short 1967:95).[19]

The initial interpretation of these findings—that they reflected very different opportunities for gang members compared with those for boys from the same neighborhoods as the gang members, and compared with those for middle-class boys—remains valid. However, we believe the data speak even more clearly to deficits in social capital among gang members, and very likely to deficits in collective efficacy among the significant adults in their lives. The final sentences in the Rivera and Short article are apposite (1967:97):

> Within the *same* urban communities there are profound gang-nongang differences in the *types* of intergenerational contacts that occur. Non-gang boys are given guidelines and advice that are likely to enhance their life chances; gang-nominated adults may live in the same community but they do little to help boys they know to live, as adults, in a better world.

We know that workers spent a great deal of their time mediating between gang boys and adults in other institutional contexts. Because we have only begun systematic examination of the data for this purpose, this chapter discusses only one such context, and that only illustratively: namely, gang member–detached worker–police relationships. Police relationships were especially important because the boys were so often in trouble. The YMCA workers took special pains to get to know local police with whom they were in contact in order to work more effectively with the boys. In contrast, Klein reports that the detached workers in his studies were often actively hostile toward police, taking sides with gang members against them (Klein 1971, 1995).

Although relationships between the police and the YMCA workers were not always smooth, little if any evidence of active hostility has emerged from the data. The philosophy of the YMCA program was grounded in what came to be known as opportunity theory, based on Cloward and Ohlin's work (1960).[20] The theory that African American gang youth, in particular, lacked both legitimate and illegitimate (in the form of organized crime) opportunities was explicit in the program, as was the view that the resulting conflict subculture had to be dealt with.[21]

Our hypothesis is that the workers' efforts were a major factor in preventing even more conflict behavior than otherwise would have occurred. And, we suggest, careful study of the results of such efforts across institutional domains can provide a different, and more valid, indication of program "success" than conventional measures based on police arrests. Police arrests are, of course, important, but they are subject to variation in police policies and practices that often are beyond the control of community intervention efforts, even when the police are participants in such efforts. This is not an anti-police argument—far from it, as the police should be important participants in all community-based programs. But police policies and practices are subject to political and other pressures beyond local communities and their problems, as well as those within neighborhoods. Most importantly, police handling of crime and crime-threatening incidents on the street, as well as citizen complaints, involves a great deal of discretion, which in turn leads to a great deal of variation in arrest data.

Many gang intervention "old-timers" will object that "social capital promotion" is merely a different label for what they have been doing all along. There is a large element of truth to this claim, but such efforts have not been systematically documented or evaluated. Jim Short recalls accompanying a worker many years ago from one of the community committees of the Chicago Area Project to a precinct station where the worker spoke with the officer in charge about a local boy who was in trouble. The discussion resulted in an agreement that the boy would come, with his parents, to the station on the following Saturday morning in order to decide what should be done about his behavior. The worker wanted to avoid a police record for the boy, and the officer agreed that if the meeting went well, it might be possible to do so. This was, of course, a bygone era, and conditions—and police policies and practices—have changed. But community- and problem-oriented policing also have evolved, and in retrospect the Chicago Area Project worker's strategy looks very like the sort of networking that is at the heart of social capital, as well as the "indigenous," "restorative justice" movement that is now being experimented with in many parts of the world (Braithwaite 2005).[22] We have much to learn from these and other "quasi-experiments," most of which are never documented or evaluated.

Incidents involving worker and gang relationships with police occur frequently in our narrative data. Absent systematic analysis of the data, excerpts from a few worker interviews and observer reports must suffice here. The first excerpts describe typical patterns of worker relationships with rival gang members and local police:

Wardell and White and Robert had run one of the Braves in[to] the police station. I got down there, and they were explaining the situation. They had chased this boy from the Y, from the playground. He came over from the projects to play basketball. In the station, the beef was that Wardell went over in the projects late [Wednesday] night with his girl in a car, and about thirty or forty of the Braves crowded around the car and were going to do him in. If it wasn't for some police officers, he probably would have been done in. So, they checked on it, and sure enough, there was a report in at the station that they had broken up something in the projects and had his name listed as one of the boys who was in the car. So, this was the main reason that he chased the boy in the police station. [Wardell, age 19] said, "If we can't go over in the projects without being chased out of there, without getting beat up and everything, neither can they come in the Maxwell Street area to shop or anything." He wasn't gonna let no 16-year-old boy jack him up. Furthermore, this boy was in the crowd that was going to do him in yesterday. The boy said he wasn't there. Of course, you don't know who to believe in a big situation like that. It is true that they do try to catch the Cobras in the projects there, and we see Braves consistently everyday shopping or walking around coming into the Maxwell Street area. They're not being molested. Officer Davis said, "Let D. [worker] straighten it out." He was passing the buck on me.

The other officer wanted to know who I was, and he said, "Okay, okay, you handle it." I said, "Hell, all I can handle is the Cobras. I can keep the Cobras from going over there, but I couldn't handle the Braves at all." So, they said, "Okay, we'll handle the Braves. You just handle your group." So, we walked out of the station. When we were in there talking, Wardell's mother came over with Wardell's sister, Wardell's baby. I stopped them about 15 yards before they got into the office. I told them I was taking care of everything. So, we all walked out of the station, and as we were walking out, some of the other Braves ran in the station. So, the boys turned around and looked at them, and I said, "Ah, just forget it. They're just checking on their boy, that's all." I got Wardell to go home. He promised me that he wasn't thinking about going over.[23]

Next, this worker notifies the police about a possible gang fight and takes pains to ensure that members of his gang do not take weapons to a scheduled softball game:

We played the Imperials out there. They [Egyptian Cobras] figured there'd be a big fight between the Egyptian Cobras, Vice Lords, and Imperials, so they all wanted to take their stuff. Isaac wanted to go get a shotgun, Wardell wanted to take his .22, and Bobby pleaded with me for them to take something, because he said, "Man, you just can't trust them out there." I said, "Man, just trust me" because I already contacted Maxwell [Police] Station and told them everything, that we were going over to play the Imperials and we were going over to play ball and we didn't want to fight. I just wanted to insure my boys' safety, at least while they're there and out of the area. I thought if they could contact Marquette Station and tell them that we would be there that they might have a (squad) car waiting for them . . . for us. They said they'd call, and the sergeant called while I was there. He's a young fellow. They have a lot of young desk sergeants now. He was real nice to me, real polite. He knew the group I was working with and everything. He called and said they'd have a car waiting, but no car showed. Wardell wanted to take his .22, but it doesn't have a barrel on it. I made him take it back upstairs. He took it back and came back telling me I could search him if I wanted to. I told him, "I don't want to search you. I believe you." We went over there and played ball. We beat the Imperials 15 to 10. We had three carloads full—Buck's car, Blue's car, and mine.

Another incident reports on a worker's actions when he is informed that members of his gang have been taken to the police station and a rumble is threatened:

Wednesday night, this one cop . . . told me, "Look, you know we got some of your guys in the station." I said, "No, who?" He said, "They were picked up earlier in the afternoon—James M. and some more guys." I said, "Okay, I'll run over there and see who it is." I left there and went over to the police station. I saw M. and Calloway and went over to the police sergeant there at the desk who knows him. He told him, "Look, I understand you're expecting a rumble out here tonight between the Vice Lords and the Warriors-Cobras." I said, "The Seniors are not participating in this. I'm speaking for my boys." The police officer appreciated this and said, "If you guys aren't participating in this, get the hell on out of the area. We don't want to catch you over there because we're going to pick up everybody we catch walking over there that are members of these groups." I said, "I'm getting ready to take them to the wrestling matches." So, the officer said, "Okay, you do that." They wouldn't let me talk to M. because he was up on armed robbery. . . . So, I took the group on to wrestling, got back later on that evening, and found out that no rumble had taken place but that four Warriors were jumped on during the course of that time. I don't know the Warriors' names, but I did get the word from some of the boys that the Warriors were beaten up that evening over by the BBR. This was four separate incidents . . . everyone they caught walking through there straggling, they'd beat him up. They didn't have to be Warriors, because they don't know who is in the Warriors group, but everyone they caught walking their so-called territory, they beat up.

An observer's report suggests the manner in which another worker handles a gang member's relationship with police concerning weapons:

In the restaurant were two Midgets, James (a new member) and Bobby. While Fred and I were eating, James got up from where he was sitting and put an iron table leg behind the telephone booth and slipped his gun under the counter to the girl (it was a zip gun) and went back to his seat. A few moments later, two members of the roving juvenile squad came into the restaurant. One was a Negro named C. and the other one was white (I forgot his name, so he's called X hereafter). C. had known Fred when he was on the park district police force and Fred was working on the South Side, so the first thing that was said was an exchange of greetings by Fred and C. and information about their both working on the West Side. C. then introduced X as his partner and asked if I was Fred's partner. Fred said yes and introduced me as L. L. The policeman then turned to the boys who were watching the proceedings in silence. C.: I saw this fellow [James] hide something behind the telephone booth and counter before I came in. James: Just my stick. (C. goes and gets the iron table leg and then says): You got your initials carved in it. James: (He explains how the iron pipe is a table leg and that the marks were caused by fitting the leg into its proper place in the table.) C.: So, you put it back in the table sometimes. James: Yeah. (Laughter from the people in the restaurant). X: Haven't I seen you someplace before? (Talking to Bobby). Bobby: No sir. The policemen exchanged a few more words with Fred and then left the store, with C. returning the pipe to James. Fred told me that he took Lester by James R.'s house and then took him home. About five minutes later, James got his gun back from behind the counter. When he did this, Fred told him that he shouldn't carry the gun, because, if he (Fred) had not been in the restaurant and had (not) known C., he might have gone to jail. Fred then asked him why he was carrying the gun, and James said, "So Jimmy G. won't catch me in a hallway anymore." I could not hear much of what was said after that, except that Fred told James that it was his job to take care of things like when he got hit. He also told James that, if he wouldn't carry the gun, he would make a deal with him—if G. bothers him again, he would arrange for James to go to the police or fight if that's what he wanted to do. After a few more minutes of discussion, James did leave the building and returned a few minutes later and told Fred that he had taken the gun home.

Finally, a spontaneous interracial incident involves police and cooperation of YMCA workers across racial lines. The incident reveals the worker's overidentification with his gang members and resolution of a conflict situation based on earlier positive relationships between workers and police:

Saturday night [members of the white gang with whom he was working] got into it with three Negro youths between 78th and 77th on Halsted and they were all arrested. One Negro had his throat cut by P.M. with a beer can. The white boys were driving south on Halsted, and the Negro boys were walking North, and K. or A. yelled out, "Hey, black son of a bitch," and the Negroes stopped and yelled back at the car and then the car stopped and everybody piled out and they stood in the middle of the street for about 10 minutes arguing back and forth. Finally, R. S. said, "Well, let's either fight or forget it," and this Negro turned on him real fast to find out who said it, and R. S. hit him and then one of the Negroes said, "I'm from the West Side. I'm a member of the Vice Lords" and all this jazz. When I saw the blue lights go flashing up to the corner I made it. So, the Negro youths were pointing out the white youths who had been involved to the police. There were about four squad cars, and I charged up and said, "What is happening, fellows?" I didn't know any of these cops that were on the scene, and one of them had his nightstick out and he put it on my arm and said, "Who the hell are you?" and I said, "Who the hell are you? Let me tell you something. You put that nightstick on my arm, you better have more than one riot squad out here because you're going to need them." This other copper in front of me said, "Are you the father of any of these boys?" and I said, "I work with these boys." And, he said, "You better get out of here and get to higher ground. You ain't got no business here." I proceeded to get good and hot, and I almost got busted too. As it turned out, they were afraid to, because they weren't sure. So, they were all taken to the station, where the lieutenant who was on duty straightened it all out, because they owed me a favor. It turned out to be a station adjustment after a hell of a long session. What worried me, on the way to the station, [the boys] told me that this one Negro youth made this statement, "I'm from the West Side. I'm a Vice Lord." So, as soon as we got to the station, I called the answering service and told them to get a hold of either B. R. or J. O. (other workers) and get them down to the station immediately, and I barely got into the Lieutenant's office and we started to chin a little bit that O. appeared through the door and said, "What the hell is going on?" I said, "I want you to take a look at these three punks and find out if any of them are Vice Lords," and of course they weren't and the Negroes were going to sign a complaint against the white boys, which would have been all right, except that the white boys in turn were going to sign a cross complaint against the Negroes, and they would have all spent the weekend in jail on a disorderly. So, I had O. talk to the colored boys privately. The one boy still wanted to sign a complaint and so I had him talk to this boy again privately and this time he didn't want to sign a complaint. I guess O. told him, "Look, punk, you ain't a Vice Lord, but I am." So, finally, at 3 a.m., we all got to leave the station. The [wounded] boy wasn't cut badly, but he had a nice gash, the width of his neck, but it was superficial. It looked bad and just as we were leaving the station the lieutenant said, "When did you get that?" and he said, "Oh, about three weeks ago, boss." "God damn, that looks awful fresh."

Although the worker's failure to deal effectively with the harassment issue was clearly counter to the objectives of the program, his reference to prior relationships with the local police lieutenant is consistent with the tenor of worker-police relationships in our data. Few worker-police contacts appear to have been as contentious as appears in this incident. As the other incidents suggest, workers typically cultivated good relationships with police and frequently called upon them when serious trouble was anticipated or appeared to be imminent. More-systematic analysis of our narrative data will flesh out the nature of such relationships.

We did not call the workers' efforts to bridge gaps in gang members' relations with adults "social capital building," but arguably that is what they were doing.[24] Our present research agenda includes systematic documentation of the nature of such activities across institutional domains and, to the extent possible, their results in the lives of gang members. We know, for example, that workers were active in helping boys to stay out of trouble at home, in school, and in their relationships with neighbors, local businesses, and others, and among themselves. The boys often sought advice from workers about such matters, and in other "growing up" contexts, including how to meet and how to behave with "nice girls"—despite, or perhaps because of, their sexual precocity (Short and Strodtbeck 1965).

Other studies likewise suggest the relevance of social capital for the problems and prospects of street gang and clique members. Mercer Sullivan's (1989) fine research monograph *"Getting Paid": Youth Crime and Work in the Inner City* described the superior community networks of members of his white clique—compared with those of the Latino and black cliques—with respect to getting jobs, for example. Getting jobs for gang members was another way in which the Chicago YMCA project compensated for the lack of job connections among members of black gangs. Getting jobs proved easier than keeping the boys on the job, however, an indication of the lack of social skills in interpersonal relationships, an important aspect of *human capital* that often hinders the acquisition of social capital (Short and Strodtbeck 1965, chapter 10; Hughes 2007).

Research Designs and Culture

Even the most rigorously designed research program confronts problems of reliability and validity. The message we want to convey is that criteria employed to measure gang-member behavior should not be conceded to police arrests (or even convictions), lest their validity be compromised by the processes that produce police and court data.[25] These processes go beyond such problems as police discretion and changing policies and practices, including, for example, both police resistance to program efforts and program personnel resistance to police, as Spergel's documentation of the Little Village project clearly demonstrates (Spergel 2007; Spergel, Wa, and Sosa 2006).

Research integrity demands more than changing measures of effectiveness, however. *Comparative research designs* are an article of faith among most of us who do research. Klein has written eloquently on the topic (Klein 2006). A cautionary tale, however, is found in ethnographic research.

Mark Fleisher, a distinguished anthropologist who has studied prisons and prisoners, inner-city youth gangs, and the homeless, notes (in personal correspondence) that the lack of support for research in other parts of the world has resulted in greater attention by anthropologists in this country to gangs and the homeless as "natives" who are studied "in every which way." But he questions whether they "understand street culture" and "how homelessness fits into prison and jails, adolescent episodic and literal homelessness, youth gangs, etc. They don't conceptualize the street as an indigenous culture that is a product of mass society and a culture that has multiple components that fit nicely together." Too often, such misunderstanding is patronizing of clients "for their own good." Culture, with all its contextual richness and complexity, is thus another theoretical and empirical challenge for understanding street gangs and evaluating interventions.

Recent work in a very different cultural setting confirms and elaborates such problems. Maureen Cain, who does research in Trinidad and Tobago, as well as the Caribbean, is highly critical of what she identifies as opposite, but equally distorting, tendencies among scholars and change agents.[26] Some of us, she charges, romanticize and patronize *others* who differ from ourselves as wayward, unknowing, and requiring our guidance and advice in order that they might find their "proper place in the world" (Cain 2002:71).[27] Others, without either romantic blinders or patronizing, nevertheless presume "the 'sameness' of key cultural categories, practices and institutions."[28] Both of these approaches, she argues, distort reality and therefore compromise the validity of research as well as the efficacy of programmatic efforts. The second may be the most relevant for those of us who have extensive experience with gangs—which, in our view, is the best antidote to romanticizing them—for it may distort perceptions and understandings by both the "others" who are studied and those who are doing the studying, as it may of those who minister (and seek to control) as well as the "others" whose communities, institutions, and behaviors are the objects of change. On the basis of her experience in the Caribbean and the United Kingdom, Cain argues that the presumption of sameness leads scholars from advanced Western societies to make "static" comparisons that lack knowledge of and appreciation for the complex and dynamic character of culturally different groups.

The point to both Fleisher's and Cain's concerns is that we must be aware of—and beware of—romanticizing and patronizing youth gang members and residents of their communities, and of too readily assuming that we understand the social and cultural contexts within which we work as researchers and practitioners. Understanding these contexts must be the first order of business for both researchers and practitioners (Hughes 2006).[29]

A related concern goes beyond technical research problems such as these. It might be called the "What's in it for our clients or those whom we study?" issue—what's in it for the gang youngsters, their parents, and other community residents? Problems with medical experimentation in recent years have alerted us to what we should have been sensitive to—and some have been—long ago. This is perhaps the most important of all the ethical responsibilities faced by those of us who study and work with people and their problems, even more than the "informed consent" so prized by institutional review boards and governments. The seemingly obvious answer—that we want to keep kids out of trouble and help them live more satisfactory lives—risks being perceived as patronizing.

There is no easy solution to this problem. Our argument is that among our interests in studying and working with gang members, individually and collectively, and with their communities should be the acquisition of social capital by gang members and the promotion of collective efficacy among community residents. Spergel and his associates did not call what they were doing "social capital and collective efficacy building," but as we read their descriptions of the Little Village project, a good argument can be made that this was what they were doing and that it may account for such success as they report (Spergel, Wa, and Sosa 2006). In retrospect, we believe they might have been more sensitive to this aspect of their evaluation. This is a challenge worthy of all community-oriented ameliorative programs. We believe that study of processes of social capital and collective efficacy building can be a powerful means of ensuring the integrity of the research that is associated with such programs.

Legitimating Disciplines and Programs

The social sciences lack the prestige of the "hard sciences" and their engineering and medical applications. The reasons are not difficult to discern. Our concepts and methods of research are less precise than those of the hard sciences. The professions that are built on the latter are much better organized and financed, their research designs are more rigorous than ours, and they are demonstrably more successful in problem identification, study, and praxis, compared with social work and other professions whose praxis is based on social science research. Still, the vital importance of systematic and disinterested (in the sense of *independent*) research for our enterprise is undeniable—as it is for theirs.

Note that independence is more than avoiding biases associated with relationships between researchers and those who are responsible for policies and practices. Independence of measures and evaluation of performance require scientifically and theoretically relevant concepts, rather than those based on criteria imported from outside the disciplines that inform our work. Progress has been made in developing new measures. The National Crime Victimization Survey has become a valuable supplement to "crimes known to the police," and collection of special data on homicides has added greatly to the usefulness of police data. Self-reports, as noted, have improved over the years and have been useful, in tandem with police data, for many purposes.

But more clarity is needed, and institutions other than those that make up the criminal justice system must be involved, though ideally each component of that system should be involved as well. Institutions change only incrementally, but there is evidence of willingness to change the ways community services are delivered, as well as the practice of and interaction among police, courts, and prisons. The suggestion that measures of social capital and collective efficacy should be developed in order to assess the performance of gang intervention programs is not far removed from objectives set forth for community- and problem-oriented policing and the small-schools movement, for example (Bureau of Justice Statistics 1993). Researchers and practitioners are clients of one another, as are the objects of our research and our praxis. Only by working together can we enhance our legitimacy and our effectiveness.

Notes

This chapter was presented at the Spergel Symposium by Short, with Hughes as discussant. The final product, with thanks to editor Robert Chaskin for his perceptive suggestions for revision, is collaborative.

1. Academic definitional arguments are found in many places, e.g., Albert Cohen's "Foreword and Overview" to Ronald Huff's first edition of *Gangs in America* (1990); Bob Bursik and Harold Grasmick's *Neighborhoods and Crime* (1993); Spergel's *The Youth Gang Problem*; and Malcolm Klein's *The American Street Gang* (both published in 1995). I admit to having been party to these arguments, e.g., in *Poverty, Ethnicity, and Violent Crime* (1997; see also Short 1998).

2. The Eurogang program is a consortium of researchers from several European countries and the United States.

3. Defining "integrity," the Oxford English Dictionary uses terms such as "uncorrupted," "not being marred or violated." Webster's Unabridged says "a sound, unimpaired, or perfect condition." Although these terms reflect common usage, as will be apparent from the following discussion, our primary concern is with the *validity* of research methods and interpretation.

4. Einstein is reported to have said that he wasted more time trying to understand quantum mechanics than he ever spent on relativity!

5. These problems are sometimes referred to as the "Heisenberg effect," so-called because of the contributions of German physicist Werner Heisenberg.

6. Variations within these broad categories are interesting and perhaps of theoretical importance (see Hughes and Short 2005), but that is the subject of more research.

7. Other micro-level influences that were associated with nonviolent dispute resolution included intra- as opposed to inter-gang disputants, peer backup, and victim acquiescence (see Hughes and Short 2005).

8. Even the most enthusiastic supporters of detached-worker programs agree that total supervision of young people is neither desirable nor possible. Kids do have to "grow up," and total supervision is not conducive to doing so.

9. Short (1997:117–118) also notes that gangs vary in their history of cohesiveness, that Jansyn's gang appears to have been more cohesive than were the gangs in the Chicago YMCA program, but that the latter often became more cohesive in response to status threats.

10. The argument can, of course, be extended to the effectiveness of other gang- and violence-oriented programs.

11. Portes's excellent review traces the origins and applications of social capital and further develops its theoretical structure and limitations.

12. Bursik, following Bursik and Grasmick (1993), terms the first of these networks "private," the second "parochial," and the third "public" (2002:74).

13. "Social capital" has been defined and used in a variety of ways. Portes defines social capital as the "ability to secure benefits through membership in networks and other social structures" (1998:8).

14. In addition to its sociological and economic roots, collective efficacy owes much to Bandura's (1986) work (see also Portes and Sensenbrenner 1993).

15. "Bridging" social capital is distinguished from "bonding" social capital. Portes notes that the latter often has downsides, such as increasing group cohesion around antisocial norms and blocking access to community and institutional resources.

16. Franklin Zimring and Gordon Hawkins (1997) argue that lethal violence, rather than crime, is "the problem," and John Hagedorn argues that gangs must be dealt with as "social actors," requiring "a policy of both intolerance of violence and tolerance of informal, nonviolent economic activity" (Hagedorn 2006:192). Such arguments are, of course, controversial, as are their merits with respect to gangs. Note, however, that Spergel's claims for the success of the Little Village project and those modeled after it are that *violent crime* was reduced among targeted youth, although other crimes—notably drug crimes—were not (Spergel, Wa, and Sosa 2006). We suspect that political and social acceptability would be the primary obstacles to policies that neglected crimes other than violence. Programs specifically *targeting* violent crime would be more acceptable.

17. This study involved interviews with 294 gang members (89 white, 205

African American), 164 non-gang boys from the gang neighborhoods (75 white, 89 African American), and 79 middle-class boys from non-gang neighborhoods (53 white, 26 African American) (Short, Rivera, and Marshall 1964). Eight adult roles—detached youth workers, religious figures, politicians, teachers, professional people, policemen, adults making money illegally, and neighbors—were rated on three-point scales measuring contact with and interest in teenagers, their "clout" (pull), and an evaluation as to whether they were "right guys" or "suckers."

18. For this phase of the program, interviews were obtained from samples of adults who had been named by members of only one white and one black gang and their non-gang counterparts. We attempted to interview all multiple nominees and random samples of single nominees. Cost considerations dictated this strategy.

19. Differences were especially striking for adults named by black gang members, compared with their lower-class, non-gang-member-named adults, ranging from 11.5 percent for truancy and spending a lot of time away from school to 52.6 percent for "hadn't learned much from his earlier school work and was finding it difficult to catch up."

20. The director of the YMCA program, Richard Boone, was a close friend of Lloyd Ohlin's.

21. For a description of the evolution of this program, see Cooper (1967). Cooper's identification of informal group process as a key element in the YMCA program was in large part the result of the associated research program at the University of Chicago (see Short and Strodtbeck 1965).

22. John Braithwaite is the leading theorist of restorative and indigenous justice, the major point of which is to bring offenders, victims, and local community representatives together in order to promote reintegration of offenders with community norms and practices and, hence, desistance from further offending (see Braithwaite 2005). Translation of these goals in terms of social capital and collective efficacy seems straightforward.

23. Later in the interview, the worker observed that when two groups like the Cobras and the Braves were playing each other, "they should have police there because the slightest little thing might start a big fight."

24. Regrettably, these efforts were not systematically documented in the original Short and Strodtbeck study, nor can we document the extent to which such social capital efforts were successful or enduring. Possible clues may be found in Short and Moland's (1976) follow-up of the original Nobles and Vice Lords.

25. We do not here address the use of self-reports as measures of behavior, methods for which have improved and become more common. Our argument is that self-reports and police reports alike should be triangulated whenever possible by observational and other methods.

26. Cain is a reader in sociology of law and crime in the law faculty at the University of Birmingham.

27. Conversations with Walter Miller, when Jim Short first met him, led Jim to the conclusion that he romanticized the Boston gangs he studied. His later work, surveying police and others regarding the prevalence and the nature of gangs around the country, disabused him of romanticism, however; and Jim does not believe that Walter patronized gang members or felt that they required his advice in order to find their proper place in the world.

28. Cain terms these tendencies "orientalism" (following Said 1978) and "occidentalism."

29. Almost as an aside, Cain writes that romantic patronizing of others "usually means a relatively subordinate place in an uncontrolled global market, a market which, however, requires, as it always has, long-term order and predictability, and the security of property in all its sites of production and exchange, in order to function effectively" (2002:71). The extent and the nature of globalizing influences on youth gangs throughout the world are subjects of extensive and sometimes heated debate (see Hagedorn 2006; Short and Hughes 2006).

References

Bandura, Albert. 1986. *Social Foundations of Thought and Action: A Social Cognitive Theory*. Englewood Cliffs, N.J.: Prentice-Hall.

Braithwaite, John. 2005. "Between Proportionality and Impunity: Confrontation—Truth—Prevention." *Criminology* 43:283–305.

Browning, Christopher R., Tama Leventhal, and Jeanne Brooks-Gunn. 2005. "Sexual Initiation in Early Adolescence: The Nexus of Parental and Community Control." *American Sociological Review* 70:758–778.

Bureau of Justice Statistics. 1993. *Performance Measures for the Criminal Justice System* Washington, D.C.: U.S. Department of Justice.

Bursik, Robert. 2002. "The Systemic Model of Gang Behavior: A Reconsideration." In C. Ronald Huff, ed., *Gangs in America III*, 71–81. Thousand Oaks, Calif.: Sage.

Bursik, Robert and Harold G. Grasmick. 1993. *Neighborhoods and Crime*. New York: Lexington Books.

Cain, Maureen. 2002. "Orientalism, Occidentalism, and the Sociology of Crime." In David Garland and Richard Sparks, eds., *Criminology and Social Theory*, 71–102. Oxford, England: Oxford University Press.

Cloward, Richard A. and Lloyd E. Ohlin. 1960. *Delinquency and Opportunity*. New York: Free Press.

Cohen, Albert K. 1990. "Foreword and Overview." In C. Ronald Huff, ed., *Gangs in America*, 7–21. Newbury Park, Calif.: Sage.

Coleman, James S. 1988. "Social Capital in the Creation of Human Capital." *American Journal of Sociology* 94:S95–S120.

Coleman, James S. and Thomas Hoffer. 1987. *Public and Private High Schools: The Impact of Communities*. New York: Basic Books.

Cooper, Charles N. 1967. "The Chicago YMCA Detached Workers: Current Status of an Action Program." In Malcolm W. Klein, ed., *Juvenile Gangs in Context: Theory, Research, and Action*, 183–193. Englewood Cliffs, N.J.: Prentice-Hall.

Decker, Scott H. and Frank M. Weerman, eds. 2005. *European Street Gangs and Troublesome Youth Groups*. Lanham, Md.: AltaMira.

Granovetter, Mark S. 1973. "The Strength of Weak Ties." *American Journal of Sociology* 78:1360–1380.

Hagedorn, John M. 2006. "The Global Impact of Gangs." In James F. Short, Jr., and Lorine A. Hughes, eds., *Studying Youth Gangs*, 181–192. Lanham, Md.: AltaMira.

Huff, C. Ronald, ed. 1990. *Gangs in America*. Newbury Park, Calif.: Sage.

Hughes, Lorine A. 2005. *Violent and Non-violent Disputes Involving Gang Youth*. New York: LFB Scholarly Publishing.

———. 2006. "Studying Youth Gangs: The Importance of Context." In James F. Short, Jr., and Lorine A. Hughes, eds., *Studying Youth Gangs*, 37–45. Lanham, Md.: AltaMira.

———. 2007. "Youth Street Gangs." In Marilyn McShane and Frank P. Williams III, eds., *Youth Violence and Delinquency: Monsters and Myths*, 1:41–59. Westport, Conn.: Praeger.

Hughes, Lorine A. and James F. Short, Jr. 2005. "Disputes Involving Youth Street Gang Members: Micro-social Contexts." *Criminology* 43:43–76.

Jansyn, Leon. 1966. "Solidarity and Delinquency in a Street Corner Group." *American Sociological Review* 31:600–614.

Klein, Malcolm W. 1971. *Street Gangs and Street Workers*. Englewood Cliffs, N.J.: Prentice-Hall.

———. 1995. *The American Street Gang: Its Nature, Prevalence, and Control*. New York: Oxford University Press.

———. 2006. "The Value of Comparisons in Street Gang Research." In James F. Short, Jr., and Lorine A. Hughes, eds., *Studying Youth Gangs*, 129–144. Lanham, Md.: AltaMira.

Klein, Malcolm W., Hans-Jurgen Kerner, Cheryl L. Maxson, and Elmar G. M. Weitekamp, eds. 2001. *The Eurogang Paradox: Street Gangs and Youth Groups in the U.S. and Europe*. Boston: Kluwer.

Klein, Malcolm W. and Cheryl L. Maxson. 2006. *Street Gang Patterns and Policies*. New York: Oxford University Press.

Papachristos, Andrew V. 2005. "Interpreting Inkblots: Deciphering and Doing Something About Modern Street Gangs." *Criminology and Public Policy* 4:643–652.

Papachristos, Andrew V. and David S. Kirk. 2006. "Neighborhood Effects on Street Gang Behavior." In James F. Short, Jr., and Lorine A. Hughes, eds., *Studying Youth Gangs*, 63–84. Lanham, Md.: AltaMira.

Portes, Alejandro. 1998. "Social Capital: Its Origins and Applications in Modern Sociology." *Annual Review of Sociology* 24:1–24.

Portes, Alejandro and Julia Sensenbrenner. 1993. "Embeddedness and Immigration: Notes on the Social Determinants of Economic Action." *American Journal of Sociology* 98:1320–1350.

Rivera, Ramon J. and James F. Short, Jr. 1967. "Significant Adults, Caretakers, and Structures of Opportunity: An Exploratory Study." *Journal of Research in Crime and Delinquency* 4:76–97.

Said, Edward W. 1978. *Orientalism*. New York: Pantheon.

Sampson, Robert J. 2002. "Transcending Tradition: New Directions in Community Research, Chicago Style." *Criminology* 40:213–230.

Sampson, Robert J., Jeffrey D. Morenoff, and Felton Earls. 1999. "Beyond Social Capital: Spatial Dynamics of Collective Efficacy for Children." *American Sociological Review* 64:633–660.

Sampson, Robert J., Stephen Raudenbush, and Felton Earls. 1997. "Neighborhoods and Violent Crime: A Multilevel Study of Collective Efficacy." *Science* 277:918–924.

Sanchez-Jankowski, Martin. 1991. *Islands in the Street: Gangs and American Urban Society*. Berkeley: University of California Press.

Short, James F., Jr. 1997. *Poverty, Ethnicity, and Violent Crime*. Boulder, Colo.: Westview.

——. 1998. "The Level of Explanation Problem Revisited—The American Society of Criminology 1997 Presidential Address." *Criminology* 36:3–36.

Short, James F., Jr. and Lorine A. Hughes, eds. 2006. *Studying Youth Gangs*. Lanham, Md.: AltaMira.

Short, James F., Jr. and John Moland. 1976. "Politics and Youth Gangs." *Sociological Quarterly* 17:162–179.

Short, James F., Jr., Ramon Rivera, and Harvey Marshall. 1964. "Adult-Adolescent Relations and Gang Delinquency." *Pacific Sociological Review* 7:59–65.

Short, James F., Jr. and Fred L. Strodtbeck 1965. *Group Process and Gang Delinquency*. Chicago: University of Chicago Press.

Simons, Ronald L., Leslie Gordon Simons, Callie Harbin Burt, Gene H. Brody, and Carolyn Cutrona. 2005. "Collective Efficacy, Authoritative Parenting, and Delinquency: A Longitudinal Test of a Model Integrating Community- and Family-Level Processes." *Criminology* 43:989–1030.

Spergel, Irving A. 1995. *The Youth Gang Problem: A Community Approach.* New York: Oxford University Press.

——. 2007. *Reducing Youth Gang Violence: The Little Village Gang Project in Chicago.* Lanham, Md.: AltaMira.

Spergel, Irving A., Kwai Ming Wa, and Rolando Villarreal Sosa. 2006. "The Comprehensive, Community-Wide Gang Program Model: Success and Failure." In James F. Short, Jr., and Lorine A. Hughes, eds., *Studying Youth Gangs*, 203–224. Lanham, Md.: AltaMira.

Sullivan, Mercer L. 1989. *"Getting Paid": Youth Crime and Work in the Inner City.* Ithaca, N.Y.: Cornell University Press.

Zimring, Franklin E. and Gordon Hawkins. 1997. *Crime Is Not the Problem: Lethal Violence in America.* New York: Oxford University Press.

Part III

(Re)considering Contexts, Orientations, and Interventions

7

Multiple Marginality and Human Development

Applying Research Insights for Gang Prevention and Intervention

JAMES DIEGO VIGIL

Like their peers in other communities, Chicano youth, especially adolescents, must face up to challenges they may experience, such as in their families and schools, and in addition struggle with other concerns, such as ethnic identity. Also like their peers in other communities, the vast majority of these youths mature their way through their problems and become able to live productive and rewarding adult lives. However, in neighborhoods afflicted by a history of racial and ethnic prejudices and the typically correlated phenomenon of poverty, a significant number of Chicano youth encounter especially stark choices. Moreover, these conditions have persisted despite repeated efforts to change them. Thus new strategies are needed to broaden the options of youths in such situations.

To point the way toward determining these strategies, in this chapter I outline key features of the human developmental process as it is reflected among youth and adolescents in low-income barrios in Southern California, and the interplay between social forces and personal propensities that shapes their trajectories. All youth in these neighborhoods must appraise and come to grips with the many environmental, socioeconomic, racial, and cultural forces that exist there. However, it is the poorest of the poor and the most culturally conflicted individuals and groups that must command our attention. It is these youth who are most prone to street socialization and to becoming gang members.

With this population, various aspects of human development have taken different and often destructive turns. Examining the social, emotional, cognitive, and physical processes of their lives shows when and where choices were made, and how conditions induced them into street socialization and thus an unconventional life path. In these neighborhoods, the street gang has become a competitor to other sources of identity formation, often replacing family, school, and other conventional influences.

Chicano street gangs are now made up, as they have been since their inception more than six decades ago, primarily of groups of male adolescents and youth who have grown up together, usually as cohorts in a low-income neighborhood of a city. Yet only about 10 percent of the youth in most of these neighborhoods join gangs (Esbensen and Winfree 2001; Short 1996; Vigil 1988a). Those who do so participate together in both conventional and antisocial behavior (Thornberry 2001). The antisocial behavior, of course, attracts the attention of authorities as well as the general public (Bursik and Grasmick 1995; Curry, Richard, and Fox 1994; Decker and Van Winkle 1996).

For all youth, making the passage from childhood to adulthood involves a marginal status crisis known as the psychosocial moratorium, where ambiguity and confusion characterize self-identification processes (Erikson 1968; Vigil 1988a, 1988b, 2002b). Ego formation, group affiliation, and adoption of role behavior dominate during this time. For about a tenth of the youths in poorer neighborhoods, because of attenuated, stressful family situations and uncaring schools that fragment and render their egos fragile at a pre-adolescent phase, the further construction of a self-identity becomes problematic during adolescence. To reiterate, it is those youths with the weakest familial guidance toward conventional life ways and the least financial support (in these neighborhoods where household finances are almost always marginal) that are most apt to become gang members (Vigil 2007).

It is no accident that these misshapen egos find solace in the group, where together with other similarly fragile egos, like pieces of a puzzle, they find a wholeness and completeness to aid survival and also a feeling of security that they have seldom experienced before. What else to do but accept the role gestalt that the group has fashioned over the years for similarly disaffected and unaffiliated youth? In short, to understand the developmental processes of gang affiliation and identification, one must intertwine ego, group, and role psychologies in ways that show connections and interactions, especially backing into their past lives in order to assess their present street lives. It is social situations and conditions that influence and shape personal human development paths.

Ethnographic Research and the Emergence of "Multiple Marginality"

The discovery and examination of these developmental dynamics were undertaken in a series of studies that utilized a community orientation to "street ethnography." Community members of varying status—household principals, merchants, social agency workers, and youth, for example—were included in the interviews and observations that focused on youth out on the streets (Vigil 1979, 1983, 1988a, 1997). Informed by the accumulation of new studies and evidence since the 1970s (Klein 1971, 1995; Klein and Maxson 2006; Moore 1978, 1991), my work involves interactions and ongoing discussions with community residents to advocate for policy formulations and changes. Particularly helpful were the statistical insights of Malcolm Klein and the methodological creativity and qualitative depth of Joan Moore in fashioning new research approaches. The much earlier work on the problem of street gangs in any ethnic group, much less Chicanos, was scant, to say the least. This work focused on the 1940s pachuco/a generation (Griffith 1948; McWilliams 1949; Tuck 1956), and none addressed the current, historically significant gang phenomenon in Los Angeles, which has become the gang capital of the world. In 1978 I conducted research with Joan Moore and the Chicano Pinto Research Project (CPRP), a team that valued community researchers, many of whom had been former gang members and/or *pintos* (convicts) or *tecatos* (addicts). This work, and the mentoring interactions that were an important part of it, led to new places, personal contacts, and more ethnographic approaches to investigate urban street youth.

In sorting through these ideas in earlier publications, I have used an analytic model I call multiple marginality (Vigil 2002a; Vigil and Yun 2002). This integrative framework argues that breakdowns in social control, including the socialization process normally centered in the conventional family, are caused by complex and multifaceted dynamics and that therefore consideration must be given to factors such as the ecological, socioeconomic, sociocultural, and sociopsychological marginality that additively affect some members of particularly low-income, ethnic-minority groups. These factors all intersect strongly with one another and lead to strains in social control and to the maladaptive, destructive behavior of some youth. To understand any of the forces at work here, it is necessary to understand all of them. The breakdown of social control unfolds in the throes of these larger forces, and an examination of the loss of social control must take this into account.

Essentially, I argue that the street gang is an outcome of marginalization, that is, the relegation of certain persons or groups to the fringes of society, where social and economic conditions result in powerlessness—a point made by earlier researchers (Miller 1958; Moore 1978, 1991; Shaw and McKay 1942; Thrasher 1963 [1927])—but with the added weight of actions and reactions suggested by a "multiple" marginality. This process occurs on multiple levels as a product of pressures and forces in play over a long period of time. Some of the gang members that I have known have come from such stressed and unstable circumstances that one wonders how they have survived. The phrase "multiple marginality" reflects these complexities and their persistence over time, the cumulative and additive nature of which simply overwhelms some youth.

Macrohistorical and macrostructural forces—those that occur at the broader levels of society—lead to economic insecurity and lack of opportunity, fragmented institutions of social control, poverty, and psychological and emotional barriers among large segments of the ethnic minority communities in Los Angeles. These are communities whose members face inadequate living conditions, stressful personal and family changes, and racism and cultural repression in schools (Moreno 1999). Most members of these communities successfully cope with adverse circumstances and achieve productive, conventional ways of life, but, as noted, the gang draws a smaller subset.

A comparison of the specific environments of gang members (especially the most committed ones) with those of barrio youth who are not in the gang (and even some who are fringe gang members) shows a wide difference in their backgrounds (Huff 2002; Vigil 1988a, 1993a, 1993b). Gang members are usually reared in poorer homes, in mother-centered family situations with more siblings, and in marginal, unstable economic conditions, including periods of unemployment and reliance on welfare (Vigil 1988a). A recent, more detailed study comparing gang and non-gang families in a public housing development (Vigil 2007) indicates this is true even among residents of a community sometimes stigmatized as a haven for welfare recipients, criminals, and drug users. Gang households in the housing development, for example, were poorer, much larger, and more likely to be headed by single females. There were also indications of greater economic stress in the gang families, including a significantly smaller proportion of those households having access to a car.

No wonder, then, that youth in such circumstances end up in gangs and engage in gang violence. Perhaps more surprising is that some, even in these unpromising circumstances, avoid serious involvement with the local gang. It is also true that most of the time spent by gang members is in the usual cavorting activities found in most adolescent and youth groups: casual repartee and joking, drinking beer and wine, playing sports, meeting at the local hangout, and catching up with the news of the street groups and gangs of the area. Such activities add to the gang's attractiveness to street-socialized youth, just as similar activities reinforce group loyalties in more conventional youth groups. The media, police, and public care little about such normal, conventional patterns, and focus more on the unacceptable activities: the drive-bys, the random wild shootings, and the criminal lifestyles represented by some gang members. Often unnoticed by gang observers and authorities are the values (i.e., ought-tos) and norms (i.e., blueprints for action) that guide gang members' thinking and behavior. The following examples give some indication of how this works for older, traditional East Los Angeles gangs: protection is valued, and thus watching other gang members' backs is encouraged; gang loyalty is important, and claiming a "turf" generally demonstrates it; respect is crucial, and deference to most older gang members is shown; and emotional support is given as if gang members were family members.

Violence against others in the form of rampant gang fighting and slayings, and against oneself through the careless use and abuse of drugs and other chemical substances, represents the destructive, debilitative habits that separate gangs from other adolescent peer networks. Put another way, there are public and private destructive acts, meaning the *locura* (quasi-crazy) orientation common in the gang can take an internal and external path, as self- and other-directed violence often dominates gang activities.

Nevertheless, even these activities can be understood as an altered type of "storm and stress" response during adolescence, when daring, excitement, courage, and adventure are valued by peers. Indeed, it is doing these "gang" things that earns you the respect and recognition as a dependable gang member with *huevos* (balls). Notwithstanding their attempts to conform to such expectations, however, most youth remain conscious of, and concerned with, the detrimental effects of this behavior. It should be underscored that often the negative results of such behavior accelerate the "maturing out" process, hastening one's exit from the gang (Vigil 1988a, 1996). These human sentiments show, as Edgerton has noted in his study of deviance generally, that those who engage in such individual and group behavior must be viewed not as "freaks in a side show" but as "principal performers in the everyday dramas of life" (1978:444).

Gang Socialization: A Developmental Perspective

If we follow a human developmental model as suggested earlier, examining the social, emotional, cognitive, and physical aspects of growth and maturation, we can pinpoint areas that augur for a gang lifestyle and the recruitment of gang members. All of these developments, of course, unfold in the context of street socialization and the larger forces suggested by multiple marginality.

First, it is fairly obvious that the *social dimension* of the gang is perhaps its most important aspect. In particular, the "desire to be well liked" is common across most adolescent groups, but this human aspiration takes different turns and twists among gang members. For one thing, it is a street-based arena that dictates how one becomes well liked, by whom, and why, among other motivations and strivings.

The initial years of adolescence, the "psychosocial moratorium," which Erikson (1968) defined as a time of confusion and ambiguity regarding one's identity, are filled with reasons why one would wish to become well liked if one were in a gang. Fictive kin are gained by joining, libidinal ties are formed that sometimes last for life, and older gang role models add to the multiple-aged peer group of the gang and the desire for friendships. All of this eases the integration of the ego into the group (that is, enables the youth's self-concept to largely merge with his gang identity). In addition, it leads youth to seek admiration from "tough" males they seek to emulate, to calm ambiguities about their feared and real selves, and to seek approval and acceptance by engaging in dangerous acts and behaviors. The list can go on. However, let me provide at least one example.

Adolescents usually wish to avoid—and, in fact, often strongly dismiss—adult supervision. When you are street socialized and need to survive the pressures and temptations of the streets, you nonetheless need caretakers and teachers to guide you through these "mean streets." Here is where older gang members, key parties of the multiple-aged peer group, play a significant role. As developmentally delayed adults, having never matured out of the gang (some even remain gang members into their forties), they are both feared as potential predators and respected as potential protectors. Much of the gang behavior of youth stems from this fear, with youth tending to emulate those they fear most while simultaneously seeking protection from them. These are the *veteranos* (veterans, or "OGs"—Original Gangsters) who are the street power brokers that everyone must contend with, including the many more youth who are not gang members. Left to the world of the streets, who do you think you would want to have like you?

On the *emotional dimension*, the second category, the crisis passage of puberty is accompanied and strongly affected by bodily changes and hormonal adjustments and imbalances. Having taught junior high school in the 1960s, I can honestly state that many of my students would change moods and personalities from day to day, sometimes acting very mature and adult and then shifting back to childlike behavior. Becoming more self-conscious of these developments in the context of street life, where the pressures and demands are sometimes overwhelming, they may experience a tremendous amount of ambiguity and confusion during this time. Among these youth a stark developmental tension often exists between early household socialization, frequently dominated by females, and the new street socialization under the aegis of the male multiple-aged peer group. Youth may become even more peer-dependent in order to summon the emotional stability necessary to maintain the gang front, which is part of the role-psychology of the gang (Vigil 1988b).

Wanting friends to like you and relying on them almost exclusively for guidance and direction can also wreak havoc on the *cognitive dimension* of a gang member (the construction of his identity), the third developmental category. Gang members exhibit many physical and mental inconsistencies that reflect this tendency. One classic story that I retell to capture this quality is the young teenager who for years had submitted to his mother's combing his hair as he was about to leave the house in the morning. One morning, as he recounted in discussing his early decision to join the gang, he decided to take the comb from his mother and from that day forward fix his hair to suit his new gang style. Countless stories have been conveyed to me about dressing for the situation, either *cholo* (today the gang attire is cutoff jeans just below the knee and white gym socks almost to the knee with a white T-shirt at the top and inexpensive tennis shoes at the bottom) when with gang members, or more conventionally when visiting family or friends (especially non-*chola* girlfriends) whom they want to impress. In keeping with such contrasting behavior, some gang members often maintain gang and non-gang associations; many follow a kind of "Jekyll and Hyde" character split. In fact, although more common among Asian American gang members, the shifting task of being schoolboys by day and streetboys by night is a balancing act that shows the precarious involvement and flexible identity that youngsters cultivate for the gang life. For some of them, it is not uncommon to hide their schoolbooks in their locker or to make sure they are never seen carrying books home: such conventional behavior would show fellow gang members that they are not serious about belonging to the gang. Finally, faking defiance in front of fellow gang members might be one way of acting unconventional in order to impress their gang "audience."

Much of what was said about the emotional state of mind during puberty also applies to the final human development dimension, *physical changes*. While the interior of a person is undergoing mostly masked changes, it is much more obvious when physical appearance makes a telltale statement about ambiguity and uncertainty. The voice changes, the height increases, the bodily alterations that remake the person, and especially the sense of confidence associated with control and management of these physical developments all send a message to onlookers that a nearly intact person is there or that a work in progress is in the making. These changes occur at a different pace for different individuals, and those for whom no or few changes are evident at a given stage create the impression that they are not growing up, causing more confusion.

Added to this variability is the need to show mastery by achieving or shining in some capacity. For males, sports become a very important avenue and outlet for such status recognition; females gain attention by adding makeup and dressing in the more junior adult styles. In contrast to the dominant society, where teenagers are socialized in conventional areas of accomplishment, such as academics and formal social outlets, the streets dictate a different arena for many barrio youth. Showing "toughness" is a particularly important characteristic for street children, and a few are actually very tough, even overly combative. These individuals are usually the ones who have experienced early childhood traumas or are unsure of themselves and overdramatize this toughness. Several gang members have mentioned to me how they have to show a hard exterior to measure up, often changing their demeanor to fit the occasion. Physical appearance counts in a street world where protective posturing often deters potential aggressors.

On the other hand, many more street youth are often tentative and uneasy in how they demonstrate and manage this toughness, especially those who are lagging in all or most of the developmental categories. When youth lack assurance on how to effect this image and behavior, and are not particularly damaged by early emotional setbacks that would instill a sense of rage, they may shakily demonstrate a tough posture, though the image comes off more as a blurred, muffled pose. Such individuals typically are tolerated by other gang members, but their opinions carry little weight and they are sometimes relegated to "go-fer" roles. Those who succeed in attaining an image of toughness, on the other hand, whether they are really tough or are faking it, are rewarded with the admiration of fellow gang members and the street community in general. In any event, the concern with image management for street survival creates personal inner tension for some gang members.

Monster Kody (Shakur 1993), in his autobiographical account of his street experiences, unabashedly states that youth achieve the level of Ghetto Hero among all parties concerned when they measure up. Respect and status are gained, and from that point on you can walk the neighborhood with your head held high—except that the high level you have achieved places you in another ranking: it marks you for others to gain status by knocking you off your perch to replace you. In contrast, though manly strength and image count at this adolescent developmental phase, many youth are quite resourceful at shining as partygoers, drug dealers, or gang street organizers—the "shot callers" who determine when violence is initiated, by whom, and against which rival gang.

In sum, certain developmental processes unfold on their own, such as hormonal and physical transformations. Others, in contrast, depend on the ecocultural system in which a person lives—home, school, the streets—and the role models found there. For example, how the ego is shaped and grows determines whether overreliance on the group is necessary for further development, in which case the person becomes peer-dependent and surrenders to the group (Erikson 1968). To complicate matters, aside from developmental issues, it is fairly obvious that most adolescents and youth have specific needs and engage in many normal activities. These outlets can be striving for friendship, selection of social gatherings, participation in the daily gossip of their cohort, and even drinking alcoholic beverages and taking drugs. In short, developmental processes and normal adolescent patterns pertain to almost all youth. However, the streets present different obstacles and dictate different options that skew such processes and normal activities for some youth.

Survival in the streets becomes an overriding force that all barrio youth must contend with, especially those who are primarily street socialized. Being and acting tough becomes a modus vivendi that bodes well for protection, bringing friendships and social routines and rhythms that fit the culture of the streets. As a coping strategy for youth who lack conventional paths for development and normal behavior, the street values and norms that dominate thinking and behavior make perfectly good sense.

Prevention, Intervention, and Suppression:
Multiple Marginality Frames Development

The interaction of gang dynamics and developmental human processes discussed thus far can serve as the basis for generating new strategies to combat gangs and the processes that create gang members. To do this effectively, I argue, we need to address each of the dimensions—social, emotional, cognitive, and physical—with attention to the impacts of multiple marginality and a sensitivity to the developmental process.

In a developmental approach, gang *prevention* activities must begin in the early childhood years, before age 8 or 9. Communities and agencies must take a proactive stance in addressing the primary problems of the general population, especially for this age group, where ego awareness and a need for praise dominate social and emotional maturation. Moreover, the cognitive and physical growth of children this young demands that they be allowed to learn by active participation, which also provides an outlet for their high energy, which must be harnessed and channeled. Prevention strategies for these youngsters thus would involve supervised activities, including arts, physical exercise, and reinforcements for participating, thus competing with the allure of the streets and gang activities.

Children aged 9 to 12 or 13 are at the stage when *intervention* should enter the picture, especially for youth who are peripherally but not yet deeply connected to the streets. Intervention needs to take into account youths' social needs at this stage, including engaging with friends without adult supervision and a desire to be well liked. Given that youths at this age are more self-conscious emotionally, care should be taken in how their independence is handled. Finally, cognitive and physical processes show many inconsistencies, and a need to achieve and shine is a strong drive in this age group and must be considered in designing and implementing intervention strategies. Thus, supervised activities like those mentioned in relation to prevention efforts would be accompanied by greater emphasis on counseling to address these youths' inconsistent and distorted socialization.

When all else fails, between the ages of 13 and 20, *suppression* is the strategy we must rely on to stop the spread of delinquency and criminal behavior. For those youths in this age range who have not yet become identified with gangs or whose involvement has been no more than peripheral, prevention and intervention efforts should of course still prevail. The suppression target here is youth who have joined gangs and are showing consistent gang involvement. Most of the older dedicated gang members whose gang careers I have documented had in fact joined the gang by age 13 or 14 (Vigil 1988a). Rehabilitation (or habilitation, because most of these children have never been adequately socialized in conventional ways) should concentrate on emotional and cognitive areas, but social and physical problems are not far behind in importance.

In light of these developmental phases and personal traits, it behooves us to employ a broader strategy, one that considers each facet of the multiple marginality that characterizes the experience of the youth we are concerned with here. Because society is an interwoven network of small and large institutions, private and public, a strategy that is comprehensive and that encourages coordination and cooperation among key groups and organizations is the path to take.[1] A limitation of such comprehensive efforts, however, is that most are not based on a human developmental scheme that follows the dimensions and stages of development highlighted in this chapter. Although we recognize that a comprehensive model is a step in the right direction, it is important to underscore that a multidimensional strategy must also adhere to the linkages and sequencing among factors, and the actions and interactions that bind them. The multiple marginality model alluded to earlier as the causative pathway to gangs and gang members can be reintroduced to formulate an applied research strategy—a holistic approach that utilizes community feedback to guide and inform policy choices—to effectively combat gangs. Moreover, developmental issues can be integrated in this version of a comprehensive strategy.

First, the social life of a person begins in the place where they are born and reared, and, as noted, gang members emerge in some of the most deteriorated, run-down sections of a region (city or otherwise). The incomes and occupations of their parents, and of their grandparents before them, are also among the lowest paid and hold the lowest status, all of which contributes to a social life of limitations based on lack of resources and opportunities for education and social mobility. Place and status often are detrimentally associated with family structure and organization, where strained household relations and interactions, as well as living arrangements, reflect attenuated social control. This is further coupled with a poor learning-readiness home situation and the commonly recognized inferior schooling available in poor areas. Finally, the self-identity processes are seriously strained and fragmented given the fact that a small but sizable portion of youth in gang neighborhoods is street socialized and inducted into a gang pattern early on.

As in the multiple marginality model, where place, status, social control, cultural changes, and self-identity unfold simultaneously, the other emotional, cognitive, and physical developments are also affected along with social growth and stability. For instance, living in an obviously visually distinct and spatially separate disadvantaged neighborhood can have untold consequences on the emotional, cognitive, and physical integrity of a person, and volumes of research underscore how such neighborhoods can contribute to compromising the mental and physical well-being of residents (Hannerz 1969; Liebow 1967; Rainwater 1970; Suttles 1968). Similarly, cognitive and physical personal transformations are affected by environmental constraints and surroundings.

These factors have important implications for intervening to address the gang problem in the neighborhoods in which gangs thrive. What I argue here is that prevention, intervention, and suppression efforts must be cognizant of the multiple factors involved in the emergence of gangs and gang members and, in addition, the human development processes that mark a life under these situations and conditions. Each step of a person's life must be considered to determine which prevention or intervention approach would make a difference. Barring success in these early efforts, how and why does suppression enter into the equation? Concrete lessons learned during the "War on Poverty" efforts of the 1960s, as well as more recent illustrative efforts to combat gang problems, can help in addressing these questions.

The 1960s War on Poverty was the last time our country embarked on a large-scale initiative to eradicate poverty and the problems associated with it. Among these problems was the growth of street gangs in mostly poor neighborhoods. In communities across the country, young professionals, some still in training, were recruited along with local residents to establish and operate prevention and intervention programs. For example, two programs were established to "steal" time from and redirect the energies of the youth in a barrio, Jardin (garden), about 20 miles east of downtown Los Angeles. Teen Post, a social and recreational program, was located in a large building in the area, and a staff of four or five adults, including the author, was charged with educating, training, and transporting twenty to thirty male and female at-risk teenagers on outings and field trips. Most of the daytime hours of the youth were supervised by the Teen Post workers during a forty-hour week. There were roughly about 135 Teen Post sites in the greater Los Angeles area serving local ghettoes and barrios. This program utilized a multidimensional strategy to occupy the teenagers' time by providing social outings and cultural enrichment, such as visits to exciting places, such as the Hollywood Bowl, scheduled educational mentoring, and personal counseling. Most developmental processes were covered in this umbrella approach, with special emphasis on new socialization routines and efforts to stabilize the emotional tensions of the youth. Youth in these programs ranged from 14 to 20 years of age.

In addition to this neighborhood settlement house arrangement, there was also the Neighborhood Youth Corp (NYC), which paid adolescents the minimum wage for twenty-five hours a week to involve them in local self-help activities, such as assisting senior citizens, cleaning up empty lots and alleys, and generally painting and sprucing up the neighborhood, all activities that gave youth a new inner map for a conventional orientation to life as well as physical actions and social interactions that helped lead to positive results. Overall, Teen Posts and NYC made a difference on all human development themes—social, emotional, cognitive, and physical. As a general consequence, gang activities were considerably curtailed during this period (1966–1969): buying their time and guiding them in conventional ways made a difference. It was during this same period that Head Start was initiated and proved to make a major difference in preparing children for schooling. Indeed, this program became so successful and popular that it continues to this day (Garces, Thomas, and Currie 2002), although fund-ing fluctuates with each new presidential administration.

The evaluation of similar prevention, intervention, and suppression efforts also led to new insights. The Lights of the Cambodian Family was a Long Beach program started during the "Weed and Seed" era of Bush the Elder. The major thrust of this program, which focused on 5-year-olds, was to make the children proud of their language and culture at an early age at the local public school, and to bridge the cultural gap between parents and children while involving the parents more deeply in the schooling enter-prise. It was thus an omnibus effort that aimed at instilling sociocultural pride and shoring up self-identification processes. The focus on encour-aging the first-generation parents to talk to and work with their second-generation children certainly helped bond families.

Another cultural intervention program in East Los Angeles was Mujeres y Hombres Nobles (Noble Women and Men), in which high school youth were taught some of the roots of Mexican culture, emphasizing education and a conventional lifestyle. The purpose was to set up a learning environ-ment that shepherded the educational trajectories of at-risk adolescents by providing additional counseling, mentoring, and parental training. Train-ing the varied staff of teachers, counselors, social workers, and parent vol-unteers was a continuing goal as well.

Pro Force bike patrol was a 1991 government-sponsored drug suppres-sion intervention program. The Pico Gardens public housing area was reconnoitered at all hours by housing police to help reduce drug use and trafficking, more a deterrent to than a redirection and reconfiguration of youth's unconventional pathways. Surveying the residents' perceptions of the program's effectiveness indicated that the bike patrols worked when they were present. However, because the small housing department police force had to be shared with other housing project neighborhoods, there was little continuity in maintaining a lid on either drug use or sales. In a somewhat similar vein, the Los Angeles Sheriff Department's Commu-nity Oriented Policing Services (COPS) program from 1997 to 2000 con-ducted training workshops and conferences, developed and administered surveys to workshop and conference attendees (mostly law enforcement officers), and generally consulted on police-community issues. Overall, there was tremendous community support for some of the outreach efforts initiated by the Sheriff's Department. Law enforcement seemed to be split on this strategy: a majority was open and supportive of fashioning such new strategies, though a sizable minority preferred the old "hook and book" technique that had prevailed for generations. When funding for COPS disappeared, most of the initiatives were abandoned. However, on the basis of my observations and interviews, I believe that law enforcement generally would embrace similar creative efforts that would make its job easier and more efficient, if appropriate funding and follow-through were available. Obviously, a creative suppression initiative drove COPS, with the expectation that once community-police relations were improved, law-and-order decorum would prevail in the maintenance of social control.

During the same period, IMPACTO (Imaginando Mañana: Pico-Aliso Community Teen Outreach) was launched. IMPACTO was a joint Robert F. Kennedy Foundation and Housing Authority program aimed at 10- to 14-year-olds. It was a combination of prevention and intervention strategies that included mentoring, parental counseling, recreation, sports and field trips, liaison with California Youth Authority camps to aid reentry for youthful offenders, and a safe house for youth in two contiguous public housing tracts. Thus the program addressed social, cultural, and psychological facets of the multiple marginality model as well as most aspects of the human developmental process, particularly the cognitive and emotional. After a dozen years, IMPACTO is still in existence, and even though the wider neighborhood is rife with street gangs and gang violence, many children have been positively affected by the program.

The L.A. Bridges program began at about the same time, formulated by several gang experts, gang workers, and city officials, including the author. Some of the members of this L.A. City Council ad hoc advisory committee later participated in workshops and lectures in various neighborhoods to publicize the purpose and goals of the program. Its intent was to target gang-infested areas by making the local middle school the headquarters for programs and activities that brought teachers, parents, and police to the same table. In doing so, it would have attempted to address the four human developmental themes discussed here. With just over $10 million to spread among 29 schools, L.A. Bridges became diluted, largely because city council politics entered into its implementation by including middle school neighborhoods that did not have a serious gang problem. Hampered by such a broad, unfocused objective, L.A. Bridges is being phased out, and its services to children, parents, teachers, and law enforcers in the selected neighborhoods will be integrated into a yet-to-be-named new anti-gang program.

Finally, another outreach program, Inner-City Games, was started (mostly with private funding) by Danny Hernandez in East Los Angeles (Hollenbeck Youth Center), with the goal of capturing the time and energies of youth after school and during summer hours. Arnold Schwarzenegger joined in by helping to expand the program to other cities, and he took a public leadership role touting the positive benefits of youth outreach programs. For a while, Schwarzenegger became the poster boy for the program, which was not surprising given his political ambitions at the time. Though computer classes and training were a part of Inner-City Games, it was mostly a sports, recreational, and field trip operation that "stole" time from youth 7 to 17 years of age and aimed to inculcate values by emphasizing a particular virtue (e.g., loyalty, honesty, and discipline) during each event or activity. Depending on the private funding (Las Vegas was more well-heeled than San Jose, for instance), some of the programs were able to provide food and refreshments for the children to further entice them to join Inner-City Games after school or during the summer.

For anthropologists particularly, but also for the early gang researchers, the quest for an understanding of urban gangs began when researchers started following peasants and sharecroppers into cities. The multiple marginality model thus incorporates immigration as a major factor. Immigration and the experiences of immigrants as they adapt and adjust to city life form the basis for all else that follows, including especially the maladaptation that so often occurs. In each period, place, and cultural milieu of an immigrant people, there are issues of access, exposure, and identity with regard to the dominant culture that need to be addressed. For example: Do newcomers live near members of the dominant culture? Are public institutions the same in immigrant enclaves as they are in upscale areas? What are the processes of identification with the new culture? There are many areas in which immigrants, and especially their children, find themselves betwixt-and-between, beginning with where they settle, what jobs they fill, and how and why their social and cultural values and practices are challenged and, typically, undermined and revamped.

The analytic framework that I have termed multiple marginality (Vigil 1988, 2002) lends itself to a holistic strategy that examines linkages among the various factors that contribute to gang formation and involvement, the actions and interactions between them, and the cumulative nature of urban street gangs. Multiple marginality also takes into account the role of the social environment in shaping personal identities with which the individuals interact. To broaden and deepen the picture, many other factors need to be considered, such as ecological, socioeconomic, sociocultural, and sociopsychological dynamics, particularly in light of the immigrant experience. It is this complexity and the reverberations within it that make conventional human development so troublesome and problematic for barrio youth generally and gang members specifically. Already filled with potential minefields and difficulties, social, emotional, cognitive, and physical developmental trajectories are considerably undermined in such situations and conditions. To prevent youth whose backgrounds are laden with such difficulties from joining gangs is a tall order. Even later interventions can tax our resources. However, somehow, some way, someone must take the steps to address this complexity and the challenges faced by street youth who are multiply marginal.

Note

1. The Comprehensive Community Model (or "Spergel Model," as it is widely known) was developed at the University of Chicago and applied to several cities in the United States (Spergel 1995, 2007). It is perhaps the best-known example of this approach, although its shortcomings and limitations have been carefully noted (Klein and Maxson 2006). See also chapters 2, 3, and 8 of this volume for more extended discussion of the Spergel Model and other comprehensive community approaches to youth gangs.

References

Bursik, R. J., Jr. and H. G. Grasmick. 1995. "Defining Gangs and Gang Behavior." In M. W. Klein, C. L. Maxson, and J. Miller, eds., *The Modern Gang Reader*, 8–13. Los Angeles: Roxbury.

Curry, G. D., A. B. Richard, and R. J. Fox. 1994. *Gang Crimes and Law Enforcement Recordkeeping*. Washington, D.C.: U.S. Department of Justice, National Institute of Justice, Research in Brief.

Decker, S. H. and B. Van Winkle. 1996. *Life in the Gang: Family, Friends, and Violence*. New York: Cambridge University Press.

Edgerton, R. B. 1978. "The Study of Deviance: Marginal Man or Everyman?" In George D. Spindler, ed., *The Making of Psychological Anthropology*, 442–476. Los Angeles: University of California Press.

Erikson, E. 1968. "Psychosocial Identity." In D. Sills, ed., *International Encyclopedia of the Social Sciences*, 7:61–65. New York: Macmillan and Free Press.

Esbensen, F. and L. T. Winfree, Jr. 2001. "Race and Gender Differences Between Gang and Nongang Youths." In J. Miller, C. L. Maxson, and M. W. Klein, eds., *The Modern Gang Reader*, 106–120. 2nd ed. Los Angeles: Roxbury.

Garces, E., D. Thomas, and J. Currie. 2002. "Longer-Term Effects of Head Start." *American Economic Review* 92 (4): 999–1012.

Griffith, B. 1948. *American Me*. Boston: Houghton Mifflin.

Hannerz, U. 1969. *Soulside: Inquiries Into Ghetto Culture and Community*. New York: Columbia University Press.

Huff, C. R., ed. 2002. *Gangs in America*. 3rd ed. Thousand Oaks, Calif.: Sage.

Klein, M. W. 1971. *Street Gangs and Street Workers*. Englewood Cliffs, N.J.: Prentice-Hall.

——. 1995. *The American Street Gang: Its Nature, Prevalence, and Control*. New York: Oxford University Press.

Klein, M. and C. Maxson. 2006. *Street Gang Patterns and Policies*. New York: Oxford University Press.

Liebow, E. 1967. *Tally's Corner*. Boston: Little, Brown.

McWilliams, C. 1968 [1949]. *North from Mexico*. New York: Greenwood.

Miller, W. B. 1959. "Lower Class Culture as a Generating Milieu of Gang Delinquency." *Journal of Social Problems* 14:5–19.

Moore, J. W. 1978. Homeboys: Gangs, Drugs, and Prison in the Barrios of Los Angeles. Philadelphia: Temple University Press.

——. 1991. Going Down to the Barrio: Homeboys and Homegirls in Change. Philadelphia: Temple University Press

Moreno, J. F. 1999. *The Elusive Quest for Equality: 150 Years of Chicano/Chicana Education*. Cambridge, Mass.: Harvard Educational Review, Harvard University Press.

Rainwater, L. 1970. *Behind Ghetto Walls: Black Families in a Federal Slum*. Chicago: Aldine.

Shakur, S. 1993. *Monster: The Autobiography of an L.A. Gang Member*. New York: Atlantic Monthly Press.

Shaw, C. and R. McKay. 1942. *Juvenile Delinquency and Urban Areas*. Chicago: University of Chicago Press

Short, J. 1996. "Personal, Gang, and Community Careers." In C. R. Huff, ed., *Gangs in America*, 3–11. 3rd ed. Thousand Oaks, Calif.: Sage.

Spergel, I. 1995. *The Youth Gang Problem: A Community Approach*. New York: Oxford University Press.

——. 2007. *Reducing Youth Gang Violence: The Little Village Gang Project in Chicago*. Lanham, Md.: AltaMira.

Suttles, G. 1968. *The Social Order of the Slum: Ethnicity and Territory in the Inner City*. Chicago: University of Chicago Press.

Thornberry, T. P. 2001. "Risk Factors for Gang Membership." In J. Miller, C. L. Maxson, and M. W. Klein, eds., *The Modern Gang Researcher*, 32–43. 2nd ed. Los Angeles: Roxbury.

Thrasher, F. M. 1963 [1927]. *The Gang*. Chicago: University of Chicago Press.

Tuck, R. 1956. *Not with the Fist: Mexican Americans in a Southwest City*. New York: Harcourt Brace.

Vigil, J. D. 1979. "Adaptation Strategies and Cultural Life Styles of Mexican American Adolescents." *Hispanic Journal of Behavioral Sciences* 1 (4): 375–392.

——. 1983. "Chicano Gangs: One Response to Mexican Urban Adaptation in the Los Angeles Area." *Urban Anthropology* 12 (1): 45–75.

——. 1988a. *Barrio Gangs: Street Life and Identity in Southern California*. Austin: University of Texas Press.

——. 1988b. "Group Processes and Street Identity: Adolescent Chicano Gang Members." *Ethos* 16 (4): 421–445.

——. 1993a. "The Established Gang." In S. Cummings and D. Monti, eds., *Gangs: The Origins and Impact of Contemporary Youth Gangs in the United States*, 95–112. Albany: State University of New York Press.

——. 1993b. "Gangs, Social Control, and Ethnicity: Ways to Redirect Street Youth." In Shirley B. Heath and Milbrey W. McLaughlin. eds., *Identity and Inner-City Youth: Beyond Ethnicity and Gender*, 94–119. New York: Teachers College Press.

——. 1996. "Street Baptism: Chicano Gang Initiation." *Human Organization* 55 (2): 149–153.

——. 1997. *Personas Mexicanas: Chicano Highschoolers in a Changing Los Angeles*. Fort Worth: Harcourt Brace.

——. 2002a. "Community Dynamics and the Rise of Street Gangs." In M. M. Suarez-Orozco and M. M. Paez, eds., *Latinos! Remaking America*, 97–109. Berkeley and Cambridge, Mass.: University of California Press and the David Rockefeller Center for Latin American Studies, Harvard University.

——. 2002b. *A Rainbow of Gangs: Street Cultures in the Mega-City*. Austin: University of Texas Press.

———. 2007. *The Projects: Gang and Non-Gang Families in East Los Angeles*. Austin: University of Texas Press.

Vigil, J. D. and S. C. Yun. 2002. "A Cross-cultural Framework to Understand Gangs: Multiple Marginality and Los Angeles." In C. R. Huff, ed., *Gangs in America*, 161–174. 3rd ed. Thousand Oaks, Calif.: Sage.

8

A Community Youth Development Approach to Gang Control Programs

JEFFREY A. BUTTS AND CATERINA GOUVIS ROMAN

Youth gangs are a top priority of U.S. law enforcement and a prominent concern of the American public. Even the words associated with youth gangs produce visceral reactions. The terms "gang violence" and "drug gang" evoke horrific images of violence in the streets, drive-by shootings, and, most tragically, innocent victims struck by bullets fired indiscriminately at one gang by another. With every incident of gang-related violence, the public demands tougher laws to crack down on gangs and to punish gang members.

As with many crime problems, however, popular solutions rarely lead to effective policies. The most popular approaches for dealing with gang violence rely heavily on law enforcement. Gang injunctions, targeted curfews, large-scale drug arrests, and warrant sweeps focus on suppression, that is, on getting gang members off the streets. These efforts may be successful in the short run, but they are rarely effective in the long run. Real, lasting progress in the fight against gang violence requires preventive approaches that address a wide range of factors, including the community-level, collective, and structural factors behind gang involvement, as well as the individual characteristics that lead young people to join gangs, such as the belief that gang membership will enhance their personal safety and lead to financial gain and social status.

Given this evidence regarding effectiveness and arguments regarding the importance of prevention, it is not surprising that academic experts argue for better prevention strategies, but federal, state, and local governments also support prevention programs (Wyrick 2006). Even law enforcement professionals often prefer to address gang problems through job training and educational supports for young offenders rather than by relying on suppression alone (Spergel and Curry 1993). After decades of effort, however, prevention is still struggling to become an established component of public policy regarding youth gangs and gang violence.

A key reason for the limited growth of gang prevention strategies is that youth gang programs are rarely evaluated, and without convincing evidence of effectiveness, such programs eventually lose the enthusiasm of political sponsors (Zahniser 2008). One reason they are not evaluated is that many gang prevention programs lack the theoretically oriented conceptual frameworks that are required to conduct a high-quality evaluation. Programs are often assembled from a grab bag of existing resources and program models—get a little education here, a little job training there, add a dash of drug treatment, and throw in a pinch of counseling. To make real progress in gang control, especially with prevention programs that focus on the youngest gang members and those at risk of gang involvement, researchers and practitioners must cooperate to build comprehensive interventions using frameworks that are theoretically, conceptually, and administratively sound.

This chapter describes a potential path to a stronger conceptual framework for youth gang prevention and early intervention that draws upon one of the most well-established gang reduction efforts to date, the Comprehensive Community Model developed by Irving Spergel at the University of Chicago, as well as two increasingly prominent perspectives in the criminal and juvenile justice system: positive youth development and the community justice approach. The chapter begins by reviewing the Comprehensive Community Model and other recent gang control initiatives. Next, it describes the concepts and principles of positive youth development and community justice. The discussion concludes by considering the potential of these two frameworks for improving gang control efforts.[1]

The Case for Gang Prevention and Early Interventions

Skeptics might advise policymakers to abandon all gang control programs, reasoning that gang members are too deeply involved in criminal behavior to be rehabilitated. Indeed, youth who join organized gangs are likely responsible for a disproportionate share of violent crime. Several studies have attempted to identify the proportion of all youth violence that is attributable to gang members. The resulting estimates, based on single-site studies, are often shocking, with gang members responsible for up to 50 or 60 percent of all violent youth crime (Thornberry 1998). Researchers also find, however, that individual involvement in gang activity varies greatly. Scholarly work on youth gangs usually begins by noting the obvious fact that gang membership increases a young person's involvement in criminal behavior, especially the number of violent acts (Klein 1971; Klein and Maxson 1989; Thornberry et al. 2003). Yet many (even most) gang youth are never more than peripheral members of their gangs, and most are involved for only short periods. In fact, the average period of gang involvement is around one year (Thornberry et al. 2003). It would therefore be grossly inaccurate to portray all youth gang members as irredeemable.

During the 1990s, investigators associated with the federally sponsored Program of Research on the Causes and Correlates of Delinquency examined individual rates of offending among self-reported gang members and compared their behavior with the behavior of delinquent youth not involved in gangs (Battin-Pearson et al. 1998). The results suggested that gang membership doubled the rate of violent offending. Gang-involved youth in Seattle, for example, averaged 0.8 violent offenses per year according to court records, whereas non-gang youth were involved in 0.3 violent offenses per year.

Other analyses from the Causes and Correlates study, however, suggested that gang youth were not inherently more criminal. Gang membership increased a youth's participation in criminal behavior during the time when that youth was actually involved in gang activities, but before and after a period of gang activity, the behavior of gang members was not substantially different from the behavior of other young offenders (Thornberry et al. 2003). It is for these reasons that law enforcement professionals see many young gang members as potentially salvageable. The challenge for policymakers and practitioners is to design interventions that actually work for these youth.

The Comprehensive Community Model

Many gang control programs in the United States have their roots in a model known as the Comprehensive Community Model. Developed at the University of Chicago by Dr. Irving Spergel, the Comprehensive Community Model is an interagency and interdisciplinary model that utilizes five strategies for working with gang-involved youth and their communities: (1) community mobilization, which encourages involvement from local citizens as well as key leaders of organizations, (2) opportunities provision, which offers specific programs to gang-involved youth, (3) social intervention, in which program staff "reach out" to youth and provide them with needed services, (4) suppression, and (5) organizational change and development, which revolves around the development and implementation of policies and procedures to provide better resources to gang-involved youth. Key goals of the model include not only the reduction of gang-related crime and a decrease in community-level crime rates but also an increase in community capacity through the creation of integrated service systems for gang-involved youth.[2]

Successes and Failures of the Comprehensive Community Model

Spergel's Comprehensive Community Model was first implemented in the 1990s in Little Village, a Chicago neighborhood with long-standing gang problems (Spergel 2007). Early results of the model were promising. As these early successes came to light, the U.S. Department of Justice's Office of Juvenile Justice and Delinquency Prevention (OJJDP) sponsored similar programs in five other cities: Bloomington-Normal, Illinois; San Antonio, Texas; Mesa, Arizona; Tucson, Arizona; and Riverside, California. Other federally sponsored gang initiatives rooted in the Spergel Model (described below) were added soon thereafter, including the Gang-Free Schools and Communities Program (GFSCP) (OJJDP 2005) and the Gang Reduction Program (GRP).

The Little Village demonstration focused on two of the largest, most violent gangs in the Chicago area. Still, program participants reported lower participation in violent crime relative to a comparison group (Spergel 2007). Analyses using official police data confirmed these findings. Following implementation of the model, community residents reported feelings of increased safety, decreased fear of victimization, and perceived decreases in community crime levels. Successful job referral and placement of program youth were associated with gang members' spending less time with their gang friends and more time with family and significant others. Successful employment was associated with reduced levels of violence and drug arrests (Spergel, Wa, and Sosa 2006). Despite these successes, researchers found that the rate of decline in arrests for gang violence dropped off during the last two years of the project. Spergel and his colleagues attributed the decline to reluctance by the city administration and police department to institutionalize the Comprehensive Community Model. One major stumbling block was the limited coordination of neighborhood organizations and government agencies.

Evaluations at additional model sites, also conducted by Spergel, found some successes (reduced levels of recidivism, reductions in crime, reductions in arrests for violent behavior) in two jurisdictions: Mesa, Arizona, and Riverside, California. At both of these sites, the program was implemented with general fidelity to the model, but not all programmatic elements of the model were incorporated. The programs in Tucson, Bloomington, and San Antonio, on the other hand, saw no statistically significant differences between program and comparison youth in arrests or self-reported offenses, and in Tucson and San Antonio there were no overall reductions in gang crime relative to comparison areas (Spergel 2007). Spergel and his colleagues attributed a large portion of the disappointing outcomes at these three sites to poor model implementation. The evaluators stated that the sites failed to implement some of the most important components of the model, including strong city and county leadership, interagency street-team coordination, and participation by criminal justice agencies. In addition, there was not enough emphasis on youth opportunities and services to balance suppression efforts. Without a truly collaborative approach, it was difficult for communities to craft intervention strategies that were tailored for the individual circumstances of youth (Spergel 2007).

Evolution of the Comprehensive Community Model

As findings from the six Comprehensive Community Model sites were emerging, juvenile justice officials at the U.S. Department of Justice began adapting and expanding successful aspects of the model into new initiatives, including the Gang-Free Schools and Communities Program (GFSCP) and the Gang Reduction Program (GRP). The GFSCP was funded by OJJDP and launched in 2000 at four sites: Miami-Dade, Florida; East Cleveland, Ohio; Pittsburgh, Pennsylvania; and Houston, Texas. The community-based initiative followed core strategies defined by the Comprehensive Community Model but with a particular emphasis on reducing gang activity in schools (NYGC 2008; OJJDP 2005). Program strategies included an anti-gang curriculum, school-based monitoring of gang activities, and the explicit goal of lowering gang activity in schools as well as in the community at large (Sheppard 2002).

The primary goal of the GRP was to reduce youth gang crime and violence in communities through an integrated application of proven practices in prevention, secondary prevention, gang intervention, and gang suppression. Similar to the Comprehensive Community Model, the GRP included among its key objectives assessing community needs and identifying resources (both human and financial) and building community capacity to deliver appropriate services based on identified risks of youth, families, and community members, including gang members. GRP adds three new aspects to the Comprehensive Community Model: an emphasis on the recruitment of faith-based partners, the recruitment of private-sector partners, and sustaining multi-agency collaborations (NYGC 2008). By 2007, GRP programs in Los Angeles, Milwaukee, North Miami Beach, and Richmond were in their third year of operation. In order to maximize resources, the programs were encouraged to co-locate with other federally supported prevention and intervention programs, such as Weed and Seed, Safe Schools/Healthy Students, and Project Safe Neighborhoods.

The strategies in the GRP framework included: (1) primary prevention, (2) secondary prevention, (3) intervention, and (4) gang suppression. Primary prevention strategies in GRP relied on the provision of one-stop service and resource centers for health and support services that would be available to all families. Secondary prevention involved the identification of at-risk youth and the provision of more-intensive supports and services for families already known to the social services sector. Interventions focused on aggressive outreach to gang-involved youth by a multidisciplinary team that included probation, law enforcement, schools, mental health agencies, child protective services, and other community organizations. Suppression efforts in GRP included targeted enforcement and prosecution to remove the most dangerous gang-involved youth from the community as well as graduated sanctions for less serious offenders. The framework was organized around the principle of collaboration and the coordination of resources across a variety of organizations to fill identified gaps in services at the local level. Specific interventions, however, were not required by OJJDP. The GRP sites were responsible for developing an overall strategy that targeted the needs of each community.

Interim evaluation results of GRP did not show significant reductions in crime across all sites. Using time series analysis, the GRP evaluation considered different crime outcomes at each site. At the time of the analysis, sites had been providing services and suppression in their target areas for approximately two years. The early results revealed that only one site, Los Angeles, showed a significant reduction in crime rates, with gang-related incidents, gang-related violence, and calls for police service due to shots fired all decreasing significantly after the implementation of GRP. Smaller declines in those measures were found in the comparison area (and no evidence of displacement was identified). In Milwaukee and North Miami Beach, no significant changes in the outcome measures were found after GRP implementation. In Richmond, the period after implementation actually saw significant increases in serious violence and gang-related measures. Although the comparison area in Richmond also saw increases in two of the measures, the increases were smaller than those in the target area (Cahill et al. 2008).

It is still too early to determine whether the Comprehensive Community Model tenets used by GRP will lead to reductions in crime at all sites. Since the interim evaluation data have been analyzed, there has been some indication that Richmond has seen a decrease in serious violence and gang crime. In addition, it should be noted that the sites' activities included substantial prevention components, but with only a two-year follow-up period to date, it is too early to assess the effectiveness of these efforts. The evaluation also includes the collection of three waves of survey data from site coordinators and committee members. The survey (designed by one of the authors of this chapter) was developed to gauge collaboration and coordination among partnership agencies within sites and across sites. Results will assist interpretation of outcome evaluation findings when final evaluation analyses are completed in late 2008.

Other Gang Control Models

Other important anti-gang strategies have been inspired by the successes of violence reduction projects in Boston and Chicago. The Boston Gun Project focused on systematic assessment and analysis of crime problems and relied on practitioner knowledge to target the underlying motives behind youth gun violence and homicide (Kennedy 1998). The strategy was developed to reduce all youth homicides, but it could also be considered a gang control strategy because program staff soon discovered that many of the youth they identified for intervention were involved in gangs. Though the project targeted specific community problems that were identified through data analysis, it was also informed by the insights of an interagency working group assembled to communicate a deterrence message to youth audiences, with appropriate follow-through and real consequences.

Initiated by a multi-agency working group in 1995, Boston's problem-solving partnership determined from a research and planning phase that youth violence in Boston was concentrated among a small number of chronically offending, gang-involved youth (Kennedy, Braga, and Piehl 1997; Kennedy, Piehl, and Braga 1996). The working group crafted an intervention that responded to the particular nature of the violence in that the programmatic activities implemented were tailored to directly address the motives and behavior patterns that were behind a large portion of the violence. The intervention, which came to be known as Operation Ceasefire, delivered an explicit deterrence message and stressed that such violence would not be tolerated. Outreach workers delivered the message to a small audience of youth gang members through formal meetings and direct contacts with gang members and inmates in juvenile facilities. The message was, in essence: "We know who you are, we are watching, and we will not tolerate violence; if you choose violence, the consequences will be as severe as state and federal law will allow—which is very severe."

One key to the strategy was making sure the members of an interagency working group followed through on the promised responses to violence. The intent of the project was to interrupt the cycle of violence and to provide a necessary lull that could enable neighborhoods and community institutions to function better (Kennedy 1998). A formal evaluation of the Boston Project revealed that the intervention accounted for a 63 percent drop in the number of Boston youth homicides, a 32 percent decrease in shots fired, and a 25 percent decline in gun assaults. These reductions were significant when compared with violent crime trends in other U.S. cities (Braga et al. 2001).

At least partly as a result of the successes of Operation Ceasefire, the National Institute of Justice within the U.S. Department of Justice funded projects in ten additional cities to replicate the Boston Gun Project. The new efforts benefited from strong support by federal prosecutors. The projects evolved into the deterrence-oriented, problem-solving partnerships known as the Strategic Approaches to Community Safety Initiative (SACSI). An evaluation of SACSI in Winston-Salem found that the initiative's Boston-style notification meetings were not as successful in reducing individual-level violent behavior as they had been in Boston but that aggregate crime levels still fell in a way that might be attributable to the intervention (Easterling et al. 2002). Other reports suggested that the positive effects of SACSI included a drop in homicides in Minneapolis and a decrease in drive-by shootings in Portland (Dalton 2003). The evaluators of SACSI in North Carolina recommended that future efforts include the use of a theoretical logic model that could account for the many factors potentially influencing behavior change (Easterling et al. 2002). Essentially, the evaluators believed that specification of the norms and behavior patterns of violent offenders could be used to tie the implementation of particular activities to intended outcomes (through a theoretical understanding of the causes of violence and programmatic aspects that could lead to desistance from crime and violent offending).

The deterrence-heavy strategies found in the Boston Gun Project and SACSI were modified further to develop another federally supported initiative, Project Safe Neighborhoods (PSN). Beginning in 2001, PSN efforts were funded in ninety jurisdictions across the country. For the most part, PSN has relied on interagency task forces and enforcement-related suppression, including the federal prosecution of offenses (as opposed to local prosecution) and the development of gang member lists that could be used in police targeting and gang crackdowns. Only a few rigorous evaluations have been conducted of PSN efforts and related focused deterrence strategies. The National Academies' Panel on Improving Information and Data on Firearms found that the evidence on the effectiveness of the focused deterrence strategy was limited (Wellford, Pepper, and Petrie 2005). Since that time, two evaluations of PSN-related focused deterrence strategies have found significant reductions in crime in the jurisdictions studied (Braga et al. 2008; McGarrell et al. 2006; Papachristos, Meares, and Fagan 2007). Braga and colleagues stated that the PSN Task Force (Lowell, Massachusetts) was extremely successful in engaging the community in their efforts and helped to create a sense of joint ownership. The authors wrote: "Given the potentially harsh law-enforcement levers that can be pulled as part of a focused enforcement program, we feel that community involvement is critical in replicating and sustaining such intensive violence prevention initiatives" (Braga et al. 2008:157).

Finally, Chicago's CeaseFire, an effort of the Chicago Project for Violence Prevention (CPVP), emerged as another possible best-practice model in comprehensive anti-gang strategies. The CPVP was established in 1995 with the goal of reducing violence in the Chicago metropolitan area. It relied on strategic public health approaches by working to change behavioral norms and to provide alternatives to violent behavior through neighborhood intervention and direct mediation (Chicago Project for Violence Prevention 2004). The CeaseFire effort began in 1999 and eventually involved twenty-five neighborhoods, mostly in the City of Chicago. The project did not try to suppress violent behavior directly among large groups or communities. Instead, it focused on reducing risky activities by those most likely to be affected by gun violence, either as perpetrators or as victims. The project hired street-level workers (often former offenders) to identify and mediate conflicts between gangs and to intervene in the cycles of retaliatory violence that often erupt after shootings. As it neared its tenth anniversary, CeaseFire was weakened by political turmoil and funding disruptions, but an evaluation revealed that the project was beginning to have effects. Time series analyses suggested that shootings and gang violence were lower than might otherwise have been expected in neighborhoods where CeaseFire was implemented (Skogan et al. 2008; chapter 4 of this volume).

Improving Comprehensive Community Approaches to Gang Control

Creating effective gang control programs is always challenging. Effectiveness is elusive and positive impacts are not easily sustained even when they do occur. It is also not easy to interpret the outcomes of previous efforts. The successes and failures of previous programs, however, represent the best source of information for developing new approaches. When all negative and positive outcomes of prior programs are considered, they begin to form a more coherent picture from which we can generate essential lessons for communities that need to prevent youth from joining gangs and wreaking havoc on their communities. It is clear from previous efforts that relying on suppression alone will not produce long-term success. Interventions must include vigorous law enforcement to mitigate the negative consequences of gang activity, but they also have to focus on positive forces. In particular, gang control programs must: (1) reduce the allure of gang membership by ensuring that individual youth have access to services, positive supports, and work opportunities, and (2) create gang-resistant neighborhoods by cultivating the organizational and community structures that lower the incidence of gang violence.

These insights, largely drawn from social disorganization theory (Shaw and McKay 1942) and its descendants (Bursik and Grasmick 1993; Sampson, Raudenbush, and Earls 1997), helped to fuel the development of comprehensive gang reduction models. Identifying these theoretical insights as the basis for intervention, however, is not the same thing as designing and implementing specific strategies to achieve gang reduction objectives. Forging a clear path between goals and their achievement requires a conceptual framework or an explicit "theory of change" (Weiss 1972). The Comprehensive Community Model encourages gang control programs to provide positive activities for youth and to include community stakeholders and neighborhood participants in carrying out program strategies, but how should communities set priorities and choose specific action steps?

It may be useful to look outside the gang control field to find suitable frameworks. Since the development and initial publication of the Comprehensive Community Model, researchers and practitioners working in the justice system and other related areas have continued to create new fields of practice that could help to refine the implementation of the Comprehensive Community Model. Two frameworks in particular could have special relevance for future efforts to implement the model: (1) positive youth development and (2) community justice. As structured, the Comprehensive Community Model emphasizes three strategies in which positive youth development and community justice could be embedded: community mobilization, opportunities provision, and social intervention. We are not advocating a totally new approach to gang control. We believe that if the foundational principles of positive youth development and community justice are moved to the forefront of the Comprehensive Community Model, future gang control efforts that adhere to the model will be more practical and potentially more effective.

Positive Youth Development

Infusing the Comprehensive Community Model with the ideas of positive youth development (PYD) could improve its overall effectiveness by making individual-level prevention efforts more targeted, more practical, and even more cost-effective. The PYD framework suggests that young people develop and flourish not only when they are free of risk factors and problem behaviors but also when they are meaningfully connected to an appropriate mix of pro-social opportunities, relationships, and developmental assets. Youth with access to an effective mix of these developmental resources are less likely to experience school failure, substance abuse, and delinquency (Catalano et al. 2004; Scales and Leffert 2004). The PYD approach suggests that interventions should enhance the positive features in a youth's environment, and not simply try to reduce the negative aspects.

The ideas behind PYD are informed by research on adolescent development, but PYD is not a theory of development. It is a set of practice principles. Researchers study adolescent development to track the processes of individual growth and maturation and to identify the factors that lead to healthy social development and a productive transition from childhood to adulthood. Practitioners rely on this knowledge to shape the set of practice principles known as positive youth development. The goal of PYD is to ensure that youth are meaningfully engaged in an array of pro-social and developmentally appropriate services, supports, and opportunities. Conventional gang prevention models have addressed these ideas before, but they have not done so in a targeted way.

The PYD framework may offer a means of adding clarity and focus to gang prevention efforts, but considerable work would still be necessary to craft such a strategy. As yet, there is no single PYD model that has been proven to be effective, particularly with young offenders. A growing evidence base, however, suggests that a PYD-informed approach could be an effective method for working with youth at risk of gang involvement. Most adolescent offenders need the same things all adolescents need. They need to experience meaningful and lasting attachments to pro-social adults and peers so that they can develop social competencies and a sense of belonging. They need help with school, or at least experience with learning new skills and what it means to be valued by others for having learned those skills. They usually need work experience and job readiness. They need to be engaged in civic and community activities, and they would likely benefit from involvement in music, art, and other forms of personal expression. They also need outlets for physical activity and to learn that there are ways to have fun without breaking the law. Most youth from wealthy and middle-class communities have ready access to these resources. The idea behind positive youth development is to devise ways of providing these resources for all youth, even those from poor, distressed, and violence-ridden neighborhoods.

Researchers and practitioners have developed a number of models to express these concepts. One of the most well-known frameworks is the Search Institute's menu of forty developmental assets, a list of individual and contextual factors that encourage youth to avoid harmful behavior and to engage instead in activities promoting positive development (Scales and Leffert 2004). The Search Institute's model is far from perfect for gang prevention, as some of the proposed assets reflect class bias (e.g., young people should "read for pleasure three or more hours per week") and others rely on conventional notions of morality that may not be acceptable to all youth and families (e.g., young people should "spend one hour or more per week in activities in a religious institution"). The forty developmental assets, however, helped to shape contemporary practices in youth development.

Another influential framework views positive youth development as a set of critical outcomes or goals based on the idea of thriving, a condition marked by healthy relationships that encourage youth to see past their own self-interest and to appreciate their community and society (Lerner, Fisher, and Weinberg 2000). The framework emphasizes interactions between individuals within varying contexts, such as family, school, and community. As young people navigate and manage these interactions, they begin to acquire what several frameworks have called the five C's—competence, character, connection, confidence, and caring/compassion. Society benefits as young people develop the capacity to nurture and sustain socially equitable institutions.

These and other PYD frameworks vary in their language and in the way they package their core ideas, but they share a number of common elements (figure 8.1). All PYD frameworks stress that youth development is enhanced when young people are able to acquire a critical set of attributes, skills, and relationships that are associated with healthy transitions to productive and socially engaged adult lives. All PYD frameworks also agree that ensuring positive developmental outcomes for youth requires that communities create sustainable structures that provide youth and families with access to a wide range of activities, supports, and opportunities—not simply services.

FIGURE 8.1

Common Concepts in PYD Frameworks

Focus on strengths and assets rather than deficits and problems.

Keeping youth away from drugs, criminal activity, premature sexual behavior, and other risks does not, by itself, prepare them for a productive future. PYD approaches emphasize the building of youth assets, or the skills and competencies that will allow them to take on new roles as they transition from childhood to adulthood.

Strengths and assets are acquired through positive relationships, especially with pro-social and caring adults.

Relationships and interactions between youth and trusted adults are one of the key mechanisms through which healthy development occurs. Trusted adults include parents and family members, but also teachers, neighbors, local business owners, and members of the community. Relationships with pro-social peers can also facilitate development, but positive relationships with adults are the primary focus of the PYD approach.

The development and acquisition of youth assets occur in multiple contexts and environments.

Unlike older views of adolescent development that placed almost exclusive emphasis on the family, PYD frameworks see youth development opportunities in all of the worlds that adolescents inhabit. Schools, workplaces, community organizations, social programs, and neighborhoods are all part of a youth's natural environment, and all offer opportunities for the acquisition of developmental resources.

Source: Butts, Mayer, and Ruth 2005.

Positive youth development could be effective as a conceptual framework for the prevention and intervention components of gang control programs, but even within suppression-focused tactics, there should be an awareness that positive youth development activities could provide diversion opportunities for youth who come in contact with law enforcement but might not be headed for lengthy prison terms. The concepts of PYD could provide a new and compelling, theoretically inspired framework for designing and delivering intervention strategies. Without a new framework, practitioners and community leaders are likely to revert to traditional ways of conceptualizing youth justice interventions. Most interventions for young offenders are based on the (usually unstated) theoretical assumption that youth involved in criminal behavior suffer from emotional or psychological pathologies. Because "good kids" don't break the law, youthful offenders must have mental health problems or drug abuse issues that cause them to misbehave, and these problems need to be treated by "behavioral health" professionals. This common, but empirically dubious, assumption limits the vision of policymakers and practitioners seeking new solutions for combating youth crime. The PYD approach could offer a practical alternative to the individual-pathology medical model that tends to dominate thinking about youth justice interventions.

Medical model treatments are appropriate for some youth in the juvenile justice system, but most (more than two-thirds) youth having contact with law enforcement and the courts are not afflicted with emotional problems, mental health disorders, or drug addiction (McReynolds et al. 2008). Youth become involved in criminal behavior for a variety of nonpathological reasons, including fear for their own safety, simple thrill seeking, defiance of authority, material desire or greed, a rational reaction to chronic school failure, and a general social environment that is conducive to, and even accepting of, a wide range of illegal behavior. Youth motivated by these factors are not likely to respond well to therapeutic treatments that require them to comply with psychological treatment protocols and to submit to the invasive (albeit well-intentioned) attention of helping professionals. Forcing them into therapeutically oriented, medical-model programs could increase the antisocial posture of youth rather than reduce it.

Why then do we assume that the best way to keep youth away from crime is to provide them with therapy? For the most part, that assumption takes root in the absence of a compelling alternative, but it is also partly the result of a common misunderstanding of research about adolescent offenders. In recent years, some mental health advocates have argued that three-quarters of all juvenile offenders suffer from mental health and/or drug abuse problems. Such statements are based on either the self-interest of treatment providers or a misunderstanding of the relevant research (Cocozza and Skowyra 2000; Grisso 2007). The most inflammatory statements are made by those who claim to draw their evidence from studies of detained and incarcerated youth. The results of such studies, however, cannot be used to generalize about the prevalence of mental health disorders among all juvenile offenders, a fact that the study authors themselves have often pointed out (Teplin et al. 2002).

Researchers investigating broader samples of youthful offenders, including those not incarcerated, find that the proportion of youth with detectable diagnoses is considerably lower than 70 to 80 percent. McReynolds and her colleagues (2008), for example, measured the incidence of mental health disorders and substance abuse problems among youth referred to a Florida juvenile assessment center that serves as the first processing stop for the wide array of youth arrested by law enforcement for any offense, which yielded a study sample that was a much better representation of youth offenders in general. Among these youth, 29 percent had some form of diagnosable disorder. Even that figure, however, was reached only by including every conceivable degree of mental health problem, including mild depression. By this standard, the same statement could be made about 21 percent of *all* U.S. adolescents (U.S. DHHS 1999).

Wasserman and her colleagues (2005) employed the same screening tool used in the McReynolds study to detect mental health problems among a sample of youth referred to a juvenile probation intake department. In other words, the youth had moved further into the juvenile justice process than those in the assessment center sample. In the probation sample, researchers found that 46 percent of youth had some form of diagnosable disorder. The pattern is clear. As one looks deeper into the juvenile justice process—from initial contact, to probation intake, to youth in detention—the incidence of mental health and substance abuse problems increases. Is this because mental health issues cause crime, or does the juvenile justice system simply react more aggressively to youth who not only violate the law but also have higher service needs because of mental health and drug problems? We argue that the latter explanation is more likely to be accurate.

The same observation can be made about drug abuse problems. In the Teplin et al. detention study (2002), for example, half the youth had a "diagnosable" drug abuse problem, whereas just one in four youth in the Wasserman et al. (2005) study of probation intake had "substance use disorders." The incidence of substance abuse problems was just 10.5 percent in the McReynolds et al. (2008) study of the juvenile assessment center population, which is just slightly more than the incidence (5.6 percent) among all teens (Butts, Zweig, and Mamalian 2004:155). Moreover, most of the drug problems identified among youth in the juvenile assessment center involved alcohol and marijuana rather than substances such as cocaine and methamphetamine. Substance "abuse" disorders involving drugs beyond alcohol and marijuana were detected in just 0.8 percent of the sample, and substance "dependence" disorders involving other substances were noted in only 1.2 percent of the study youths (McReynolds et al. 2008:323).

Do mental health problems and drug abuse cause youth to become involved in crime? If so, clinical treatment programs that address these problems are probably sufficient as an intervention strategy for gang control. Or, as seems far more likely, are the higher rates of mental health disorders and drug abuse problems among young offenders a result of social and structural factors that affect the impoverished and disadvantaged communities from which a disproportionate number of juvenile offenders originate? If this is a more accurate interpretation, interventions to reduce criminal offending among the youth most at risk of gang involvement need to provide far more than clinical or medical-model treatment.

In fact, a broad consensus of epidemiological studies suggests that mental disorders are associated with disadvantaged social status, including income and education levels (Kessler et al. 2006). Research on adolescent mental health has shown that perceived community safety has a significant effect on the appearance of mental disorders (Aneshensel and Sucoff 1996). The incidence of disorders is generally higher among youth from poor and disadvantaged communities—the very areas where youth are more likely to be arrested and to become involved in the justice system. Thus the increased incidence of mental health problems among youth in the justice system is at least partly a result of the economic and social conditions of the neighborhoods in which they live, rather than of inherent individual differences between offenders and non-offenders. Mental health treatment and substance abuse treatment are certainly important components of crime prevention, but they are not sufficient by themselves as an overall strategy for reducing youth violence and ensuring public safety.

Policymakers and practitioners need to develop a model of intervention that makes sense for young offenders who come into contact with law enforcement and justice agencies and do not have treatable mental health or substance abuse disorders. A comprehensive model of gang control should include strategies for working with multiple types of youth. A sound gang control program could draw upon the principles of positive youth development and provide developmental resources that enhance multiple facets of a youth's life, as well as offer individualized treatment or counseling when necessary. Spergel and colleagues have indicated that provision of socioeconomic opportunities by outreach workers, police, and probation was associated with a significant level of success in the Comprehensive Community Model sites that were most effectively implemented (Spergel, Wa, and Sosa 2006). A successful PYD approach to gang control would identify the best type of developmental and socioeconomic resources for individual youth, peer groups, or even entire gangs, and then rely on those resources as the basis for intervention. Without some understanding of the complex forces at work in neighborhoods—and often particular to neighborhoods—and the norms and behavior patterns of the targeted youth, any efforts will fall short in reducing community crime rates and individual levels of offending. An adherence to the principles of community justice, described in more detail below, would provide the foundation for understanding local neighborhood processes and incorporating the needs of the community into every facet of PYD–focused gang control—from initiative or program development and planning, to implementation, maintenance, and sustainability.

Community Justice

Public safety interventions often acknowledge the importance of community, but achieving true partnerships between justice systems and communities requires explicit attention to a conceptual model of community engagement. For instance, the Comprehensive Community Model includes community mobilization—a key tenet of community justice—as one of its core strategies. Programs built on the Comprehensive Community Model give credence to community mobilization by including residents or local leaders on the steering committee and creating or linking activities with those of block watches and other community groups. In reality, however, community mobilization practices have not been a central component in some previous demonstrations of the Comprehensive Community Model. A summary of the evaluation findings for the Little Village program and the five OJJDP-funded sites (1995–2000) reveals that the evaluation team (Spergel and colleagues) does not believe community mobilization to be more than "moderately important" to program success, yet the sites that were not successful in reducing individual-level and community-level crime had lower community-mobilization implementation levels, on average, than the three sites that were successful (Spergel, Wa, and Sosa 2006:216). Community mobilization must be brought to the forefront of comprehensive gang control efforts. We argue that this can be done by adhering closely to the principles underlying the community justice framework.

The community justice model that has emerged over the past several decades sees the development of public safety as a participatory process in which stakeholders come together to join in collective problem solving, to promote community capacity, and to heal the harm associated with crime and violence (Clear and Karp 1999). In a community justice framework, the community is viewed as a full and active partner within a democratic paradigm. Citizens and residents help to build a broader constituency for the performance measurement process, to clarify a community's priorities, and to encourage public accountability for program performance (Wray and Hauer 1997). Generally, community justice initiatives aim to articulate the voice of the community and improve the quality of life for everyone—across a wide range of stakeholders. The community voice is generated through a process of public deliberation about the common good (Thacher 2001) and a dialogue within the community (Pranis 1998), as opposed to individual declarations of self-interest. Through public deliberation, new information is generated about social problems and the capabilities of government and the community to solve them. True partners in community justice efforts can exchange information, discuss and debate problems, and arrive at agreed-upon strategies for collective action. A partnership, by nature, brings together different groups and organizations to develop a common mission. Solutions to crime and disorder are developed from community-driven, proactive problem solving, and not from professionally defined and bureaucratically delivered interventions.

Traditionally, crime prevention efforts are designed and implemented by government agencies. At best, public agencies request community "input" about their plans and policies. Their stated goals may include problem solving with community partners, but these partnerships rarely involve the integration of residents and community organizations into decision-making structures. True community justice partnerships involve equality and power sharing among partner entities.

Achieving equality in voice and decision making across large crime prevention collaboratives is difficult in and of itself (Roman, Jenkins, and Wolff 2006), but it is perhaps more difficult when demonstration or program funds flow outward from government agencies. Agencies that hold the funding also are more likely to hold the reins in directing programmatic efforts. It should be noted that the Comprehensive Community Model demonstration sites funded by OJJDP, including GRP and Gang-Free Schools and Communities Program sites, involved, for the most part, "lead agencies" that were government agencies, as opposed to community-based collaboratives or nonprofits. Strategies that arise internally from the community are more likely to generate trust between partners, needed resources, and success in accomplishing community objectives.

Community justice partnerships depend on community organizations, including agencies and associations that have a clear stake in supporting the quality of life in a neighborhood and that meet or communicate regularly and can be identified by others. A simple neighborhood block association that meets once a month and has ten volunteers could be as much of a community partnering entity as a formally established nonprofit agency with a hundred staff members and a board of directors. Organizations could even be "virtual" groups that meet and communicate only via the Internet.

For community justice initiatives, the process begins with defining the immediate parties to criminal incidents and/or criminogenic situations (Bazemore and Pranis 1997; Karp and Clear 2000). The range of stakeholders who experience or are affected by criminogenic situations may be quite broad. They may be offenders, victims, or supporters of victims or offenders. They may be residents, students or teachers, property owners, service providers, local government officials, criminal justice practitioners, civic leaders, business owners, or others who use or build community resources and are affected by the quality of life in the community. Because community justice initiatives aim to articulate the voice of the community and to improve the quality of life for everyone who uses or provides resources to the community, the number and type of relevant stakeholders can be quite diverse, and organizing them into a coordinated effort can be very difficult.

For the most part, however, adherence to the principles of community justice initiatives would involve inclusion of those who are affected because of geographical proximity and/or an emotional connection to the issue. By inclusion, we mean that the initiative or strategy makes sustained efforts to reach out to stakeholders during all phases of the program or initiative, not just during development.

Three key facets of the community justice paradigm may be particularly relevant for gang control efforts: mobilization, capacity building, and leadership. These constructs appear to be central to the success of community justice partnerships as a whole (Roman, Jenkins, and Wolff 2006).

MOBILIZATION

Within the context of gang control, experts routinely advise communities that their strategies must take into account the community context and be tailored to address the underlying causes of gang violence in targeted communities, as well as the particular nature of gang crime. In response, communities usually attempt to assemble information on the level and types of violence being committed and the demographic characteristics of the youth and young adults participating in gangs and gang-related crimes. These data-gathering steps are important, but community mobilization is more than understanding community context. Community mobilization for gang prevention is a dynamic process that involves the community as an active agent—whether this is through one community agency or large partnerships—working to build the *internal* capacity of the community to respond to gang violence. The key is having knowledgeable and respected community leaders and residents involved not just in identifying the problem but in designing responses and in maintaining and sustaining the strategy. The Comprehensive Community Model appears to succeed in bringing the community to the table during the program development stages but is less effective with sustaining engagement and collaborative problem solving across time (Roland, Roman, and Coggeshall 2007; Roman, Jenkins, and Wolff 2006; Spergel, Wa, and Sosa 2006).

Community mobilization around gang prevention can involve a wide range of possible objectives, such as building a broader constituency concerned about gang problems, helping to clarify community priorities, developing grassroots strategies to prevent at-risk youth from joining gangs, or providing known gang members with jobs or the skills necessary to obtain legitimate jobs.

CAPACITY BUILDING

Community justice partnerships and strategies may identify the development of community capacity to combat crime as an immediate, intermediate, or long-term goal of a partnership, and undertake specific activities that help to build capacity for joint action and to solve problems. Although community capacity or capacity building may have many definitions (Chaskin 2001), we use the term "community capacity" to refer to the skills and resources necessary to move communities toward their collectively defined goals. Community goals, by definition, are more than a collection of individual, self-interested goals, and collective action entails individuals acting together with a concern for a particular problem.

Capacity building is connected to and, in fact, inherent in successful community mobilization. A community's capacity is its ability to take *collective action toward defined community goals*: in this case, toward a coordinated anti-gang strategy or prevention program. Mobilization will not succeed without buy-in and a focused commitment from community members to fight gang problems in a concerted manner.

Community justice partnerships must overcome the common myth that either communities have capacity or they don't, and that those without existing capacity will have great trouble developing it. Capacity can be developed. It can be developed through the cultivation of informal community assets (such as neighbors and residents) and connections to formal organizations and institutions both inside and outside the community. Community stakeholders who do not seem interested in tackling gang problems—for whatever reason—can be educated about issues related to youth gangs and the consequences of remaining inactive, which will help to galvanize their commitment.

LEADERSHIP

Not surprisingly, community leaders must play a key role in successful community mobilization and capacity building. Strong leaders can articulate the community's voice through identification and development of core values and the expression of a unifying purpose. The type of leadership that is particularly relevant to community justice principles is transformational leadership. Transformational leadership (Bass 1985; Burns 1978) pertains to the capacity of leaders to instigate positive change and the vision of leadership as a part of a democratic process. Transformational leaders build interconnectedness, mobilize and empower the informal community, and articulate the community voice (Hickman 1997). With regard to the gang problem, transformational leaders would generate consensus and interest in the common good by leading communities through the process of deliberation around community priorities by providing the public with information about the local gang problem and the far-reaching consequences of gang violence.

As a result, new, on-the-ground interest and information are generated about gang problems and the capabilities of governments and communities to solve them. This is a method of getting all community stakeholders interested and, more importantly, ready to tackle gangs. Stakeholder buy-in means partners are willing to provide much-needed skills or resources and to be held accountable for inadequate follow-through. Community leaders set the tone for anti-gang strategies by advocating continued respect for youth rights, opposing unduly repressive punishments, and advocating just and balanced procedures. Transformational leaders would help assure diversity so that any coordinated coalition or partnership represents all members of a community (Hickman 1997).

The broader the constituency fighting gang problems is, the more likely it is that programmatic efforts can be implemented on a broad scale, or at least on a scale large enough to make an impact. Having a range of stakeholders, including community leaders, social service and faith-based agencies, businesses, schools, youth, and even local and federal government leaders, provides the expertise needed to tackle the tough multidimensional problems associated with gangs. Large anti-gang partnerships or coalitions may be fraught with problems such as turf battles, lack of accountability, and an unwillingness to share information. To overcome these issues, community stakeholders must be dedicated to a common mission and committed to achieving shared goals. Programs with clear missions and transformational leaders will be better able to determine which partner agencies and organizations should be involved, including which public government agencies are needed to expand community capacity to achieve intended goals. The Comprehensive Community Model attempts to have a broad range of stakeholders on the steering committee, but there are few checks and balances in place to monitor dedication to a common mission, maintenance of diversity, and adequate representation of grassroots and community.

Bringing More Comprehensiveness to the Comprehensive Community Model

A comprehensive model of gang control that is built around the core concepts of positive youth development and community justice could refine the Comprehensive Community Model and perhaps make a real difference for families and communities. Such an approach would be familiar to law enforcement agencies and community organizers accustomed to relying on Spergel's Comprehensive Community Model. It could be consistent with the key strategies of the model, but it could add insights and principles that would facilitate program development and the maintenance of programmatic efforts. Key principles and components could include the following:

- The effectiveness of a community youth development effort depends on effective organization of a diverse range of stakeholders and the concrete experiences of each member in contributing to community solutions.
- Interventions to facilitate youth development should be community-focused but also community-led.
- Improving the life prospects of youth requires systematic efforts to improve the conditions of their families and neighborhoods as well.
- The preferred strategy for reducing youth involvement in crime should be civic engagement and social attachment.
- Resources and opportunities for youth should be individualized and targeted to meet the interests and capacities of youth and their families.
- "Case conferencing," or the development of a multi-agency and multidisciplinary intervention team that meets regularly to discuss individual youth and/or families and develop appropriate resources and actions to assist them should be a centerpiece of any comprehensive strategy.

- Resources meant to divert youth from criminal involvement must make sense to youth and be appealing to youth.
- Efforts to control youth gang involvement must include strategies for economic independence in order to be effective and sustainable.
- Youth participation in the design and implementation of gang control strategies should be extensive and sustained, not symbolic.
- Periodic review of efforts and activities should be undertaken by the lead agency or "steering committee" to ensure community involvement and ongoing mobilization tactics.

The central challenge for policy and practice is how to make these concepts a concrete and permanent feature of gang prevention and control. Positive youth development and community justice are both broad concepts. Without a theory-driven, goal-oriented strategy for embedding the concepts into the Comprehensive Community Model, the ideas could become diluted. Which pieces of each framework are the most feasible for gang prevention and control? Which are the most practical, or the most effective? The construction and implementation of such an approach must be based upon continual experimentation and feedback between practitioners and researchers.

As a first step in this strategy, policymakers and funding entities should help youth development and community justice innovators turn their attention to the needs and abilities of practitioners in the field of youth gang prevention. Practitioners need program models and intervention frameworks that are designed for their targeted problems. The young people most at risk of gang involvement present special challenges for community organizers and youth workers. Many of these youth come from highly disadvantaged communities, and they have embraced values and behaviors that make them resistant to the conventional, pro-social messages embedded in popular youth gang prevention models. Gang control efforts need action frameworks that are designed with these youth and their specific communities in mind.

Next, the community youth development approach would have to be implemented in a variety of settings and on a relatively small scale in order to build up a record of program effects. To demonstrate the efficacy of the approach, funders would have to support small, targeted experiments. One experiment might test the differential effects of using civic engagement with at-risk youth, and another might focus on the unique effects of adult role models, physical activity, etc. Practitioners working to create the new approach would have to chart their own course.

Finally, as the lessons of small experiments accumulate, funding agencies and policymakers would have to support an expanded effort to blend the results into the Comprehensive Community Model. Local officials and community leaders would need to know exactly what the new approach entails and be able to implement the components of the model carefully and with proven fidelity to a research-oriented framework. Then the model would have to be tested with rigorous evaluation designs. To make real progress, practitioners and researchers must work together to generate strong findings that are replicated over time and in multiple settings. With sufficient time and resources, a vigorous effort to create a community youth development approach to the Comprehensive Community Model of gang reduction could produce significant benefits for youth, families, and their communities.

Strong local leadership, community mobilization, and a focus on growing community capacity are promising tools that could lead to successful gang control efforts. Ensuring youth access to pro-social assets, facilitating their participation in neighborhood problem solving, and promoting their attachment to community institutions may be more effective strategies for reducing the allure of gang membership for young people than conventional, suppression-focused programs. Together, the conceptual frameworks of community justice and positive youth development may be effective approaches for building sustainable and long-term gang control efforts that support the social development of adolescents and provide positive returns to communities. The basic ideas underlying these frameworks are not new. They are embedded implicitly within many anti-gang programs and strategies implemented throughout the United States, including Spergel's Comprehensive Community Model. Communities have to make these concepts explicit and to rely upon them in designing and refining youth gang interventions. Public officials at the local, state, and national levels will always support anti-gang efforts that have at least some promise of effectiveness. Government and private funding can provide solid footing for innovative ideas to blossom. The real key to successful gang prevention and gang control programs, however, must be the energy of community-based organizations and the positive leadership of youth themselves.

Notes

1. Following Klein and Maxson (2006), we use the term "gang control" as an umbrella term covering the wide array of anti-gang programming that may include prevention, intervention, enforcement, and suppression, as well as comprehensive programs that involve more than one of these elements.

2. For more detail on the workings of this model, see Spergel, Wa, and Sosa 2006 and chapter 3 of this volume.

References

Aneshensel, Carol S. and Clea A. Sucoff. 1996. "The Neighborhood Context of Adolescent Mental Health." *Journal of Health and Social Behavior* 37 (4): 293–310.

Bass, Bernard M. 1985. *Leadership and Performance Beyond Expectations.* New York: Free Press.

Battin-Pearson, Sara R., Terence P. Thornberry, J. David Hawkins, and Marvin D. Krohn. 1998. "Gang Membership, Delinquent Peers, and Delinquent Behavior." *OJJDP Juvenile Justice Bulletin.* Washington, D.C.: U.S. Department of Justice, Office of Juvenile Justice and Delinquency Prevention. [NCJ171119].

Bazemore, Gordon and Kay Pranis. 1997. "Restorative Justice: Hazards Along the Way." *Corrections Today* 59 (7): 84.

Braga, Anthony A., David M. Kennedy, Elin J. Waring, and Anne M. Piehl. 2001. "Problem-Oriented Policing, Deterrence, and Youth Violence: An Evaluation of Boston's Operation Ceasefire." *Journal of Research in Crime and Delinquency* 38 (3): 195–225.

Braga, Anthony A., Glenn L. Pierce, Jack McDevitt, Brenda J. Bond, and Shea Cronin. 2008. "The Strategic Prevention of Gun Violence Among Gang-Involved Offenders." *Justice Quarterly* 25 (1): 132–162.

Burns, James M. 1978. *Leadership.* New York: Harper.

Bursik, Robert J., Jr. and Harold G. Grasmick. 1993. *Neighborhoods and Crime: The Dimensions of Effective Community Control.* New York: Lexington Books.

Butts, Jeffrey A., Susan Mayer, and Gretchen Ruth. 2005. *Focusing Juvenile Justice on Positive Youth Development.* Chicago: Chapin Hall Center for Children at the University of Chicago.

Butts, Jeffrey A., Janine M. Zweig, and Cynthia Mamalian. 2004. "Defining the Mission of Juvenile Drug Courts." In Jeffrey A. Butts and John Roman, eds., *Juvenile Drug Courts and Teen Substance Abuse*, 137–184. Washington, D.C.: Urban Institute Press.

Cahill, Meagan, Mark Coggeshall, Ashley Wolff, Erica Lagerson, Michelle Scott, Elizabeth Davies, Kevin Roland, David Hayeslip, and Scott Decker. 2008. *Community Collaboratives Addressing Youth Gangs: Interim Findings from the Gang Reduction Program*. Technical Report. Washington, D.C.: Urban Institute.

Catalano, Richard F., M. Lisa Berglund, Jean A.M. Ryan, Heather S. Lonczak, and J. David Hawkins. 2004. "Positive Youth Development in the United States: Research Findings on Evaluations of Positive Youth Development Programs." *Annals of the American Academy of Political and Social Science* 591 (1): 98–124.

Chaskin, Robert J. 2001. "Building Community Capacity: A Definitional Framework and Case Studies from a Comprehensive Community Initiative." *Urban Affairs Review* 36 (3): 291–323.

Chicago Project for Violence Prevention. 2004. *Program Description*. Chicago: Author.

Clear, Todd R. and David R. Karp. 1999. *The Community Justice Ideal: Preventing Crime and Achieving Justice*. Boulder, Colo.: Westview.

Cocozza, Joseph J. and Kathleen Skowyra. 2000. "Youth with Mental Health Disorders: Issues and Emerging Responses." *Juvenile Justice* 7 (1): 3–13.

Dalton, Erin. 2003. *Lessons in Preventing Homicide*. Project Safe Neighborhoods Report. East Lansing, Mich.: School of Criminal Justice, Michigan State University. Available online (www.cj.msu.edu/~outreach/psn/erins_report_jan_2004.pdf). Accessed April 25, 2008.

Easterling, Doug, Lynn Harvey, Donald Mac-Thompson, and Marcus Allen. 2002. *Evaluation of SACSI in Winston Salem: Engaging the Community in a Strategic Analysis of Youth Violence*. Report submitted to the National Institute of Justice, Washington, D.C. [NCJ202977].

Grisso, Thomas. 2007. "Progress and Perils in the Juvenile Justice and Mental Health Movement." *Journal of the American Academy of Psychiatry and the Law* 35 (2): 158–167.

Hickman, Gill Robinson. 1997. "Transforming Organizations to Transform Society." In *Transformational Leadership Working Papers*. College Park, Md.: University of Maryland, Kellogg Leadership Studies Project, James MacGregor Burns Academy of Leadership.

Karp, David R. and Todd R. Clear. 2000. "Community Justice: A Conceptual Framework." In Charles M. Friel, ed., *Boundary Changes in Criminal Justice Organizations: Criminal Justice 2000*, 2:323–368. Washington, D.C.: U.S. Department of Justice, National Institute of Justice. [NCJ-182409].

Kennedy, David. 1998. "Pulling Levers: Getting Deterrence Right." *National Institute of Justice Journal* 236:2–8.

Kennedy, David M., Anthony A. Braga, and Anne M. Piehl. 1997. "The (Un)known Universe: Mapping Gangs and Gang Violence in Boston." In David Weisburd and Tom McEwen, eds., *Crime Mapping and Crime Prevention*, 219–262. New York: Criminal Justice Press/Willow Tree.

Kennedy, David M., Anne M. Piehl, and Anthony A. Braga. 1996. "Youth Violence in Boston: Gun Markets, Serious Youth Offenders, and a Use-Reduction Strategy." *Law and Contemporary Problems* 59 (1): 147–196.

Kessler, Ronald C., Wai Tat Chiu, Lisa Colpe, Olga Demler, Kathleen R. Merikangas, Ellen E. Walters, and Philip S. Wang. 2006. "The Prevalence and Correlates of Serious Mental Illness (SMI) in the National Comorbidity Survey Replication (NCS-R)." In Ronald W. Manderscheid and Joyce T. Berry, eds., *Mental Health, United States, 2004*, chapter 15. Rockville, Md.: U.S. Department of Health and Human Services, Substance Abuse and Mental Health Services Administration (SAMHSA), Center for Mental Health Services (CMHS).

Klein, Malcolm W. 1971. *Street Gangs and Street Workers*. Englewood Cliffs, N.J.: Prentice Hall.

Klein, Malcolm W. and Cheryl L. Maxson. 1989. "Street Gang Violence." In Neil Weiner and Marvin Wolfgang, eds., *Violent Crimes, Violent Criminals*, 198–234. Thousand Oaks, Calif.: Sage.

——. 2006. *Street Gang Patterns and Policies*. New York: Oxford University Press.

Lerner, Richard M., Celia B. Fisher, and Richard A.Weinberg. 2000. "Toward a Science for and of the People: Promoting Civil Society Through the Application of Developmental Science." *Child Development* 71 (1): 11–20.

McGarrell, Edmund F., Steven Chermak, Jeremy M. Wilson, and Nicholas Corsaro. 2006. "Reducing Homicide Through a 'Lever-Pulling' Strategy." *Justice Quarterly* 23 (2): 214–231.

McReynolds, Larkin S., Gail A. Wasserman, Robert E. DeComo, Reni John, Joseph M. Keating, and Scott Nolen. 2008. "Psychiatric Disorder in a Juvenile Assessment Center." *Crime and Delinquency* 54 (2): 313–334.

National Youth Gang Center. 2008. *Gang-Free Schools Initiative*. Available online (www.iir.com/nygc/gang_free_schools.htm). Accessed April 2008.

Office of Juvenile Justice and Delinquency Prevention. 2005. *Program Summary: Gang-Free Schools and Communities Program*. Available online (http://ojjdp.ncjrs.org/programs/ProgSummary.asp?pi=6&ti=&si=&kw=&PreviousPage=ProgResults). Accessed April 2008.

Papachristos, Andrew V., Tracey L. Meares, and Jeffrey Fagan. 2007. "Attention Felons: Evaluating Project Safe Neighborhoods in Chicago." *Journal of Empirical Legal Studies* 4 (2): 223–272.

Pranis, Kay. 1998. *Engaging the Community in Restorative Justice*. Washington, D.C.: Office of Juvenile Justice and Delinquency Prevention, U.S. Department of Justice, Balanced and Restorative Justice Project.

Roland, Kevin, Caterina Gouvis Roman, and Mark Coggeshall. 2007. "Collaboration and Partnership Functioning Within the Gang Reduction Program." Paper presented at the American Society of Criminology annual meeting, November 14–17, 2007, Atlanta.

Roman, Caterina Gouvis, Susan Jenkins, and Ashley Wolff. 2006. *Understanding Community Justice Partnerships: Testing a Conceptual Framework and Foundations for Measurement*. Final Report to the National Institute of Justice. Washington, D.C.: Urban Institute.

Sampson, Robert J., Stephen W. Raudenbush, and Felton Earls. 1997. "Neighborhoods and Violent Crime: A Multilevel Study of Collective Efficacy." *Science* 277:918–924.

Scales, Peter C. and Nancy Leffert. 2004. *Developmental Assets: A Synthesis of the Scientific Research on Adolescent Development*. 2nd ed. Minneapolis: Search Institute.

Shaw, Clifford R. and Henry D. McKay. 1942. *Juvenile Delinquency in Urban Areas*. Chicago: University of Chicago Press.

Sheppard, David. 2002. "National Evaluation of the Gang-Free Schools Initiative Research Design." Draft manuscript. Bethesda, Md.: COSMOS Corporation.

Skogan, Wesley G., Susan M. Hartnett, Natalie Bump, and Jill Dubois. 2008. *Evaluation of CeaseFire-Chicago*. Research report submitted to the National Institute of Justice, U.S. Department of Justice. Evanston, Ill: Northwestern University, Institute for Policy Research.

Spergel, Irving A. 2007. *Reducing Youth Gang Violence: The Little Village Gang Project in Chicago*. Lanham, Md.: AltaMira.

Spergel, Irving and G. David Curry. 1993. "The National Youth Gang Survey: A Research and Development Process." In C. Ronald Huff and Arnold Goldstein, eds., *The Gang Intervention Handbook*, 359–400. Champaign, Ill.: Research Press.

Spergel, Irving A., Kwai Ming Wa, and Rolando Villarreal Sosa. 2006. "The Comprehensive, Community-Wide Gang Program Model: Success and Failure." In James Short, Jr., and Lorine A. Hughes, eds., *Studying Youth Gangs*, 203–224. Lanham, Md.: AltaMira.

Teplin, Linda A., Karen M. Abram, Gary M. McClelland, Mina K. Dulcan, and Amy A. Mericle. 2002. "Psychiatric Disorders in Youth in Juvenile Detention." *Archives of General Psychiatry* 59:1133–1143.

Thacher, David. 2001. "Equity and Community Policing: A New View of Community Partnerships." *Criminal Justice Ethics* 20 (1):3–16.

Thornberry, Terence P. 1998. "Membership in Youth Gangs and Involvement in Serious and Violent Offending." In Rolf Loeber and David P. Farrington, eds., *Serious and Violent Juvenile Offenders: Risk Factors and Successful Interventions*, 147–166. Thousand Oaks, Calif.: Sage.

Thornberry, Terence P., Marvin D. Krohn, Alan J. Lizotte, Carolyn A. Smith, and Kimberly Tobin. 2003. *Gangs and Delinquency in Developmental Perspective*. Cambridge, England: Cambridge University Press.

U.S. Department of Health and Human Services. 1999. *Mental Health: A Report of the Surgeon General*. Rockville, Md.: U.S. Department of Health and Human Services, Substance Abuse and Mental Health Services Administration, Center for Mental Health Services, National Institutes of Health, National Institute of Mental Health.

Wasserman, Gail A., Larkin S. McReynolds, Susan J. Ko, Laura M. Katz, and Jennifer R. Carpenter. 2005. "Gender Differences in Psychiatric Disorders at Juvenile Probation Intake." *American Journal of Public Health* 95 (1): 131–137.

Weiss, Carol H. 1972. *Evaluation Research: Methods for Assessing Program Effectiveness*. Englewood Cliffs, N.J.: Prentice-Hall.

Wellford, Charles, J. Pepper, and Carole Petrie, eds. 2005. *Firearms and Violence: A Critical Review*. Committee to Improve Research Information and Data on Firearms. Committee on Law and Justice, Division of Behavioral and Social Sciences and Education. Washington, D.C.: National Academies Press.

Wray, Lyle and Jody Hauer. 1997. "Performance Measurement to Achieve Quality of Life: Adding Value Through Citizens." *Public Management* 79:4–9.

Wyrick, Phelan. 2006. "Gang Prevention: How to Make the 'Front End' of Your Anti-Gang Effort Work." *United States Attorneys' Bulletin*. Washington, D.C.: Office of Juvenile Justice and Delinquency Prevention.

Zahniser, David. 2008. "L.A. Rethinking Its Anti-Gang Programs—As Villaraigosa Plans to Drop L.A. Bridges, the Effectiveness of Such Initiatives Remains Unknown." *Los Angeles Times*, April 21.

[9]

Taking Criminology Seriously

Narratives, Norms, Networks, and Common Ground

DAVID M. KENNEDY

Professor Irving Spergel's (1995, 2007) community-based approaches to gangs have been model examples of the weaving together of what should not be, but usually is, separate. Though we are not accustomed to speaking in these terms in academic settings—an odd matter, to which I will return—Spergel's Comprehensive Community Model has been infused with an innate, and sophisticated, sense of "justness." In an area in which policy and operations tend to be polarized by extreme analyses, interpretations, and imagery, the Comprehensive Community Model has merged, both intellectually and practically, what are so often sundered: sympathy and accountability, help and authority, formal and informal, public and private, street and tower. This is not merely a technical question, but also one of norms, morals, and politics. Professor Spergel has consistently been able to articulate, in a way that is rare among those who make and influence policy, that gangs and gang members are appropriately to be both sympathized with and feared; are deserving of both help and control; are both members of their communities and threats to those communities; are both victims—

immediately and more largely—and offenders. The success of the community model, and its ability to mobilize and sustain large coalitions of disparate actors, is more than a matter of theoretical insight and operational prowess. It is a matter of the moral salience of the community framework, the way in which that salience is immediately recognizable to actors with typically more polarized opinions, and the ways in which all those actors are given an appropriate place to do their appropriate work. Aristotle taught that "all virtue is summed up in dealing justly," and Professor Spergel's work has been conspicuously, and importantly, just. Its very real virtues—its successes in engagement with gangs and gang members, its contributions to theory and practice, its contribution to our understanding of what is fit and possible in community action—flow in no small part from that palpable justice.

I want to push this notion further. On the question of "what works" in addressing the social problem of youth gangs—if the question is, what works as we would want it to work—the answer today, I think, is that nothing does. On the ground, we want approaches that dramatically decrease gang violence, drug dealing, domestic and sexual assault, community damage, and gang formation and involvement—and that can be readily adopted and adapted by various communities. At the intellectual and political level, we want discussions, understandings, and policies that are nuanced, responsible, and absent polarized caricatures, whether sympathetic or vile. Neither, I submit, do we have.

I think, though, that we might be able to achieve them. And I think that the most productive path from here to there may be in focusing explicitly on norms, values, even justice. Beyond that, I think criminology—dusty, venerable, off-the-shelf criminology—has a great deal to offer in helping us relearn how important these things are, how they operate in practice, and how we might make them very practical indeed.

Norms and Narratives

Let us begin with the utterly commonplace: norms matter. Crime, criminology, and criminal justice are notoriously areas in which thinking and acting tend to focus on the poles of the individual and society, but between these poles is a vast and rich—and shifting—landscape. We know, for example, that there are likely to be gangs in poor, minority areas of many cities. We know that those gangs will tend to attract the most active young offenders, and that while engaged with the gang those offenders will tend to offend even more. These things we can take as givens. We cannot take as givens, however, whether these offenders in these gangs believe that one must commit a violent assault to join the gang, must kill a parent to leave the gang, will earn approbation or onus for using cocaine while in the gang, must respond to disrespect with lethal violence, or which acts do and do not count as disrespect. These are norms, which shift quite dramatically from time to time and place to place, and they have large and concrete effects on how people behave.

Beyond norms, narratives matter. We cannot, for example, take as givens how members of the community articulate their support or tolerance for, or opposition to, gangs and gang behavior, or how they understand and interpret the actions of police. We cannot take as givens how police articulate their understandings of gangs and of the communities in which gangs are found, or how those views are understood and interpreted by communities and gang members. It makes an enormous difference, for example, whether gang members see the police as conscious actors in a racist conspiracy to oppress minority communities or as agents of legitimate community interests. It makes an enormous difference whether the police see gang violence as the product of considered decisions by depraved individuals or as desperate actions by those trapped unwillingly in desperate conditions. It makes an enormous difference whether the community sees an active street drug trade as the product of police corruption and conspiracy or as the product of well-intentioned but unsuccessful official action. It makes an enormous difference whether the police see community silence about gang activity as tolerance and support or as something else. Take these things together, and in the same community one can have extremely violent gangs believing that they exist and act with community support in opposition to racist oppression, or far less violent gangs acting in an atmosphere of moral and material opposition from both community and outside forces.

It is striking, then, that we are very rarely explicit about these norms and narratives in our thinking about addressing gangs. The literature on the theoretical and descriptive side is rich on this subject; on the action side it is almost silent. This is true even when the policies and interventions in question engage directly with gangs and communities on these very dimensions. I have to believe, for example, that in the Little Village project (Spergel, Wa, and Sosa 2006) and the other community-based interventions that flowed from it, these issues arose in important ways: one simply cannot have law enforcement, service providers, community activists, and outreach workers working together with gangs and not have these questions surface. I strongly suspect that an important element of the evolution and impact of these projects has to do with the dialogue and engagement on these issues, how the various actors' views change over time, and how this affects the work. Yet these issues, if they are in fact as present and significant as I think, rarely receive independent attention, either descriptively as part of what happens in community interventions or as possible independent opportunities for policy and action.

There are a number of reasons for this. One is that these matters do not fit neatly into the individual accountability/social structure dichotomy that so frames our thinking on gangs and crime. Nor do they fit neatly into the prevention/intervention/suppression framework that also so frames our thinking and action. We readily think, "This person needs help," or "This person needs to be controlled." We do not very readily think, "This person holds a wrong idea, which needs to be addressed." It is striking, when working in community settings where community actors, service providers, and law enforcement interact with gangs and gang members, how uncommonly anybody simply says—even about the most extreme misbehavior, such as homicide, or the most extreme idea, such as that disrespect requires homicide— "This is wrong." Threats are common, help is common, utilitarian appeals are common. Moral and intellectual engagement is vanishingly rare.

Another reason is that we are simply uncomfortable on what is frankly treacherous ground. We are comfortable, for whatever reason, saying that a person has a need and should have a particular service provided. We are less comfortable, for whatever reason, saying that a person holds a dangerous and destructive opinion and should be engaged on that point. This is all the more true when those opinions are submerged, smoldering, and laced with racial tension, as is very often the case with the norms and narratives here at issue. As a result, even when there is such engagement, as can be the case between street workers and gang members, it goes undocumented and unevaluated. The question of what potential such engagement holds is not even asked.

Group and Network Processes Around Norms and Narratives

We know, also, a number of very important things about such norms and narratives. They are inherently social matters, and they play out in particularly heightened ways in small groups and networks. They are almost always implicit, not explicit. As David Matza (1990) says, subcultures are never written down but are inferred from action. In such inference, error is easy: that gang members or the community do not speak in opposition to a drive-by does not mean that they approve, though their silence may be taken as such. We know that such perceived norms have the same practical effect as "real" ones. We know that the process of creating new norms is not linear or arithmetic; in an unstable situation, extreme norms tend to emerge and survive ("polarization" or "risky shift"). We know that particular figures emerge to hold heightened informal influence as "models" or "keynotes." We know that there is a strong tendency to infer intent and settled aspects of character from observed behavior ("attribution error"). We know that there is a strong tendency to conformity with perceived norms. All of these things, and the many others like them, mean that particular norms may emerge, hold great sway, and still be very superficial and ultimately quite changeable.

One feature of such collective behavior is that some, or even all, of the participants can reach and sustain incorrect conclusions about the views of other participants. Matza, again, is particularly insightful about this situation of *pluralistic ignorance*:

> Each member believes that others are committed to their delinquencies. But what about each member, what does he believe himself? . . . Possibly, he is transformed in the situation of company to a committed delinquent by dint of the cues he has received from others. Possibly, however, each member believes himself to be an exception in the company of committed delinquents. The intricate system of cues may be miscues. Since the subculture must be constructed from the situation of company, it may be misconstrued. (Matza 1990:52)

It may, moreover, be cued on the basis of extreme behaviors by outlying members of the group—keynotes and models—whose examples then assume normative status. Matza notes that the extreme "status anxiety" and "masculinity anxiety" prevalent in offending circles inhibits opposing and confronting, or even articulating, reservations about the behavior and norms of such outliers (1990:53, 56).

Others have framed these dynamics in terms of "referent informational influence" and "the inductive aspect of categorization" (Turner 1982, cited in Levy and Nail 1993:263). Both refer to processes in which "group members seek out the stereotypic norms which define category member-ship and conform their behavior to them. It is, in effect, a process of self-stereotyping" (Reicher 1984, cited in Levy and Nail 1993:263). Quite infor-mal and fluid—and even internally divided—groups may thus act with remarkable cohesion.

Perkins (2003), discussing these dynamics in the context of alcohol and drug abuse, identifies three driving factors also generalizable to other settings. One is "the general social psychological tendency to erroneously attribute observed behaviors of other people to their disposition, and to think the behavior is typical of the individual when the action cannot be explained by the specific context or put into perspective by knowing what the other person usually does most of the time." The second is that social communications processes highlight the extreme. "The tendency is to recall the most vivid behaviors and then conversation gravitates to the extreme incidents, in the end making them seem more common than is really the case." The third is that "cultural media reaffirm and amplify these exaggerations," something that is true of a wide variety of offending and other extreme behaviors outside the realm of substance abuse (Perkins 2003:7–8).

Norms and Narratives in the Context of Youth Gangs

These are powerful dynamics, and ones that in fact profoundly influence both gang offenders and authorities, as well as their views of one another. Authorities, faced with an outbreak of drive-by shootings, will readily conclude that they are dealing with stone-cold superpredators, an expressly characterological diagnosis: they have no way of know-ing that the shooters have never done such things before, did not want to do them this time, acted in abject fear of both their enemies and their friends, and hope fervently never to have to do anything simi-lar in the future. Authorities will remember the drive-bys, and discuss them; they will not similarly remember the vastly more frequent occa-sions in which gang tensions did *not* lead to violence. Film, rap, and the like reinforce these conceptions. Offenders, for their part, faced with authorities driving by open-air drug dealing, will readily conclude that they are dealing with police officers who are racist and corrupt, also an expressly characterological diagnosis: they have no way of knowing that the officers loathe drug dealing and its impact on the community, have been enjoined from street drug enforcement by their superiors, and have been chastised by the district attorney for clogging the calendar with arrests that the bench will simply throw out. Offenders will remember, and discuss, these and other incidents of misfeasance and malfeasance by authorities; they will not similarly remember occasions in which authorities acted to protect them and the community. Shooters who think privately that violence in response to the slights of disrespect is lunacy will look at their peers' support for such violence and believe that they are genuinely committed, not knowing that other gang members have their own doubts. Film, rap, and the like reinforce these conceptions. Such confusions, of course, virtually never get aired or addressed, much less resolved.

Where gangs in particular or crime in general is concerned, we do not usually take such norms and narratives as open to direct intervention. Yet Perkins, discussing the "social norming" approach to preventing drug and alcohol abuse, reports interventions directly aimed at the pluralistic ignorance that obtains in campus settings around drugs and drinking (Perkins 2002:169). The basic form of the intervention is to report back to students the results of research into *actual*, rather than *perceived*, student attitudes, thus correcting misapprehensions about norms. These interventions have reportedly resulted in substantial reductions in drinking and drug use. To take a narrow parallel example, if gang members truly believe that it is necessary to kill one's mother to leave the gang, and if this is not in fact true, making that fact plain to them could have a meaningful impact on desistance. Needless to say, such steps are not part of our normal gang intervention repertoire.

Formal and Informal Social Control

Formal social control is weaker than informal social control. External informal social control—the opinions of one's peers, family, loved ones, role models—is weaker than internal informal social control—guilt, shame, and the like. (I happily incorporate by reference here all the insights of the restorative justice movement, which has done an enormous service in reminding us of the salience of these facts, and in unpacking many of the ways informal social control operates and can be applied. One of my convictions is that the restorative justice movement is far more right than even it knows and, in particular, that its insights are not and should not be limited to the creation of an alternative case-processing structure aimed at minor offenses.) All are heavily influenced by the norms, narratives, and processes discussed. An arrest for a gang crime may be a deterrent to future offending if one's family and peers take it as just and fit; it may be an incentive to further offending if it is taken as an act of political oppression.

A feature of these norms is that it is not at all difficult, or unusual, to be influenced by competing values, either simultaneously or in close proximity. Whether the idea is "code switching" (Anderson 1999) or "techniques of neutralization" (Matza 1990), multiple normative strands, and various ways in which those strands are mobilized and interrelate, are common. Much of the work in restorative justice proceedings and similar enterprises is aimed at highlighting and encouraging norms that are already held by offenders. The same can be true at the community level. Sampson and Bartusch, for example, distinguish between "tolerance of deviance"— support for criminality, which is in fact very low in troubled minority communities—and "legal cynicism," or distrust of law enforcement, which is very high (Sampson and Bartusch 1998). This is frequently misread by outsiders, who see in silence about offending and hostility toward the police approval for crime and criminals, which is much less true than is perceived. One implication here is that at both the personal and the community level—as with pluralistic ignorance—the seeds of one position may be present even when another is being strongly presented.

Making It Practical

If the foregoing is true, then in doing gang work we should seek to engage directly with gangs, gang members, communities, authorities, and other parties with respect to the norms and narratives that shape their actions, and we should do so in a way that is respectful of small-group, network, and community dynamics. We should especially seek to elevate existing norms and narratives that oppose gangs and gang crime. In fact, this does frequently happen in the course of community-based gang efforts: it is intrinsically far too important not to. When it happens, however, it tends to be ad hoc and informal, and it usually doesn't get a great deal of attention.

My argument here is that this reliance on ad hoc and informal approaches greatly devalues the forces at work and the potential of making them a high priority. My intuition is that they should perhaps be the highest priority.

My first encounter with the energies at work here came in one of the face-to-face "forums" that were a feature of the Operation Ceasefire intervention in Boston. In that meeting, several dozen gang members had heard the message from law enforcement (serious violence will result in sanctions against your gang) and service providers (we have help for you) and were listening to a minister talk about the community's stake in having the violence stop. A gang member took vociferous exception, arguing that he had to sell drugs, white racism had destroyed his community and left him no choice, the CIA was responsible for the drug trade, and the like. The minister heard him out and then simply asked, "Shot any CIA agents lately?" It was an electric moment; at a stroke, a whole narrative excusing and even encouraging black-on-black violence had been vitiated. The gang members knew it as well or better than the rest of us; the tenor of the entire group, and the subsequent conversation, changed.

If we are to build on these possibilities in addressing gangs, I believe that policy and operations will have to take account of at least these core dimensions:

- the heavily racialized narrative in minority communities about history, current oppression, law enforcement, crime, and drugs;
- the heavily racialized narrative in law enforcement about minority offenders and communities;
- the unintended damage done to minority communities by mainstream law enforcement practices;
- the particular dynamics of gang networks, and the ways in which those dynamics generate actions and norms;
- the license and encouragement afforded to offenders by community silence about minority offending.

Doing so requires adding to the existing menu of community-based interventions a set of deliberate strategies by authorities and communities to act on norms and narratives.

In a process spearheaded by the police, we worked in High Point, North Carolina, and subsequently in several other jurisdictions to operationalize these notions. The focus was on overt (open-air, crack house) drug markets and related harms, such as violence, prostitution, and loss of public space to street offenders. It was not explicitly on gangs, though the offenders in question constituted loose drug crews that would be considered gangs in many (though not all) jurisdictions. The following account gives the basics of what happened, without addressing all elements of the intervention or the process (or presenting what did happen in chronological order).

Addressing Community Narratives with Law Enforcement

The police department, prosecutors, probation, and parole were engaged with respect to ways in which the minority community regards law enforcement and, especially, drug enforcement. The essence of this discussion was that—regardless of the merits—the community saw law enforcement as racist. It regularly experienced illegal and abusive treatment by law enforcement and viewed this through the lens of slavery, Jim Crow, the abuses and killings of the civil rights era, and other instances of deliberate oppression. It saw current behavior as an extension of past behavior, saw the drug war as a deliberate attack on the minority community, and did not believe the drug trade could continue without the inattention or corruption of law enforcement. It regularly saw the police taking actions, such as driving by and ignoring overt dealing, that reinforced those beliefs. Drug use, drug dealing, "hustling," and other criminality were present in the white community at far higher levels and did not get anything like the same attention from law enforcement. Forces outside the community were bringing in drugs and guns and got little attention from law enforcement. Minority youth were being put in a position of having no legitimate options except to sell drugs. The community needed serious help from outside and was not getting it, but there was plenty of money for police and prisons. Without the minority community to prey upon, the whole criminal justice system, with its jobs and profits for outsiders, would collapse.

Addressing Law Enforcement Narratives with Law Enforcement

The police department, prosecutors, probation, and parole were engaged with respect to ways in which law enforcement regards the minority community and offenders. The essence of this narrative is that the minority

community, with exceptions, embraces criminality, opposes law enforcement, cannot or will not control its youth, has no meaningful remaining leadership or social structure, and will not take even readily available
steps—such as finishing school and taking entry-level jobs—to participate
in the mainstream.

Addressing Unintended Damage with Law Enforcement

The police department, prosecutors, probation, and parole were engaged
with respect to ways in which law enforcement unintentionally did damage
in minority communities. Particular attention was given to the outcome of
decades of street drug enforcement, leading to majorities of young men with
criminal records, normative involvement with the criminal justice system,
families disrupted by prison sentences, and the like. The impact of these
issues on family and neighborhood social control, the erosion and reversal
of stigma around criminal justice sanctions, the greatly reduced utility for
those with criminal records of finishing school and taking entry-level jobs,
and the subsequent "tipping" of street culture toward oppositional norms
were explored. Because of these dynamics, some—maybe a great deal—of
what law enforcement attributed to individual and community choice was
in fact the unintended result of deliberate enforcement actions. The con-
fluence of these issues with the dire community perceptions of both legitimate law enforcement actions (such as breaking into houses to serve warrants) and illegitimate law enforcement actions (such as brutality, illegal
stops and searches, perjury, and sexual abuses) was discussed.

Addressing the Dynamics of Gang Networks with Law Enforcement

The police department, prosecutors, probation, and parole were engaged
with respect to ways in which many of the above elements resonated with
particular strength in offender groups and networks. The basic narratives
were even stronger: that law enforcement was seen as particularly racist,
corrupt, abusive, and incompetent. Beyond that, street culture required
offenders to take positions that individually they may not have agreed with,
or may not have agreed with as fully as was apparent: that jail and prison
were nothing to be feared, that they would be dead by age 25 so nothing

mattered anyway, that violence in response to disrespect was legitimate, that offending was standing up to white oppression, that one was a fool to go to school and work at entry-level jobs. The fact that attention from law enforcement was unpredictable and incoherent was explored: that while an offender might accrue a long record of arrests and sanctions, those were rare events in a long offending history, with no rhyme or reason as to how they were applied, and that because of major inconsistencies across official contacts, any given day's decision to offend could be seen as fairly rational.

Addressing Law Enforcement with the Community

The police department, prosecutors, probation, and parole engaged with the community with respect to their past behavior. In essence, law enforcement said that they knew that they had failed to control crime, especially drug crime; that they had done what they knew how to do but that it hadn't worked, and they knew it hadn't worked; that they realized that they had done enormous damage to the community in the process; that in addition to inadvertent harm, everybody in law enforcement knew that illegal and improper things happened in drug enforcement, and although not tolerated, such things had not been stopped. Particular examples of what had been taken as evidence of corruption and conspiracy were addressed, such as why officers would drive by overt drug dealing (the difficulty of making cases, the orientation of prosecutors and judges, the near-certainty of minor penalties, the pointlessness of sentences to probation, etc.). Law enforcement told the community that they would like to do something different and better.

Addressing Issues of Accountability and License with the Community

The community was engaged with respect to the position it had taken regarding drug crime and the way that this position relieved offenders of accountability and even conferred status upon them. The community did not articulate, in any consistent and effective way, that drug dealing, gun violence, and the like were wrong. Instead, it spoke about outside oppression and plots, the racism of the police and outsiders, the lack of options for young men. Offenders reasonably concluded that their conduct was tolerated or even celebrated. The community was engaged with respect to the fact that clear internal standards were the first line of defense for any healthy community. It was pointed out that these issues could be separated: that the community could insist on the historical and structural roots of current problems; that current harms were being done to it; that the community needed help; that offenders needed help; and that the community needed to articulate to offenders that their behavior was wrong.

The Intervention

The actual drug market intervention was designed in accordance with the foregoing logic. A particular geographic drug market was identified, and all active drug dealers in it were identified by law enforcement (this was seen as a proxy for attending to a particular offender network or networks). Using ordinary law enforcement techniques, criminal cases were prepared against each offender but not pursued. In each case, a warrant could have been signed but was not. Instead, law enforcement and community members together visited each offender at home, spoke with the offender and a family member (or in some instances another adult "influential" who had been identified as important in the offender's life), and told the offender that he could be under arrest, that he was not currently being arrested, but that there was to be a meeting that the offender and the family member were urged to attend. Nearly all those invited attended the meeting. At the meeting, three messages were delivered.

First, law enforcement told the offenders that they were out of the drug business—that they could be in jail already; that despite how law enforcement had always conducted itself, nobody wanted to do that; that they were going to hear from others who wanted to help them; that if they desisted, nothing more would be done; but that if they resumed dealing, they would immediately be arrested on the current charge and get special prosecutorial attention.

Second, service providers told the offenders and their families that any help they needed would be provided: drug treatment, education, job training and placement, transitional assistance, etc. Case managers were identified who would (and did) actively work with offenders and, if desired, their families.

Finally, in what was clearly the most electric and effective part of the meeting, community members—ministers, activists, local residents—told the offenders that they were loved and cherished, that the community needed them to succeed, but that they were destroying the community, what they were doing was wrong, and they had to stop. Offenders hung their heads; mothers and grandmothers cheered and shouted amen.

Impact

In each of the interventions (two in High Point, one in Winston-Salem, one in Newburgh, New York), the drug markets in question immediately evaporated after the meeting (the first of these interventions is almost two years old and is clearly self-sustaining). More formal quantitative and qualitative evaluations are proceeding, but the initial impressions are that there is virtually no overt dealing in the areas, no evidence of displacement, large reductions in reported crime, and substantial improvements in the quality of life. Each intervention has resulted in a new and continuing dialogue between community, law enforcement, service providers, and local government about the future of the community and how best to create it.

Lessons and Common Ground

We shall see if these apparent results are real and sustainable. For this discussion, the real point is the prelude to the actual intervention: the express surfacing of submerged, competing norms and narratives, an explicit attempt to air them out, and the design of a strategic intervention that was expressly intended to change norms and narratives and that took into account small-group and network dynamics. Everything else that happened was straight out of the community-based playbook.

Norms and narratives changed, I should point out, among others besides the offenders. Community members were poleaxed to see police officers admitting that they had no idea how to address the drug problem, and police officers were poleaxed to see drug dealers they had dismissed as sociopaths walking meekly into the meetings accompanied by parents they had dismissed as irredeemable. Whether these particular operations worked or not, there is, I think, something important here to work with, and to work on.

In the language of the academy, what we have here is a deliberate attempt by agents of formal social control—police, city government—to mobilize processes of informal social control. It is not the way government normally operates, but it is not theoretically or practically absurd. Once that goal is framed, norms, narratives, group and network processes, and all the rest come to the fore, and the rest of the problem is trying to figure out exactly what that terrain looks like and how—if at all—it can be navigated. It is inevitable, where gang issues are concerned, that the terrain will include extraordinarily difficult, divisive, and toxic racial, ethnic, and historical issues. It may be, though, that *not* facing these issues is the most toxic choice of all.

In more ordinary language, what we have is common ground. The clashing norms and narratives touched on here blind us to this common ground. It may be small, and it does not and cannot do away with the very real conflicts that remain, but it is precious. Nobody—not even offenders—wants the killing and the chaos. Nobody—not even police—wants anyone who does not absolutely have to go to prison to do so. Everybody wants the truly dangerous to be controlled. Everybody wants the community to improve and to succeed. Everybody wants any young person who wants help to get help. Everybody wants their mothers and grandmothers and siblings to be safe. Nobody wants the police on the street churning up bitterness and frustration. Nobody wants the past to poison the future.

Note

The symposium talk on which this chapter was based both drew from and influenced a longer treatment (Kennedy 2009), then being drafted, of many of the themes addressed here. In the interest of preserving this article in its original form, I have included some material now duplicated in that later work, and left the discussion of the High Point drug market intervention as it was at the time of the symposium. For a more current discussion, see *Deterrence and Crime Prevention*, chapter 9.

References

Anderson, E. 1999. *Code of the Street: Decency, Violence, and the Moral Life of the Inner City*. New York: Norton.

Kennedy, D. M. 2009. *Deterrence and Crime Prevention: Reconsidering the Prospect of Sanction*. New York: Routledge.

Levy, D. A. and P. R. Nail. 1993. "Contagion: A Theoretical and Empirical Review and Reconceptualization." *Genetic, Social, and General Psychology Monographs* 119 (2): 235–284.

Matza, D. 1990. *Delinquency and Drift*. New Brunswick, N.J.: Transaction Publishers.

Perkins, H. W. 2002. "Social Norms and the Prevention of Alcohol Misuse in Collegiate Contexts." *Journal of the Study of Alcohol*, supplement no. 14:164–172.

——. 2003. "The Emergence and Evolution of the Social Norms Approach to Substance Abuse Prevention." In H. Wesley Perkins, ed., *The Social Norms Approach to Preventing School and College Age Substance Abuse*, 3–17. San Francisco: Jossey-Bass.

Reicher, S. D. 1984. "The St. Pauls' Riot: An Explanation of the Limits of Crowd Action in Terms of a Social Identity Model." *European Journal of Social Psychology* 14:1–21.

Sampson, Robert J. and Dawn Jeglum Bartusch. 1998. "Legal Cynicism and (Subcultural?) Tolerance of Deviance: The Neighborhood Context of Racial Differences." *Law and Society Review* 32 (4):777–804.

Spergel, Irving A. 1995. *The Youth Gang Problem: A Community Approach*. New York: Oxford University Press.

——. 2007. *Reducing Youth Gang Violence: The Little Village Gang Project in Chicago*. Lanham, Md.: AltaMira.

Spergel, Irving A., Kwai Ming Wa, and Rolando Villarreal Sosa. 2006. "The Comprehensive, Community-Wide Gang Program Model: Success and Failure." In James F. Short, Jr., and Lorine A. Hughes, eds., *Studying Youth Gangs*, 203–224. Lanham, Md.: AltaMira.

Turner, J. C. 1982. "Toward a Cognitive Redefinition of the Social Group." In H. Tajfel, ed., *Social Identity and Intergroup Relations*, 15–40. Cambridge, England: Cambridge University Press.

Community Gang Programs

Theory, Models, and Effectiveness

IRVING A. SPERGEL

Youth gangs and the problems they create are a source of significant, if not major, concern to citizens in many local (especially larger) communities, to criminal justice agencies, social agencies, churches, and a variety of other organizations, and to government leaders in the United States. Youth gangs are also a growing problem in many smaller cities and suburban areas, as well as in developed and developing countries across the globe. We have considerable awareness and some good understanding of the varied nature and causes of youth gangs, their behaviors, and the problems they create, but we know less about the value and effectiveness of programs designed to address them.

In this concluding chapter, I attempt to interrelate and emphasize some of the rich ideas in the foregoing chapters, with brief attention to the nature and scope of the problem. My focus is on recent major approaches to understanding youth gang problems in the urban context. I identify models of intervention, assess their values in terms of several key programs, and suggest more effective approaches to program research and evaluation. In addition to my comments, I provide data and ideas from other "gang experts" about these issues.

Scope of the Problem

Youth gangs, their characteristics, and the crimes and problems they create are not clearly or consensually defined within and across U.S. jurisdictions. However, there may be fairly good reliability of the law enforcement reports of the growth, scope, and severity of the crimes that gangs account for. On the basis of law enforcement data, the National Youth Gang Center (NYGC) estimates that in 2005 youth gangs were active in more than 3,400 jurisdictions served by city (with populations of 2,500 or more) and county law enforcement agencies in the United States. A significant increase in the number of gangs and gang members is reported over a recent ten-year period (*OJJDP Fact Sheet* 2008).

A more recent NYGC report states:

A primary concern for communities is violent criminal activity by gangs. . . . Overall, larger cities [with populations of 250,000 or more] accounted for nearly 77 percent [1,746] of the recorded gang homicides across the country . . . an additional 20 percent were reported by suburban counties, while [rural counties and smaller cities] accounted for approximately 3 percent. (Egley and O'Donnell 2008:2)

U.S. Senate Bill S. 456, "Gang Abatement and Prevention Act of 2007," passed by the Senate in September 2007 (a similar bill in the House of Representatives has not yet been acted upon), includes the following assessment in its section 3 findings of gang crime. It focuses more on the serious nature of the problem:

(1) Violent crime and drug trafficking are pervasive problems at the national, State, and local level;

(2) According to recent Federal Bureau of Investigation, Uniform Crime Reports, violent crime in the United States is on the rise, with a 2–3 percent increase in violent crimes in 2005 (the largest increase in the United States in 15 years) and an even larger 3.7 percent jump during the first six months of 2006 . . .

(3) These disturbing rises in violent crime are attributable in part to the spread of criminal street gangs and the willingness of gang members to commit acts of violence and drug trafficking offenses;

(4) According to a recent National Drug Threat Assessment, criminal street gangs are responsible for much of the retail distribution of the cocaine, methamphetamine, heroin, and other illegal drugs being distributed in rural and urban communities throughout the United States;

(5) Gangs commit acts of violence or drug offenses for numerous motives, such as membership in or loyalty to the gang, for protecting gang territory, and for profit;

(6) Gang presence and intimidation, and the organized and repetitive nature of the crimes that gang and gang members commit, has a pernicious effect on the free flow of interstate commercial activities and directly affects the freedom and security of communities plagued by gang activity. . . . (U.S. Senate Bill S. 456, 2007–2008:3)

A recent Justice Policy Institute report, however, raises questions about some of the foregoing data and conclusions:

There are fewer gang members in the United States today than there were a decade ago, and there is no evidence that gang activity is growing. . . . Gang members account for a relatively small share of [total] crime in most jurisdictions. . . . Gang members may be responsible for fewer than one in 10 homicides. . . . Much of the crime committed by gang members is self-directed and not committed for the gang's benefit. . . . Gang members do not dominate or drive the drug trade. . . . Gang members account for a relatively small share of drug sales and . . . [youth] gangs do not generally seek to control drug markets. Investigations conducted in Los Angeles and nearby cities found that gang members accounted for one in four drug sale arrests. The Los Angeles district attorney concluded that just one in seven gang members sold drugs on a monthly basis. (Greene and Pranis 2007:2–3)

The definition of the gang problem varies with the interests and perceptions of the writers and representatives of organizations describing and assessing the problem, as well as with whether the focus is on juvenile, youth, or more organized or serious gang problems. The predominant interest group making assessments of the gang problem is law enforcement. There is consensus that the youth gang problem and the more organized adult gang problem, however defined, have been spreading across the United States, as well as abroad, in recent years.

Youth and adult gangs and their criminal activities, and so-called anti-state activities, have proliferated in other countries, particularly in Central America, South America, North Africa, and to a lesser extent in Europe, Australia, and Asia. The explosion of gangs and gang problems in other countries has been attributed to representations and glamorizations of gang members and the gang-member life by U.S. media. It is also claimed, in the aftermath of the civil war in El Salvador, that deported youth who had settled in Los Angeles went back to El Salvador, increasing violence and drug trafficking there and extending the problem to Honduras and Guatemala and then, upon their reentry and growth in the United States, increased youth gang-member violence in American cities, particularly on the East Coast and the West Coast (Internet Forward Communications 2008:1–4).

Also, with the large increase in illegal immigration, particularly of young people, to Western Europe from Eastern and Southern Europe, Russia and other regions of the former Soviet Union, South America, Asia, and North Africa, there has been a large increase in street crime, violent crime, and incarcerations. With community concerns and increased law enforcement activity, however, several innovative social programs are developing in some of these countries (Holthusen 2007; Specht 2000).

Explanations of the Youth Gang Problem

Ideas of special value for addressing the problem include community development theories. Chaskin (chapter 1, this volume) reviews the history of social disorganization theory and the basic community approaches created to address the gang or group delinquency problem. Shaw and McKay (1943), Thrasher (1963 [1927]), and University of Chicago social researchers in the early decades of the twentieth century "relied heavily on notions of urban growth and community dynamics" in their theories of social disorganization and how to address it on a local community basis. Industrial and economic development brought new immigrants—often low-status, peasant populations—to major urban areas. These new groups settled in marginal or transitional areas, replacing more-established low-status groups who were moving up the social and economic ladder in American society. These interstitial areas were often characterized by high levels of crime, gang formation, and social and health problems. They were somewhat separate from the mainstream culture and economic opportunities.

Chaskin writes that, according to Shaw and McKay, "crime and delinquency in these areas are responses to the disjunction between the goals promoted by society and the opportunity to achieve them available to the residents . . . as well as conflicting value orientations and weakened institutional sources of socialization and social control" (Chaskin, chapter 1, p. 7; see also Merton 1957). Social disorganization and opportunity notions were further developed in a theory of differential opportunities to explain the rise of different delinquent or gang subcultures (Cloward and Ohlin 1960; Spergel 1964).

Similarly, Vigil (chapter 7) elaborates his theory of multiple marginality, focusing on the human and social-psychological consequences resulting in these so-called transitional areas or barrios, which often become long-term ghettoes. Many of the youth in such areas are at special risk of gang involvement in their critical adolescent, maturational years because of the interplay of racial and ethnic prejudice, poverty, family disorganization, and the inadequacy of socialization institutions. Vigil (chapter 7, p. 170) states that "immigration and the experiences of immigrants as they adapt and adjust to city life form the basis for all else that follows, including especially the maladaptation that so often occurs among them," such as the gang subculture, intergang conflict, and drug crimes.

However, youth gang members and others in these transitional, barrio, or ghetto areas are not completely separated from mainstream norms and values, opportunities, and significant relationships with their mainstream providers. Bursik and Grasmick (1993) suggest that there are shortcomings in social disorganization theory, and in the explanations of the formation of gangs and delinquent criminal behaviors created. Gang youth maintain ties to family, kin, and neighbors and to "other members of the larger society." They retain ties simultaneously to law-abiding citizens and gang members. Bursik, in a later article (2002), states that there is an "underdeveloped appreciation for the complicated nature of these network dynamics in such deprived, segmented local areas." There is a lack of understanding of the interaction between "private or intimate, parochial or neighborhood and public or larger community dynamics and structures and relations." He suggests that an expanded version of social disorganization theory is needed that draws from theories of social capital, interorganizational theory, and politics (Bursik 2002:71–81).

Hagedorn and others (2007, 2008), in their versions of globalization theory, expand social disorganization theory, further explaining youth gang problems worldwide. "In the wake of a vast increase in urbanization and social and economic marginalization gangs are spontaneously created in cities all over the world" (2008:132–133).

Manwaring conceptualizes a sequence of stages in the evolution of the gang problem in many countries, although the sequence is not yet fully developed in the United States:

> Gang violence develops from (1) the level of [turf] "protection," gangsterism, and brigandage; (2) to drug trafficking, smuggling people, body parts, armaments, and other lucrative "items" . . . (3) [and then] to taking political control of ungoverned territory and/or areas governed by corrupt politicians [also militias] and functionaries. (Manwaring 2007:3–4)

Other authors have viewed youth gangs as examples of legitimate, or potentially legitimate, resistance organizations to "systems of domination [and] . . . sites of spiritual practice" in urban areas of the United States. Youth gangs are representative of oppressed, minority, marginalized groups. "The primary task is to set the oppressed and the marginalized free from all forms of domination—be it spiritual, material or cultural" (Barrios 2003:122). Youth gangs should be transformed and empowered to join other social reform organizations with links to community traditions of combating social ills present in urban ghettoes (Brotherton 2003).

Mediating Theories

Midlevel or intervening theories and concepts are important for connecting social disorganization, and other grand theories, to gang intervention models and programs at the community level. The authors in this volume provide a great deal of experience, information, and ideas about critical community programs and research strategies. Further, the ideas of Sampson, Raudenbush, and Earls (1997) and Coleman (1988), referred to by several chapter authors, are of special importance. What is significant for analysis is not only the group structure and process of gangs and the motivations and behaviors of youth that create the youth gang problem but also how local institutions, organizations, and existing related policies and programs precipitate, sustain, and aggravate the problem. Contributing to the problem is the nature of politics and patterns of interorganization relationships in either addressing or not addressing the problem (Chaskin, chapter 1; Spergel 1995, 2007).

Short and Hughes (chapter 6, this volume) stress the importance of neighborhood "collective efficacy" and "social capital" as essential policy and program means for addressing the youth gang problem and, also, the importance of their inclusion in evaluation measures in determining the effectiveness of gang programs. They state that the nature and level of shared expectations of neighborhood residents to take responsibility for each other's children and the nature of relationships with street action teams (including street workers in direct contact with gang youth) determine the level of deviancy and crime committed by such youth. The nature of relationships of residents and organizations to each other contributes to neighborhood "collective efficacy" and the development of relationships conducive to the creation of "social capital."

> The essence of social capital is the quality of a person's relationships with other people and with organizations and institutions—relationships that take place within such networks as family, friends, and neighbors, within local organizational and institutional contexts, and within public networks that "connect local residents to noncommunity-based persons or agencies that control political, economic, and social resources." (Bursik 2002:74, quoted in Short and Hughes, chapter 6, p. 132)

Chaskin (chapter 1) notes that the early notions of community organization processes of Shaw and McKay (1943) and Thrasher (1963 [1927]), which focused strictly on local efforts to address delinquency and youth gang problems, may be inadequate for dealing with the problem. Such approaches are still prevalent today and do not develop the broad citywide, state, and, especially, national perspective necessary to address the various interconnected and complicated levels of the problem. Local communities characterized by low levels of "collective efficacy," with limited access to "social capital," appear to be associated with higher levels of gang crime, especially gang violence (Chaskin, chapter 1; Sampson, Morenoff, and Earls 1999; see also Cloward and Ohlin 1960; Decker and Van Winkle 1996; Kobrin 1961; Spergel 1964, 1995).

The failure of communities and organizations to successfully address the youth gang problem has also been conceptualized as resulting from organizational goal displacement. Schools, social agencies, law enforcement, and employment agencies may express concern and obtain funds to deal with gang problems but may deal primarily with non-gang problems or low levels of the gang problem. Funds and attention tend to be directed to traditional, narrow agency missions, such as enhancement of existing, specialized prevention or suppression programs that may functionally ignore the youth gang problem. This often occurs because agencies tend to express goals or accomplishments in quantitative terms of activities employing established routines and procedures, not usually involving the more difficult groups to identify and contact.

Political or organizational interest is often the primary, rather than the objective or rational, consideration in resolving the gang problem. Government and political leaders frequently propose and utilize strategies to fight, ameliorate, or otherwise reduce the gang problem, but that may not be directed to enhance "collective efficacy" or "social capital" in high-gang-crime communities. These strategies become simply a means to co-opt local residents, leaders, and even gang members to support established or aspiring political leaders. For example, law enforcement officials and certain candidates for public office often claim that they can solve the gang problem by putting more gang members in prison for longer sentences, but in fact their essential purpose is to add more law enforcement personnel to the agency, or to achieve elective office.

Community citizens and leaders addressing the problem usually confront a variety of myths, ideologies, and political interests that are not based on adequate data or research findings, even if such data or findings exist or are available for use. Local communities are frequently without sufficient means to exchange views about community patterns, strategies, and best practices in regard to the problem.

In response to this, Kennedy (chapter 9, this volume) describes community meetings and the exchange of views about so-called facts and expectations as a means to change "norms and narratives" of conflicting community residents and law enforcement constituencies about the gang problems and how more effectively to address them.

> The community saw law enforcement as racist. It regularly experienced illegal and abusive treatment by law enforcement and viewed this through the lens of slavery . . . and other instances of deliberate oppression . . . and did not believe the drug trade could continue without the inattention

age-related and interacting social-intervention and opportunity strategies to be applied as well.

The youth development model was the key emphasis in the Los Angeles Bridges Program (Zahniser 2008) and OJJDP's Gang Reduction Programs (Cahill et al. 2008). Despite initial program designs and claims to be comprehensive in nature, these multiple strategies were not interrelated, and program components were not characterized by close collaborative operations. Such programs were committed primarily to prevention and, occasionally, secondary prevention; they did not target hard-core gang youth. They focused on younger youth and were not established necessarily in high-gang-crime neighborhoods. They also functioned to expand existing, traditional service programs that had limited contact with law enforcement personnel.

Deterrence and Suppression Programs

Butts and Roman (chapter 8, p. 175) declare that "the most popular approaches for dealing with gang violence rely heavily on law enforcement. Gang injunctions, targeted curfews, large-scale drug arrests, and warrant sweeps focus on suppression, that is, on getting gang members off the streets." The Chicago and Los Angeles police departments developed specialized gang units in the 1960s to deal aggressively with the youth gang problem. The units were separate from the youth division, narcotics, organized crime, and other units, and more recently were separate from community policing. The law enforcement gang suppression approach became the basis for special procedures of prosecution, probation, and prison officials dealing with youth gangs. Strong deterrence and punishment were incorporated in the criminal justice legislation of many states (Klein 1995; Spergel 1995; Tita and Papachristos, chapter 2, this volume).

The Boston Gun Project's Ceasefire operation in the 1990s emphasized the coordination of suppression tactics by police, prosecution, probation, and the U.S. Bureau of Alcohol, Tobacco, and Firearms. Collaboration with a ministerial group, public schools, public health, and youth agencies was also (although less explicitly) developed. Gang youth responsible for the rising gang violence problem were targeted through a variety of innovative, community-based deterrent procedures (Butts and Roman, chapter 8; Kennedy, chapter 9; Tita and Papachristos, chapter 2; see also Braga, Kennedy, and Tita 2002; Braga, McDevitt, and Cronin 2008). The Boston Gun Project model was subsequently the basis for the Project Safe Neighborhoods Program (PSN), funded by the U.S. Department of Justice and located in more than ninety federal jurisdictions across the country.

The deterrence strategy focused attention on chronic, especially violent, offenders and the convening of interagency working groups representing a wide range of criminal justice capabilities. These working groups developed assessments of violence dynamics of perpetrators and victims and of related market, weapons-use, and acquisition patterns but focused less on social service capabilities. These coordinated suppression efforts were also facilitated by partnerships between researchers and practitioners. The Boston Gun Project's "pulling levers" strategy was designed with the aid of Harvard University researchers to deter violence by having law enforcement reaching out directly to gangs, saying explicitly that violence would no longer be tolerated, backing up the message by "pulling every lever" legally available when violence occurred (Braga, Kennedy, and Tita 2002:271–272).

The "pulling levers" strategy exploits the structure of the gang by holding the collective responsible for the actions of the individuals (Tita and Papachristos, chapter 2). However, it is far from clear that crime committed by members of a gang is always motivated by the norms and behaviors of the gang as a unit. Members of the same gang may have different crime patterns and may develop different norms of behavior under a variety of circumstances. They require different diagnoses (or assessments) and different interventions, including types of deterrence and/or social-intervention procedures (Spergel 2007). Gang structures are complex, changing, and elusive, and they are still not well understood. It is possible that holding a group—criminal or social—accountable for the actions of individual members may result in cohering the group and reinforcing its activities—criminal or noncriminal (Klein 1971).

The Chicago Project for Violence Prevention (CPVP), with headquarters in the University of Illinois School of Public Health, developed its distinctive CeaseFire approach partially from the Boston Gun Project's operation, modifying it to include strong community agency and church involvement and, later, a more focused gang outreach approach using "violence interrupters" and outreach youth workers.

From 1997 until 2001, the focus was on fostering clergy partnerships and community involvement, organizing collective responses to shootings and public education. . . . [CPVP] identified high violence areas and selected community-based organizations to administer the program locally using outreach workers and activities consistent with norms of violence reduction. [Later], "violence Interrupters," specialists in contacting hardcore gang members and influentials, were [hired and] directed from the central office at the University of Illinois. . . . [Selection of sites and host organizations was at times politically driven.] (Skogan et al., "Executive Summary," 5–10; see also Skogan et al. *Evaluation of CeaseFire*, 2008, chapter 2)

Of special importance in the development of the Chicago Project was its employment of "violence interrupters," usually former gang members with prison backgrounds. They were able to resolve gang conflict situations because of their personal experience, influence, and contacts in the local communities. However, they had little formal education and no professional training. They had limited knowledge of local agency resources and made little attempt, at least early in the program, to assist youth with jobs, training, educational opportunities, or treatment resources.

In addition, there was no collaboration with law enforcement with respect to the individual clients contacted. "Violence interrupters" were highly concerned with maintaining credibility with the local community, particularly the gang members, and not sharing information on particular youth with the police (identifying information on youth was not supplied to the project evaluators). The "violence interrupters" were almost totally focused on reducing violent activity and mediating problems of conflict concerned with the drug trade (Skogan et al. 2008, "Executive Summary," 14). Also, the line between street workers and gang members for many police officers in the Chicago Project and elsewhere seemed blurred (Tita and Papachristos, chapter 2).

Both the Boston Gun Project's Ceasefire operation and the Chicago CeaseFire project focused on changing norms of behavior, i.e., reducing the violent behavior of young adults prone to violence based on their membership in gangs. The Boston Gun Project emphasized deterrence through direct contacts with youth, and warnings by a team of law enforcement officers "pulling levers." The Chicago Project emphasized deterrence based largely on direct outreach contacts with youth and reliance on the special influence of "violence interrupters." There was apparently little coordinated assessment, collaborative planning, or joint practice with other agencies in the Chicago Project regarding targeted gang youth. There were, however, meetings initiated by the project with community groups and other agencies to express aggregate-level concern and to organize marches and demonstrations against gang violence incidents occurring in the local communities.

Comprehensive, Integrated Strategies

The Comprehensive Community Model is described in Howell and Curry (chapters 3 and 5, this volume), Spergel (1995, 2007), and in materials of OJJDP and its National Youth Gang Center. It is a community-, neighborhood-, or area-wide approach involving government leaders, a variety of agencies and community organizations, public and nonprofit organizations, criminal justice, businesses, faith-based and grassroots groups, schools, and former gang members—all concerned with the gang problem and the development of programs through interactive prevention, social intervention, suppression, and, more recently, prison or correctional reentry strategies to reduce the youth gang problem, particularly the gang violence problem, as well as other kinds of criminal behavior.

The model requires productive and appropriate use of five interactive and interdependent strategies: community mobilization, social intervention, provision of social opportunities, suppression, and organizational change and development targeted to gang-involved delinquent or criminal youth, or youth at high risk of gang involvement. Three interrelated program structures are required: an advisory group or council of significant agencies, including community organizations, criminal justice and social agencies, grassroots groups, and others concerned with the gang program; an outreach team of law enforcement, probation, street workers, and related school, job-development, and specialized treatment personnel; and a lead agency coordinating the efforts of the advisory group or council and administering or coordinating the efforts of the street team. Key elements of the structure and process of the approach are: (1) lead agency and community leadership capacity; (2) program staff commitment to use of multiple, interrelated strategies focused on the gang problem; (3) local government support; and (4) use of street workers.

COMMUNITY MOBILIZATION

The model focuses on youth in specific sectors of a community with a gang problem. Local community leaders and organizations, government officials, and heads of relevant city- or county-wide agencies of the larger community must recognize that a gang problem exists and seek to address it in some collective, problem-solving fashion. Community-wide leadership and organizations beyond the target neighborhood, as well as local leadership, organizations, and community groups, must utilize outside experts, such as university researchers and program specialists, to assess the nature and scope of the problem and be available to assist in developing policies and programs to address it. The mayor's office, city council, police department, school system, faith-based agencies, universities, the business community, other criminal justice agencies, human service organizations, and grassroots groups, as well as state officials and representatives of the federal government (particularly when the gang problem is widespread and serious) are expected to be drawn into this mobilization process to aid in determining and guiding the nature of the plan and sustaining the program in the gang-problem community over an extended period.

OPPORTUNITIES PROVISION

This strategy requires the provision of special or additional access to resources of education, training, and jobs to program youth. The lead agency, executives, and policy members of the advisory board have a special responsibility to modify their existing organizational and governmental policies, and to facilitate and develop resources to implement the project through a variety of means—for example, through local and citywide business and legislative contacts and pressures. After appropriate assessment of the problems, needs, and interests of the targeted youth, the outreach street team (especially street gang workers) involve youth in making use of those resources through relationships they establish and opportunities they make available. This may involve collaboration with the other team members, as well as contact with service agencies and community groups, all under the direction of the street-team leader, lead-agency case manager, or supervisor. A job agency representative, probation officer, drug counselor, school or college counselor, teacher, family members, former gang members, and neighbors may also be involved in this process. The opportunities-provision strategy is usually closely interrelated with the social-intervention strategy.

SOCIAL INTERVENTION

This is a set of methods or procedures—interacting with those not only of opportunities provision but also suppression—to control youth and their gangs—that also requires participation in community mobilization, i.e., assisting, contacting, and mobilizing neighborhood groups and other agency program personnel to support program youth. It is a primary strategy of the outreach youth worker or street gang worker and a secondary but important strategy of other team and related staff members. It requires positive and professional relationships with targeted youth in a variety of settings in the gang neighborhood in which each youth is located or related, including his gang group and family. The street worker must be able to assess the interests, needs, and activities of each of the targeted gang youth in relation to gang structure and process, in large measure through street-team meetings and operations. The street worker's primary purpose is to help the youth, through counseling and controls, to pursue legitimate patterns of behavior and career objectives. The information about targeted youth and gangs, their characteristics and activities, is shared fully with other members of the street team, particularly with the police in relation to issues of violence and serious criminal behavior. The street worker, with other team members, informs and plans interventions and even control activities for the youth and gang associates. He makes known his street-team connections to target gangs and gang members but is careful not to appear to be or become an agent of law enforcement; he maintains his primary role as a social service worker. He does not collude with the gang or targeted youth in their criminal activity. His role is difficult and marginal, requiring that he carry out a highly complex, disciplined, and sometimes risky set of interactive strategies and relationships. It may not be fully or consistently accepted by gang youth, or even by other street-team members, especially the police.

SUPPRESSION

This set of strategies requires the use of graduated sanctions for illegitimate and illegal behavior. It is exercised formally and informally by all members of the outreach street team of workers, most formally but not exclusively by police, probation, and other criminal justice personnel. The police officer on the team also has a limited social-intervention and opportunities-provision role to play, not only through informal referrals but also through limited, socially oriented discussions—for example, asking the target youth if he is working, and even providing information to the youth about job or school personnel contacts he may know about.

The suppression strategy in the context of the model (as well as reentry of gang members into the community after prison) requires not only surveillance but also knowledge and familiarity with most aspects of the youth gang member's relationships and behaviors with family, school, girlfriends, employers, and even faith workers. It is also important that the police officer not identify or label a youth a "hard-core" gang member, particularly if he or she is young and a peripheral member. The street-team officer is expected to treat gang youth with respect and may even provide a certain level of advice—even when he arrests them. At the same time, he is expected to communicate knowledge about gang locations and gang activities to other police officers in the district unit to which he is assigned and to facilitate deterrence tactics and service approaches that he has learned and successfully used.

A special responsibility of the police officer on the team is protection of street gang workers—who provide him with confidential gang-related information—from abuse and even false arrest by other police officers in the target community. The support of the district commander, who is expected to be a member of the advisory council, is vital in facilitating the role of the team police officer and in removing abusive police officers who impede the project. Appropriate bureaucratic, midlevel police structures and department policies and procedures are also essential to support the team police officer and his work on the project.

ORGANIZATIONAL CHANGE AND DEVELOPMENT

Commitment to organizational change and development is at the core of the implementation of the four foregoing strategies. Existing policies, administrative structures, worker knowledge, norms, and practices may need to be further developed, modified, or significantly changed to achieve efficient and effective program operation and results. The organizational change and development strategy is closely related to the community mobilization strategy. Key organizations that have not been involved when they should be are recruited and persuaded to participate in the project. Organizations that seek to exploit the gang program simply to obtain funds to narrowly enhance existing program efforts that may be unrelated to the goals and objectives of the comprehensive, community-wide model may have to be bypassed or terminated from the project. A special effort may need to be made to include grassroots groups in advisory council or team unit discussions, and to persuade them to support the project.

The comprehensive, community-wide, integrated-strategies approach requires a high level of lead agency, advisory council, street team, and local government leadership involvement and support to meet the complex challenges of program development, and to overcome the obstacles of agency and sometimes local community-group resistance. Gang crises and program failures are almost inevitable and also have to be overcome. Commitment and fidelity to program concepts, and high levels of tolerance for frustration are required. The development of effective monitoring techniques and program assessment and evaluation procedures is essential to the achievement of specific organizational change that is conducive to community development aimed at successfully addressing the local gang problem.

Existing agency strategies may have to be modified. For example, emphasis on wraparound services for all youth attending human services programs may not constitute an appropriate prevention strategy, and indiscriminate police sweeps of high-gang-crime neighborhoods, with arrests of all gang and non-gang members for simply hanging around, may be inappropriate, illegal, or unconstitutional. A fairly common strategic organizational failure is the lack of interest or capacity of a program to employ former gang members or influentials as team members. Resistance by agencies because of insurance requirements and government funding guidelines may have to be overcome. Administrators and supervisors with appropriate knowledge, commitment to the comprehensive model, and experience in dealing with the gang problem are essential and need to be recruited.

Almost all comprehensive, community-wide gang-control intervention and prevention programs—including comprehensive, community-wide, multiple-strategy, integrated gang programs—may be deficient in the development of an adequate assessment of the nature of gang subcultures and gang activities, and the range of local resources that are or should be employed to address the problem in particular gang-crime neighborhoods. Adequate data systems are often not available to effectively assess the nature and scope of the gang problem and the services and controls provided by gang programs. Adequate monitoring of program implementation by independent government authorities and funding sources is usually lacking. Probably the greatest failure of comprehensive, community-wide programs is defective evaluation of program processes and outcomes for program youth. These deficiencies may well continue to account for the lack of significant progress in addressing the gang problem in the United States.

Evaluation

The authors of the chapters in this volume emphasize the critical importance of program evaluation in determining whether gang programs— particularly comprehensive, community-wide programs—have been successful. Questions raised include whether evaluations of such programs have been adequately conducted in terms of scientific criteria, and whether they are useful for policy purposes or the development of future programs. Sufficient, detailed analyses and criticisms of evaluations of major gang programs usually have not been provided. This could partially account for the weakness and ineffectiveness of gang program and policy development. A great deal more attention and support must be directed to gang program evaluation, which must become far more sophisticated and comprehensive than currently is the case, or has been in the past.

Chaskin (chapter 1, p. 15) observes that "the evidence base regarding 'what works' in gang intervention more broadly remains fairly weak, and investment in the evaluation and application of research findings to such interventions remains relatively low." Butts and Roman (chapter 8, p. 176) estimate that "a key reason for the limited growth of gang prevention strategies is that youth gang programs are rarely evaluated. . . . One reason they are not evaluated is that many gang prevention programs lack the theoretically oriented conceptual frameworks that are required to conduct a high-quality evaluation." Curry (chapter 5, pp. 111–112) states in greater detail:

Outcome evaluation has most often been a neglected part of this process. In two of the most famous gang prevention and intervention programs in the history of the United States [the Chicago Area Project and Mobilization for Youth], there was a lot of theory and effective implementation, but no effective evaluation. . . . [In the CAP (Chicago Area Project) evaluation] there was no uniform program of delinquency prevention or record keeping of service delivery across sites, let alone any effort to address issues of outcome attribution by identifying appropriate comparison communities or control groups. [In the Mobilization for Youth (MFY) project] the program directors and planners did not understand opportunity theory [which was the generating idea of MFY], the program was not executed as proposed, and although there was a little research associated with the program, there was no evaluation.

Similar criticism can be made of the New York City Youth Board's Council of Social and Athletic Clubs—a pioneer outreach youth gang program, and the longest-running such effort (1950–1965) to address the youth gang problem, particularly intergang conflict. There was no systematic attempt to document the nature and quality of services to gang youth or their families, or of contacts with other agencies and community groups. There was no elaboration of theory and no evaluation of outcome at the individual, gang, or community (delinquency or crime) levels.

Even Malcolm Klein's elaborate studies of the processes and outcomes of a Los Angeles County Probation Department's youth gang outreach program (1968) and his responding program effort (1971)—regarded as probably the best of the classic outreach gang program evaluations—had serious flaws. His evaluations did not present quantitative or clear details of the scope and quality of services provided directly to youth, and perhaps to family, girlfriends, and other adults. The Ladino Hills project field researcher may not have been available to observe the clustering and activity patterns of program youth during sufficient nighttime or weekend hours. Also, there was an apparent reduction in the size of observed program youth groups on the streets, but there was no reduction in the rate of individual program youth delinquency or serious crime, and there was no formal identification of competing programs or social movements that may have affected outcomes (Moore 1978).

Adequate research method is essential to effective policy and program development. Curry (chapter 5) and Short and Hughes (chapter 6) insist also that the development of good gang program evaluation must be based on theory and should further theory development.

Short and Hughes (chapter 6, p. 128) state further that accuracy, relevant theory, research independence, and collaboration are key factors to be considered in good gang-program research evaluation:

> Constructing as accurate and precise a picture of the gang problem as is possible is fundamental to research integrity, whether the goal is basic science, informing public policy, or evaluating program performance. . . . We believe that research integrity requires recognition of the problematic nature of gangs, and that relational processes and network interactions must be studied as a means of evaluating intervention policies and practices. . . . [Independence of research] is more than avoiding biases associated with relationships between researchers and those who are responsible for policies and practices. Independence of measures and evaluation of performance require scientifically and theoretically relevant concepts. . . . Researchers and practitioners are clients of one another, as are the objects of our research and our praxis. Only by working together can we enhance our legitimacy and our effectiveness.

Rosenfeld, Fornango, and Baumer (2005:439) add:

> Before an intervention can be deemed effective in reducing crime, the observed reduction must be plausibly linked to the characteristics of the intervention. Second, the observed reductions must have occurred where and when the intervention was present and not where and when the intervention was absent. Third, the observed reductions must be shown to have exceeded the expected rate of crime decline . . . [and not] the change that would have taken place absent the intervention.

They also include important detail about the impact of the Boston Project:

> We do not find evidence supportive of a program impact on homicide trends for Boston's Gun Project Operation Ceasefire. . . . The homicide trends during the interventions did not change significantly from the sample average, although the Boston results are marginally significant when the age range is expanded to encompass 11–24 year-olds. . . . It is difficult to identify with high confidence program effects on low base-

rate events . . . we cannot confidently conclude that a nonzero difference exists between Boston's youth firearm homicide trend and those of other large cities. (438)

Also, Skogan may have provided an unduly favorable evaluation of the Chicago CeaseFire program. In So Young Kim's appendix table A-2 (p. 2 in Skogan and colleagues' recent full evaluation, 2008), I note that, for all shots, actual shootings, and killings, the reductions in the program and comparison areas are essentially the same comparing before and after periods in all shots and actual shooting categories. The number of killings was reduced significantly more in the Auburn-Gresham program test area than in its comparison area, but the opposite occurred, because killings were reduced significantly more in the comparison areas than in the program areas of Englewood and Logan Square. There were no significant differences in any of the four other sets of the Chicago Project program and comparison test areas.

Skogan and colleagues, however, indicate the limitations of their evaluation, which are mainly due to the limitations of the program design and funding policy:

The analysis did not incorporate any measures of the *strength* [or scope] of the programs. [No identifiable records of activity with program youth were kept and/or provided to the researchers]. . . . The intervention was not neatly contained within . . . [program] official boundaries. . . . Other programs were operating in and around the study areas [whose effects could not be separated out]. . . . [A number of comparison areas were not well matched [to the program areas.] (Skogan et al. 2008: chapter 8, pp. 39–40)

A great deal more "independence" of research is needed, within a scientific framework, as indicated by Short and Hughes and informed by the other authors cited in this volume. This requires greater interest, knowledge, and commitment to scientific research than currently exists among gang program evaluations, program designers and implementers, policymakers, funders, and especially the federal government.

Many recommendations for improved community-oriented gang programs and their evaluations are made by the authors of the chapters in the volume, as well as by other scholars. I highlight only a few of them.

Regarding knowledge development, Chaskin (chapter 1, p. 16) implicitly emphasizes the need for greater complexity in gang program research:

Efforts to generate knowledge about effective interventions through evaluation research must confront the complexities of design, measurement, and method inherent in attempting to understand interventions targeting complex, variable, and highly dynamic social phenomena such as gangs. These are further complicated within the context of comprehensive community interventions.

Similarly, Howell (chapter 3, pp. 51–52) cautions that "program models . . . are often difficult to replicate in real-world settings with fidelity to the original program requirements."

Regarding program implementation, Short and Hughes (chapter 6) emphasize the importance of including detached workers or street gang workers as a basic partnership component of community-based gang control programs. The use of such workers has been sorely neglected in most such programs. Similarly, Braga, Kennedy, and Tita (2002:284) recommend the inclusion in program operations of the knowledge and relationship of grassroots and local workers who are in daily contact with gang youth in their community:

> The experiences, observations, local knowledge and historical perspectives of police officers, street workers, and others with routine contact with offenders, community and criminal networks represent an underutilized resource for describing, understanding and crafting interventions aimed at crime problems.

Kennedy (chapter 9, p. 206) also stresses the importance of not only intelligence in design but also human sensitivity, authority, and understanding in gang program and evaluation efforts:

> Gangs and gang members are appropriately to be both sympathized with and feared; are deserving of both help and control; are both members of their communities and threats to those communities; are both victims— immediately and more largely—and offenders.

Recommendations

Finally, in a time of the nationalization and globalization of social problems that used to be strictly local and less complicated, we must address the youth gang problem through comprehensive policies, programs, and evaluation research by means of:

- large-scale community-wide, integrated approaches theoretically developed and scientifically tested;
- the partnership of policymakers, community leaders, practitioners, and researchers in these efforts, from the planning stage to program initiation, and then to project or demonstration termination;
- comprehensive gang program demonstrations and evaluations that extend over five- to seven-year periods in order to provide adequate time for program and research collaborative design development, implementation of the program model, and acquisition of pre- and post-program as well as program-period data using multiple units of analysis;
- funding and close monitoring arrangements of these complex projects and programs that are led by the federal government, with assistance and involvement of local authorities and foundations;
- the development of interrelated structures for each major gang program at the policy, administration, and practitioner levels, that involve appropriate representatives of local government, criminal justice and social agencies, youth and faith-based organizations, businesses, and the local citizenry, including former gang members from the gang crime community—all concerned with the youth gang problem;
- quasi-experimental design evaluation methods so that we can discover and learn what programs, what organizational and strategy arrangements, and what services and controls are truly effective in preventing, reducing, and controlling the youth gang problem for different kinds of gang-involved youth, or youth at high risk of becoming involved in gangs, as well as their families, groups, and communities; and
- the establishment of the national Gang Research, Evaluation, and Policy Institute, preferably in the Office of Juvenile Justice and Delinquency Prevention, Office of Justice Programs, U.S. Department of Justice, with the participation of other Justice and federal agency units, local policymakers, community leaders, gang experts, and gang researchers, to promote and facilitate the testing and implementation of effective, comprehensive, integrated youth gang intervention, prevention, suppression, and community-reentry models for reducing gang crime, especially violence.

The authors of the chapters of this volume, including myself, have expressed the critical need to more effectively conceptualize, design, implement, and evaluate programs that address an increasingly complex youth gang problem. We have described the existence and need for community-based, comprehensive approaches, but we differ somewhat in emphases, types of multidisciplinary and interagency patterns, and jurisdictions to be used. All of the approaches have not as yet been adequately tested. I firmly believe that the importance of program and policy evaluation research must be fully recognized and effective scientific evaluations developed if we are to make progress in dealing with the youth gang problem.

Note

I much appreciate the interest and support of Jeanne Marsh, dean of the School of Social Service Administration, University of Chicago, and her sponsorship of the symposium from which the chapters in this volume are derived. My appreciation also goes to Professor Robert Chaskin of the school, who developed and edited this volume, and to the other presenters and participants who made valuable contributions to our knowledge of what to do about the youth gang problem. Annot Spergel and Elisa Barrios provided valuable assistance in the production of this chapter.

References

Barrios, Louis. 2003. "The Almighty Latin King and Queen Nation and the Spirituality of Resistance." In Louis Kontos, David Brotherton, and Louis Barrios, eds., *Gangs and Society*, 119–135. New York: Columbia University Press.

Braga, Anthony A., David M. Kennedy, and George E. Tita. 2002. "New Approaches to the Strategic Prevention of Gang and Group-Involved Violence." In C. Ronald Huff, ed., *Gangs in America III*, 271–285. Thousand Oaks, Calif.: Sage.

Braga, Anthony A., Pierce McDevitt, and Bond Cronin. 2008. "The Strategic Prevention of Gang Violence Among Gang Involved Offenders." *Justice Quarterly* 25 (1): 132–162.

Brotherton, David. 2003. "Education in the Reform of Street Organizations in New York City." In Louis Kontos, David Brotherton, and Louis Barrios, eds., *Gangs and Society*, 136–158. New York: Columbia University Press.

Bursik, Robert J., Jr. 2002. "The System Model of Gang Behavior. A Reconsideration." In C. Ronald Huff, ed., *Gangs in America III*, 71–81. Thousand Oaks, Calif.: Sage.

Bursik, Robert J., Jr. and Harold G. Grasmick. 1993. *Neighborhoods and Crime*. New York: Lexington Books.

Cahill, Meagan, Mark Coggeshall, David Hayeslip, Ashley Wolff, Erica Lagerson, Michelle Scott, Elizabeth Davies, Kevin Roland, and Scott Decker. 2008. *Community Collaboratives Addressing Gang Youth: Interim Findings from the Gang Reduction Program*. Washington, D.C.: Urban Institute Justice Policy Center.

Cloward, Richard A. and Lloyd E. Ohlin. 1960. *Delinquency and Opportunity*. Glencoe, Ill.: Free Press.

Coleman, James S. 1988. "Social Capital in the Creation of Human Capital." *American Journal of Sociology* 94:S95–S120.

Decker, Scott H. and Barrik Van Winkle. 1996. *Life in the Gang: Family, Friends, and Violence*. Cambridge, England: Cambridge University Press.

Egley, Arlen, Jr. and Christina E. O'Donnell. 2008. "Highlights of the 2005 National Gang Survey." *OJJDP Fact Sheet*, July (4), 2 pages. U.S. Department of Justice, Office of Juvenile Justice and Delinquency Prevention.

Greene, Judith and Kevin Pranis. 2007. *Gang Wars*. Washington, D.C.: Justice Policy Institute.

Hagedorn, John M. 2008. *A World of Gangs*. Minneapolis: University of Minnesota Press.

——, ed. 2007. *Gangs in the Global City: Alternatives to Traditional Criminology*. Urbana and Chicago: University of Illinois Press.

Holthusen, Berna, ed. 2007. *Prevention of Youth Crime in Germany*. Munich: Deutsches Jugendinstitit.

Internet Forward Communications. 2008. "Transnational Gangs: How Have Gangs Gone Global?" (www.forewardcommunication.wordpress.com, pp. 1–4).

Klein, Malcolm W. 1968. *From Association to Guilt: The Group Guidance Project in Juvenile Gang Intervention*. Los Angeles: Youth Studies Center, University of Southern California and Los Angeles County Probation Department.

——. 1971. *Street Gangs and Street Workers*. Englewood Cliffs, N.J.: Prentice-Hall.

——. 1995. *The American Street Gang*. New York: Oxford University Press.

Kobrin, Solomon. 1961. *Sociological Aspects of the Development of a Street Corner Group: An Explanatory Study*. The American Journal of Orthopsychiatry 31 (October): 685–702.

Manwaring, Max G. 2007. *A Contemporary Challenge to State Sovereignty: Gangs and Other Illicit Transnational Criminal Organizations in Central America*. Carlisle, Pa.: Strategic Studies Institute, U.S. Army War College.

Merton, Robert K. 1957. *Social Theory and Social Structure*. Glencoe, Ill.: Free Press.

Moore, Joan W. 1978. *Homeboys*. Philadelphia: Temple University Press.

New York City Youth Board. 1960. *Reaching the Fighting Gang*. New York: New York City Youth Board.

Office of Juvenile Justice and Delinquency Prevention. 2008. *OJJDP Fact Sheet*. July. 2 pages. U.S. Department of Justice, Office of Justice Programs.

Rosenfeld, Richard, Robert Fornango, and Eric Baumer. 2005. "Did Ceasefire, Compstat, and Exile Reduce Homicide?" *Criminology and Public Policy* 4 (3): 419–450.

Sampson, Robert J., Jeffrey D. Morenoff, and Felton Earls. 1999. "Beyond Social Capital: Spatial Dynamics of Collective Efficacy for Children." *American Sociological Review* 64:633–660.

Sampson, Robert J., D. Raudenbush, and F. Earls. 1997. "Neighborhoods and Violent Crime: Multilevel Study of Collective Efficacy." *Science* 277:918–927.

Shaw, Clifford R. and Henry D. McKay. 1943. *Juvenile Delinquency and Urban Areas*. Chicago: University of Chicago Press.

Skogan, Wesley G., Susan M. Hartnett, Natalie Bump, and Jill Dubois, with the assistance of Ryan Hollon and Danielle Morris. 2008. *Evaluation of CeaseFire*. Revised. Chicago: Northwestern University. Available online (www.northwestern.edu/ipr/publication/ceasefire.htwh).

Skogan, Wesley G., Susan M. Hartnett, Natalie Bump, and Jill Dubois, with the assistance of Ryan Hollon and Danielle Morris. 2008. "Executive Summary." *Evaluation of CeaseFire Chicago*. Revised. Chicago: Northwestern University. Available online (www.northwestern.edu/ipr/publication/ceasefire.htwh).

Specht, Walther, ed. 2000. *Street Children and Mobile Youth Work in Central and Southeastern European Countries*. International Workshop, October 1–3. Stuttgart, Germany: International Society for Mobile Youth Work (ISMO).

Spergel, Irving A. 1964. *Slumtown, Racketville, Haulburg: An Exploratory Study of Delinquent Subcultures*. Chicago: University of Chicago Press.

——. 1995. *The Youth Gang Problem: A Community Approach*. New York: Oxford University Press.

——. 2007. *Reducing Youth Gang Violence: The Little Village Project in Chicago*. Lanham, Md.: AltaMira.

Thrasher, Frederic M. 1963 [1927]. *The Gang*. Chicago: University of Chicago Press.

United States Senate Bill. 2007–2008. "Gang Abatement and Prevention Act of 2007." S. 456, 110th Cong.

Zahniser, David. 2008. "Villaraigosa Plans to Eliminate L.A. Bridges Gang Program." *Los Angeles Times*, April 15.

Contributors

JEFFREY A. BUTTS is executive Vice President for Research at Public/Private Ventures.

ROBERT J. CHASKIN is an associate professor at the University of Chicago School of Social Service Administration and a research fellow at Chapin Hall at the University of Chicago.

G. DAVID CURRY is a professor of criminology and criminal justice at the University of Missouri, St. Louis.

JAMES C. HOWELL is a senior research associate with the National Youth Gang Center in Tallahassee, Florida.

LORINE A. HUGHES is an assistant professor in the School of Criminology and Criminal Justice at the University of Nebraska at Omaha.

CANDICE KANE is the chief operating officer for the Chicago Project for Violence Prevention.

DAVID M. KENNEDY is the director of the Center for Crime Prevention and Control at the John Jay College of Criminal Justice at the City University of New York.

TIM METZGER is a research specialist at CeaseFire Chicago.

ANDREW PAPACHRISTOS is an assistant professor in the Department of Sociology at the University of Massachusetts, Amherst.

ELENA QUINTANA is the director of evaluation at CeaseFire Chicago.

CHARLIE RANSFORD is a data analyst at CeaseFire Chicago.

CATERINA GOUVIS ROMAN is a researcher at the Urban Institute's Justice Policy Center.

JAMES F. SHORT, JR., is a professor emeritus of sociology at Washington State University.

Gary Slutkin is a research professor of epidemiology at the University of Illinois at Chicago and founder of the Chicago Project for Violence Prevention.

IRVING A. SPERGEL is the George Herbert Jones Professor Emeritus at the University of Chicago School of Social Service Administration.

GEORGE E. TITA is an associate professor in the Department of Criminology, Law, and Society at the University of California, Irvine.

JAMES DIEGO VIGIL is a professor of social ecology at the University of California, Irvine.

Index